OTHER BOOKS BY ALICE E. SINK

On This Day In
PIEDMONT TRIAD HISTORY

ALICE E. SINK

THE
History
PRESS

Published by The History Press
Charleston, SC 29403
www.historypress.net

First published 2013

ISBN 978-1-5402-2160-5

Library of Congress CIP data applied for.

Notice: The information in this book is true and complete to the best of our knowledge. It is offered without guarantee on the part of the author or The History Press. The author and The History Press disclaim all liability in connection with the use of this book.

In loving memory of my paternal grandmother, Jenny Alice Wood Evans, for whom I was named. She taught me that diligent work was always rewarding.

CONTENTS

Acknowledgements   11
Preface   13

1. January   15
2. February   51
3. March   85
4. April   123
5. May   159
6. June   193
7. July   227
8. August   265
9. September   301
10. October   335
11. November   375
12. December   409

Bibliography   443
About the Author   463

ACKNOWLEDGEMENTS

To Banks Smither, my editor at The History Press, who gave me superior guidance and answered all of my questions (and there were many), and to Alyssa Pierce, assistant editor, who evaluated the availability and suitability of many, many images and chose the ones that were big enough and clear enough and important enough for publication. To Katie Parry, my publicist at The History Press, who always arranges my many presentations and book signings and responds to my e-mails at six o'clock in the morning, I appreciate your dedication. To Magan Thomas and Meredith Riddick of The History Press sales department, I marvel and appreciate your promptness in filling all those orders for books for businesses that want them NOW.

I could not have written this book without the online archives of the *Lexington Dispatch*, which go all the way back to the late 1880s. In addition, during the early part of the twentieth century, this newspaper printed news from the entire Piedmont Triad and provided valuable information.

Thanks also to very special Piedmont Triad individuals and the Forsyth Public Library who supplied me with personal photographs that make this book unique.

PREFACE

The Piedmont Triad of North Carolina has three major cities: Greensboro, Winston-Salem and High Point. Secondary cities over ten thousand in population include Asheboro, Burlington, Clemmons, Eden, Graham, Kernersville, Lexington, Reidsville and Thomasville. Fifty-three other municipalities under ten thousand in population call the Piedmont Triad home.

As a lifelong resident of this area and a writer, I am extremely interested in Piedmont Triad history and the unique format of this book—one page of historical truths for each day of the year. To my knowledge, everything I have written is true and documented. Specifics, illustrations and examples come from various sources that my bibliography will reveal.

I researched newspaper archives extensively. The earliest newspapers were published once a week, usually on a Wednesday. Later, reading audience popularity increased publications to twice a week—Tuesdays and Thursdays. Finally, newspapers rolled off the presses 6 or 7 days a week. The daily incidents for all 365 days are accurate; however, the exact day (for the very early stories) is as close as I could get them. For example, a weekly paper might report something that happened "last Friday" or "a couple weeks ago." If the paper were published on a Wednesday, I would count back to the previous "Friday" or "earlier week." So, the late 1800s and early 1900s necessitated my issuing an educated guess.

The daily historical events recorded in this book are a mixture of what we might call "straight" or serious news and also unique or even "quirky" news items. One recurring recorded historical event throughout the early years was the weighing of hogs at butchering time as farmers vied for the fattest hog. How times have changed! When regional newspapers were weekly and consisted of only three or four pages, the "personal" and "quirky" happenings appeared on the front page and carried large, bold headlines—with state and national news taking a back seat on the third or fourth page.

Most terms in this historical account need no definition. The term "blind tiger" is the exception. Originating in the United States in the nineteenth century, it was applied to lower-class establishments that sold alcoholic beverages illegally. The operator of an establishment (such as a saloon or bar) would often charge customers to see an attraction (such as an animal) and then serve a "complimentary" alcoholic beverage, thus circumventing the law. In addition, blind tigers sometimes referred to moonshiners and bootleggers, who sold alcoholic beverages illegally from their homes for on-site or off-site consumption. Occasionally, the term "blind tiger" referred to a mysterious place where very bad whiskey was sold, with this activity often blamed on Prohibition.

I had a great time writing this book, and I hope you have as much fun reading it. I have learned many unique and important true stories about my native Piedmont Triad.

January 1

1882: SMALLPOX EPIDEMIC IN WINSTON
The Board of Aldermen issued an edict that everyone—young and old—receive the smallpox vaccination. For those already ill with the disease or having been exposed to someone with smallpox, a pest house opened to quarantine—under guard—those persons. The cost of the pest house rental was four dollars a month.

1905: AN INTERESTING NEW YEAR BEGINNING
Fourteen-year-old Luther Beasley was found dead at the Green Street railroad crossing in High Point at about one o'clock in the morning. His mangled body had been crushed under the wheels of one of the trains on the main line of the Southern Railway. Apparently, Luther had left his home in Randleman but had told no one where he was going. It was presumed that the teen fell from a train while "stealing a ride." Complete details concerning his horrible death were not known.

Assembling at the Baptist church was the largest concourse of people that ever sought admission into that house of worship. The topic of that evening's meeting concerned citizens' disapproval of dispensaries. Several ministers made talks, pointing out the moral side of the issue. Reverend J.C. Leonard closed the meeting with an interesting talk on how to rid the town of "blind tigers." A vote was then called for, asking all persons who were opposed to "blind tigers, a dispensary, or open saloons" to stand. Reportedly, nearly every man, woman and child in the church arose.

January 2

1905: Trophy Hog and Elegant Party

Making front-page news in a regional newspaper was the butchering of a hog weighing 505 pounds. Mr. C.F. Conrad from near Pilgrim arrived at the newspaper office the day after the killing. He brought with him the bladder taken from the hog. When blown up, it measured thirty-five by four and a half inches in circumference. The editor of the *Lexington Dispatch* found this newsworthy because this was one of the largest hogs slaughtered in Davidson County that particular season.

Also making first-page news on this date was a recap of a "very delightful" New Year's reception hosted by Mr. and Mrs. C.C. Hargrave at "their splendid new residence" on First Avenue. Games such as "Pit" and "Old Maid" were played, after which "elegant" refreshments were served. Mr. Joe Thompson and Miss Fanny Wheeler won the prizes, and Mr. O.E. Mendenhall received the "booby." About forty young people were present and enjoyed a most pleasant evening.

A not-so-pleasant happening of this day was the news that Mr. C.C. Inman, a well-known farmer of Westfield, Surry County, left home on this day. His body was later found in a tobacco basement a few miles from his home. He had left home with a jug and went directly to a stillhouse several miles away. His vessel was filled with whiskey, from which he drank freely. When found, he still had one hand on the handle of the jug. He left a wife and fifteen children.

January 3

1900: A GIFT FOR THE YEAR

The State Superintendent of Public Instruction allotted each schoolchild fifteen and a quarter cents, the apportionment based on a school census. The total of the appropriation was $100,000, which would be divided among the different counties, and it was estimated that this amount of money would run the schools for only a week. Superintendent Worth announced that warrants for the payments of the funds would be sent to the various counties immediately. However, there was one catch: the warrants would not be honored until more money could be collected. Hopefully, only several weeks would lapse between issuance of the warrants and payment to the counties. Piedmont Triad's twelve counties received warrants for the following amounts: Alamance, $2,310.22; Caswell, $710.54; Davidson, $1,284.96; Davie, $601.15; Forsyth, $1,712.11; Guilford, $1,855.77; Montgomery, $604.73; Randolph, $1,520.88; Rockingham, $1,596.42; Stokes, $1,166.47; Surry, $1,458.34; and Yadkin, $805.01.

January 4

1908: The Force of Habit

A Lexington man confessed the following to a newspaper editor:

> *I came near blowing myself up. I was about to make a fire, and there were coals in the stove. I didn't have many chips, and I saw I must use kerosene to get a fire started. You know that when I take a drink of corn whiskey I always fill the glass plum full. I hate a small drink, and I despise people who do take such. Same with them who take a little chaw of terbaccer. I go whole hog or none. Well, you know, when I started to put coal oil on them coals, I knew it wouldn't do to pour it out of the can, so I taken a glass and dadblamed if I didn't fill it full, unconsciously thinking I was taking a drink. Well I poured that glassful on the coals in the stove, and it purt nigh blowed the top offen the critter! Now what you reckon would a'happened if I had poured it out of the can?*

His story, printed verbatim, made the second page of the regional newspaper.

January 5

1905: IMPROVEMENTS FOR CITIZENS

A senator from Forsyth County, Mr. Eller, recently introduced a bill to incorporate the Winston-Salem South Bound Railway Company. The road and telegraph line would extend from Winston through fifteen counties to the South Carolina line. The capital stock was listed at $125,000; however, citizens were informed that the amount could increase to $300,000. Citizens of Piedmont Triad counties, townships and cities would be given the option to vote subscriptions to stock or bonds. Another interesting aside was the fact that 250 or more convicts would be hired by the state.

In addition to expanding the railroad, citizens were asked to consider the following questions: "Shall Davidson County continue to have the worse roads in the State, or shall we get together and make improvements as the people have done in Guilford and other counties? Do the people of Davidson Country want their roads improved by local taxation or by issuing bonds? The answer was this: If so, they should get together and petition the Legislature for such relief as they want."

January 6

1905: News of Senate and House

On this day, the Senate passed a bill to reimburse State Treasurer Lacy $374, an amount embezzled by W.H. Martin, a clerk under former treasurer Worth. In addition, the House repealed the anti-jug law; however, no specifics were given concerning this action. It would seem that the repeal meant that Piedmont Triad citizens would again be allowed to possess liquor in jugs. Interestingly, House members were introduced to a bill to sanction the appointment of women as notaries public, a bill to make sixty-three hours a week's work in cotton mills and yet another bill to allow veterans who lost an arm or leg to receive pensions even if possessed of over $500 in property.

Another political truth on this day was the fact that Z.I. Walser, a Republican, said he voted for Captain R.B. Glenn for governor, this "being the first time he ever cast a ballot for a Democrat."

January 7

1905: Gay Voices and Merry Laughter

Mr. and Mrs. John Raymond McCrary entertained a number of friends at their "beautiful new home." Mrs. McCrary charmed residents with her gracious cordiality and won many friends. Mr. McCrary was to be congratulated on having won one of the belles of the Old Dominion. The house was beautifully decorated with holly and mistletoe, ferns and palms, while "glorious fires" burned in every grate. Gay voices and merry laughter of the guests "formed a picture it would be difficult to describe." A guessing contest and a number of games were played and greatly enjoyed. Miss Louise Hanes was the winner of the prize in the guessing contest, and Miss Edith Greer was the successful winner in the Cinderella game. Delicious refreshments were served after the games to the thirty-two guests.

January 8

1905: INJURED BUT STILL TICKING

Mr. George W. Conrad, a respected citizen living about five miles from Lexington, was the victim of a serious accident. He was "slopping his hogs" while standing on a platform at the hog pen, and he either fell or jumped to the ground. He landed on an old pitchfork, which had no handle. Consequently, the splintered end of the sharp fork entered into his body for several inches. The result was a dangerous wound.

That same day, an announcement was made that J. Reese Blair, Esquire, of Troy, Montgomery County, was a patient in the hospital with a pair of broken ribs as the result of a railway-automobile collision on the Aberdeen & Asheboro Railway. Mr. Blair's injuries did not prevent him from marrying Miss Ada Allen of Troy—in his hospital room. The Reverend T.G. Ellington officiated in the presence of a "considerable number of friends."

January 9

1905: MORE LARGE HOGS

Historical news at the turn of the twentieth century in the Piedmont Triad seemed to focus a great deal on big hogs. Their stories usually made the first page of the regional newspaper. January 9 was no exception. Two big hogs were killed, but the owner/informant did not report whether the weights were gross or net, stating that "either way will not change the fact that the hogs were big ones." The largest was killed by Mr. Jacob Wagoner of Thomasville township. It weighed 565 pounds. Mr. S.L. Yokley, of Lexington township, killed one that weighed exactly 533 pounds. Mr. Haley Myers, of Fair Grove, killed two hogs that together weighed 874 pounds. The largest was a 450-pounder, while the smaller one weighed 424 pounds. Interestingly, they were both less than one year old. It seemed that "hog weight" was an important and newsworthy subject for farmers.

January 10

1906: Strike at the Wenonah

Demanding an increase in wages, approximately forty to fifty employees at Wenonah Cotton Mill No. 1 left their weaving machines and walked out on a strike. They argued that they were paid by the "cut," a piece of cloth consisting of sixty yards at a rate of twenty-two cents per cut. Millworkers asked for an increase of three cents for a cut because their living expenses had greatly increased during the past few years. They revealed that they were having a very difficult time meeting their living expenses. Although two of the weaving-room workers did return to work at the old pay rate, the remaining stood firm with their request. That same afternoon, a second strike at the Wenonah Mill No. 2 involved approximately fifty weavers who claimed they had for some time been dissatisfied with the existed "schedule" (pay rate). They wanted the "cut" rate to be raised to twenty-five cents. These workers were informed there would be no increase in pay; furthermore, if they weren't willing to work at the existing pay rate, the mill would be closed immediately. That being said, all but five operators returned to work.

January 11

1905: INAUGURATION DAY

This was a red-letter day for folks in the Piedmont Triad because the new governor and other state officers were inaugurated in Raleigh at one o'clock in the afternoon. A joint legislative committee and a committee of citizens went to Winston to escort Governor-Elect Glenn to the state capitol. They left Winston on a special train, which was met by a committee that escorted present and incoming state officers to the place of inauguration. The actual ceremony took place on the east front of the capitol, with Senator A.H. Eller, chairman of a joint committee, as master of ceremonies. Troops formed at noon on Fayetteville Street in Raleigh and escorted the governor and state officers-elect to the place of inauguration. At the conclusion of the ceremonies, the governor and staff and state officers went to the balcony of the Yarborough House and reviewed the National Guard. A dress parade followed. Then, at eight

Governor-Elect Glenn and other state officers were inaugurated in Raleigh at one o'clock in the afternoon. Various carriages carrying the dignitaries passed by the Confederate Monument. *Wikimedia Commons.*

o'clock that evening, a public reception was given in the rotunda of the capitol, where the governor and incoming officers and their wives were "received."

Not all was pomp and circumstance with Piedmont Triad folks on this day. At Advance, Davie County, Bob Williams shot and killed Lewis Laird. Reportedly, the trouble started when Laird went to the Williamses' home "for the sole purpose of creating a disturbance." Laird had a pistol and fired twice at Williams; however, both balls went "wide of the mark." Williams grabbed his nearby rifle and fired on his antagonist just above the eye. Laird "died without uttering a word."

January 12

1920: HOMELESS ARMENIAN ORPHANS KNOCK AT THE DOOR
An important appeal went out to all the people to adopt
55 homeless Armenian orphans who were facing death in
a land "where hopeless natives know nothing but sorrow."
Food and clothing were desperately needed, so a campaign
of relief was waged under the direction of Mr. George L.
Harkney, chairman of the drive. Citizens were reminded
in a straightforward and honest manner of the fact that
this emergency solicitation was not a war fund but an act
of humanity for the 300,000 "naked and starving boys and
girls who are waiting for a chance to live." These homeless
and parentless children suffered because their parents were
murdered and their homes destroyed. The plea continued
with a rather subjective evaluation of this misfortune:
"Yes, all because the Armenians would not discard their
Christian faith for that of the cruel and barbarous Turks."

1936: HER BODY WAS HURLED IN THE AIR
Mrs. Ada Embler, about thirty-five, was struck by a Southern
Railway freight train at the corner of Salem and Randolph
Streets in the center of Thomasville. Reports indicated that
Mrs. Embler had seemed unaware of the approaching train
and walked directly in front of the engine. Her body was
hurled some 125 feet through the air, with death coming
immediately. Although the body was not badly mangled, it
was terribly crushed.

January 13

1913: HE WILL BE AFTER THE BLIND TIGERS

Chief W.F. Thomason of Lexington was not unknown to the blind tigers, gamblers and other "malefactors." For several years, he "harried and harassed" them, and they obviously were not eager to see him in the office, which had been vacant for some time since ex-chief Mr. J.W. Davis "took off his badge and laid down his club" several months prior. Thomason announced that although he would make no "wild promises," he would definitely do his very best to accomplish his main goal: "to rid Lexington of the tigers, the gamblers and petty thieves that now infest the town." He also advocated what he called "real law enforcement."

In contrast to reports of scandals, the regional newspaper ran a front-page obituary for a widely known and well-beloved citizen of Cotton Grove who had "passed over the river." T.M. Sheets, or Tom, as he was known throughout the area, died of what was called "congestion of the brain." Before Tom died, he had hosted a barbecue for over one hundred of his friends, who gathered at his home. When

In the early 1900s, "blind tigers," or bootleggers, were the main targets for law enforcement officers, who vowed to rid the Piedmont Triad of these unlawful folks. *Library of Congress.*

he had bought his farm in Cotton Grove township, he had "found the land a wilderness, and he left it a model farming section, dotted with handsome homes and filled with a contented, happy people." Tom Sheets did not have an enemy in "all the world," and everybody who knew him "loved him."

January 14

1910: HONOR LEE AND JACKSON

The Robert E. Lee Chapter of the Daughters of the Confederacy honored the memory of General Robert E. Lee and General Stonewall Jackson in a fitting celebration of the birthdays of these "two great Southern soldiers." Invitations to the gala event were issued to the home of Mrs. C.C. Hargrave. The agenda for the celebration was as follows: "Prayer, Reverend V.Y. Boozer; Lee's favorite hymn, 'For All the Saints Who from Their Labors Rest'; Short Address, Dr. J.C. Leonard; Song, 'The Southern Girl' or 'The Homespun Dress' by Mesdames Greer, Thompson, Grimes and Hunt; Reading, Mrs. P.S. Vann; Piano Solo, 'Dixie' by Miss Louise Hill; Reading, Miss Camille Hunt; Soldiers Chorus; Reading, Mrs. Correll; Solo, Mrs. W.G. Penry; Short address, Capt. F.C. Robbins; and 'Bonnie Blue Flag' by the Daughters of the Confederacy." The birthday celebration began at 8:30 p.m. With that long agenda, I wonder what time they finished.

General Robert E. Lee was considered a great Southern soldier. The Robert E. Lee Chapter of the Daughters of the Confederacy was extremely active in the Piedmont Triad. They sponsored gala events to celebrate his birthday. *Wikimedia Commons.*

January 15

1910: SUIT FOR ALIENATION

A High Point dispatch on the fifteenth read: "It is rumored that a very sensational and interesting lawsuit will be tried in Davidson County Superior Court in the near future." It seems that a young High Point man, H.V. Kimball, instituted suit against a prominent and well-to-do Davidson County farmer, W.M.C. Surratt, who lived near Jackson Hill. The alienation-of-affection suit came about in this manner: Kimball married Mr. Surratt's daughter. As soon as the couple went to High Point to live, the father of the bride enticed her to return to his home and leave her husband. Mr. Kimball claimed that his bride's father had attempted again and again—in the six weeks they had been married—to get her to return to her childhood home, supposedly for a visit only. But once she was there, Surratt did not let her leave, nor would he allow her husband to visit her. Kimball claimed damages to the extent of $10,000 because his happiness and contentment for the future had been destroyed. According to a newspaper article about this suit, the case would be watched with a great deal of interest.

January 16

1905: MET DEATH BY FREEZING

A "well-known character" about the city of Winston-Salem, John Dalton, was found dead about one hundred yards north of Belo's pond. Officials pieced together what they thought had happened: he was lying on his back in the road. The coroner's jury speculated that Mr. Dalton had fallen in Belo's pond, climbed out and later froze to death. Reportedly, he was about forty-eight years old and in poor health, and "drinking was perhaps his worst habit." He had been arrested for vagrancy several times, for which he served various sentences on the county roads.

Also making front-page news on this day were two positive and exciting items. One was an announcement of the groundbreaking for the Pittsburg Plate Glass Company's $10,000 factory to be built in High Point. Another concerned the Asheboro Electric Company's incorporation, with $30,000 capital, to establish an electric light plant.

January 17

1906: REMINISCES OF YE OLDEN TIMES

It seems rather strange to us today to think that Mrs. S. Abigail Irish wrote an article about the Piedmont Triad in its "olden days." Yes, we think of the 1906 as extremely olden! Mrs. Irish wrote that she wanted to relate her memories of times in Davidson County prior to antebellum days. She did so in hopes of saving for coming generations the most "toothsome" bits of history. She remembered the old flintlock musket in its rack above the pioneer's door. This brought a sense of peace to the family within the cabin and also provided them with "toothsome" game. There had been a gristmill on the Richard Cranford place, operated in very early days by David Stout, but Mrs. Irish confessed that this was "before her time; however, she was certain that the mill ground the bread stuffs for the soldiers of the Revolution." She recalled that trampling by horses was then the method of operation. Upon the bare floor would be placed

Old gristmills were built in antebellum days. As early as the Revolution, these mills ground the breadstuffs for soldiers. Later, women on horseback took their sacks of grain to the mill to be ground. *Wikimedia Commons.*

two lengths of sheaves with heads together and several sheaves thick. Then horses were driven around on it, the driver turning the straw, meanwhile, so as to bring all up to the tramping. It was not unusual for the woman of the household to take a sack of grain to the mill on the horse she rode and additional sacks on a horse that was led. She would wait for the grinding of the grain and then carry home the meal.

January 18

1910: COURT MAKES LITTLE PROGRESS

Superior court was in session but, according to front-page newspaper reports, had made little progress concerning the damage suit of Mr. W.M. Cross against the Town of Lexington. Mr. Cross alleged injuries as a result of defective machinery at the town's light and water plant while he was employed there some months earlier. The jury answered the first issue, which asked if the town was negligent, with a resounding negative. Obviously, that ended the case with Mr. Cross getting nothing, so he sued for $500. Then, another case, *John A. Lane vs. the Southern Railroad*, came before the judge. The plaintiff alleged that while he was closing or trying to close a car door, the door gave way at the top because of rotten wood. It subsequently fell on him, injuring his arm. Interestingly, it took considerable time to illustrate the proper way to open and close a wooden boxcar door. The jury was still out on Mr. Lane's case as the newspaper went to press. Finally, on this day, the court heard the case of *Eveline Goss vs. L.F. Weaver* over an acre of land. This resulted in a "non-suit."

January 19

1900: Epistles to the Editor
Mr. F.M. Simmons's January 19, 1900 letter to the editor of the *Lexington Dispatch* argued that the day of Negro control in the South had passed forever, and it could safely be asserted that no party controlled by the Negro would ever again carry a state south of the Mason-Dixon line and that the white men who "hereafter attempted to manipulate the Negro vote to further their mean and selfish ambition, and to degrade their race, would become daily and yearly more and more odious in the eyes of self-respecting white men and women." Simmons concluded his letter with the following postscript: "Let Senator Prichard and his office holding negrophilists put this in their pipes and smoke it." That same day, the *Carolinian* was quoted in the regional newspaper. The editor of the *Carolinian* asserted that the best interests of the Negro would be "subserved [*sic*] by his making himself a friendly helping mate rather than an incubus to the white man."

1908: Fire in Winston
About seven o'clock in the evening, a fire broke out in Winston. Before it could be extinguished, approximately $70,000 of property was damaged and destroyed. The blaze started in the Young Women's Christian Association, over the store of the Brown-Rogers Hardware Company. The stores of F.C. Brown and the Winston Clothing Company also incurred fire and water damage.

January 20

1905: THE SLAYER IS RELEASED
In Davie County, Bob Williams allegedly shot and killed
Lewis Laird of Advance. Williams was given a hearing
before a magistrate at Advance on this day. After hearing
the evidence, the court ordered that Williams, who had
been under arrest since the shooting, be discharged on the
ground of justifiable homicide. This is the story behind the
story: Williams and Laird were the only ones present when
they got into the trouble, and the defendant was the only
person who could tell about the shooting. He testified that
he killed Laird after the latter had fired at him twice with
a pistol. The two men were apparently about ninety steps
apart when Williams fired upon Laird. Consequently, there
was no evidence produced at the trial to show this to be
true. Williams also claimed that he was near Laird when
the shooting occurred.

January 21

1900: Yadkin College Notes

The lead paragraph of this *Davidson Dispatch* article might shock readers today: "Vaccination is not at all popular among the people at this place. No one has had the operation performed." Isn't it strange that a "vaccination" was considered an "operation"? Other news from Yadkin College (which is a town that also had a college) also illustrated historical 1900 interests and activities. The Ciceronian Literary Society members hosted a meeting with Mr. T.S. Dale as speaker. Mr. Dale graciously donated to the society five dollars toward furnishing a room. Detailed reports of various sermons preached the previous Saturday and Sunday mornings filled the newspaper column. Topics for different ministers' talks included "Living" and "Suffering of Christ." One minister, Dr. Bays, reportedly preached with "suffusing power and eloquence, painting vivid pictures, using beautiful and fitting illustrations, and making comparisons that were apt and grand." He was touted as the best preacher Yadkin had seen for years.

January 22

1913: SELF-DEFENSE?

A coroner's jury convicted Robert L. Thomas of Thomasville of shooting and killing Roomie N. Stevens in Stevens's kitchen. Although Mr. Thomas was warned by the Davidson County coroner that any statement he might make could be held against him, he willingly took the witness stand. He did admit that he killed Stevens; however, he pled self-defense. It was testified that Stevens opened fire first, striking Thomas in the right cheek. Stevens then shot his wife in the left side. Thomas, who had been stunned by the force of the bullet entering his cheek and glancing off the cheekbone, arose and began shooting at Stevens, sending two bullets into his body and causing him to fall to the floor lifeless.

1908: FACTORIES WILL NOT STOP

Rumors were denied. Factories in Lexington and High Point would not be shutting down. There were many empty houses, and men made only fifty cents a day. This certainly indicated that times were extremely difficult with furniture people, but a front-page newspaper article assured readers that the report exaggerated the conditions. In fact, a reporter went to a furniture maker when the mill was closed for Lee's birthday and asked him "point blank" what the situation was. The furniture maker laughed and said, "I have grown used to dull springs. I have been through such times as this a dozen or more springs. People lost their nerve, that's all. You know yourself that business has been abnormal for several years. Now, after all these good seasons, when a dull time comes, it scares folks to death. It don't scare me." He continued by saying that, in his opinion, none of the shops would shut down. He predicted that by March, business would be "in full blast—with more orders than we could fill."

January 23

1908: The Trial Was Deemed a Warm Number

Mr. F.R. Loftin was tried before Squire Sidney Craver in the Davidson County Courthouse on the charge of obtaining money from William Lee under false pretense. Loftin was bound over to court on a justified bond of $350. The hearing this time had to do with $81, which Lee alleged that the defendant secured from him at different times in various denominations. Lee claimed that the defendant got from him the sum of $198 and paid back only $17. Reported in a regional newspaper on the front page, the story indicated that the trial was one of the most sensational minor affairs that had ever been held in Lexington. The grand-jury room was "packed to suffocation." William Lee swore that the beginning of his trouble occurred when he suspected a boy of stealing from him and took him and his money to the mayor to see if something could be done to correct the boy. The mayor, however, was not in his office, so Lee asked Mr. Loftin, who happened to be present at that time, to count the money. There was $100. The saga deepened. Lee testified that Loftin went to his house, collecting for Loftin and Harkey's Republican bank that paid 6 percent interest while the National Bank, a "Democratic" bank, paid only 4 percent. Then Ann Lee, wife of the plaintiff, claimed that some of the money was hers. The plaintiff said that when he demanded the money, the defendant claimed it "wasn't banking hours." Character witnesses testified for both parties. No resolution was reached.

January 24

1905: Exciting Case After Two Negro Desperadoes
When Policemen Heitman and Shoaf attempted to arrest two men, Nat Crump and Roscoe Eller, for retailing liquor, the action brought dire consequences. Crump, who lived in Boone township, and Eller, a resident of Midway, arrived in Lexington together. They brought with them a keg of liquor, and they began selling drinks on a back street. When the officers tried to arrest the two men, they were in their buggy and refused to stop at the officers' commands to halt. In fact, they reportedly whipped their horse into a gallop and left town. When they arrived at the public square, the policemen shot at the two bootleggers but missed. Finally, those same policemen secured horses and chased the men for about eight miles toward Winston. At one point, the fugitives left the main road and entered a thick wooded area. The officers dutifully followed, and the escapees fired shots. After the officers shot at the men, they were, in turn, fired upon. Mr. Shoaf received a buckshot in his left cheek, inflicting a slight wound. The two policemen gave up their chase after Shoaf was wounded. Warrants were issued against the two desperadoes. According to the news article, they were "desperate characters and no doubt intended to be killed rather than captured."

January 25

1905: HAS TWO WIVES

The "strange case" of Mr. R.F. Chitty, an employee of the Elk Furniture Company, "came to light" on this day. Chitty had two living wives. The facts were reported on the front page of a regional newspaper. About four years earlier, Chitty had been married to Miss Clementine Teague of Wallburg. They lived together about a year and then separated. Mrs. Chitty refused to live with her husband, according to a statement issued by the latter. In addition, Mr. Chitty testified that he had received a letter from his wife's father stating that she was dead and also asking for his help in defraying her funeral expenses. Truly believing his first wife was deceased, Mr. Chitty married Miss Maggie Conrad. The plot thickened when relatives of Mrs. Chitty No. 1 went to Lexington to notify her husband that she was alive and well. Upon learning that Mr. Chitty had remarried and was living with wife No. 2, the relatives, a brother and a brother-in-law of wife No. l, promised that a warrant would be taken out for Chitty at once, charging him with bigamy. Apparently, this threat was not carried through, but the confusion caused Chitty and wife No. 2 to separate. Chitty indicated he would seek a divorce from his first wife because of abandonment.

January 26

1910: YADKINVILLE LADY FALLS OR JUMPS IN WELL

The wife of ex-sheriff Kelly of Yadkinville either fell or jumped into the well at her home. She was rescued by her husband, Dr. T.R. Harding and Esquire John H. James within a few minutes. A page-one regional newspaper article indicated that Mrs. Kelly had been grieving for over three months over the fate of her daughter, who had become mentally incapacitated and placed in a Morganton hospital for treatment. This had resulted in Mrs. Kelly's inability to sleep, which supposedly caused her to become unbalanced from grief and worry. The men immediately drew her to the top of the well, but just as she was within reach, she let go. She would have fallen; however, Dr. Harding grabbed her. After she was carried into the house, she remembered nothing about the incident.

January 27

1908: FIGURE ON THIS

This reporting style was popular in the Piedmont Triad during the early part of the twentieth century:

> *"Say!" said Mr. Thomas Taylor, though he didn't know he was going to get in the paper by yelling at a reporter.*
>
> *"I spent Sunday at Yadkin College," he went on, "and there's a fellow up there who says he will furnish a horse and work for any man this year for a grain of corn a day if the man will double the number of grains each day. I don't remember the figures, but it will be interesting to figure on it."*

January 28

1920: Linwood Boy Injured by Dynamite Cap

Eight-year-old Raymond Monsees, the son of Mr. and Mrs. L.J. Monsees of Linwood, was painfully injured when a dynamite cap exploded in his right hand, blowing away a part of his thumb and forefinger. He also suffered from a slight wound in his breast. The boy, taken immediately to Lexington, was examined and treated by Dr. C.R. Sharpe. After his wounds were dressed, he was "getting along as well as could be expected." Upon investigation of the accident, reports indicated that the lad found the dynamite cap near a creek, perhaps left there by men who had been dynamiting fish. Raymond thought it was a cartridge of some kind. The explosion occurred when he began scraping the sand from the cap with his pocketknife.

January 29

1905: THESE MEN WERE FOOLED
Politics has always been an interesting subject, even back
in 1905, when the following paragraph appeared in a
Piedmont Triad newspaper:

> *If an election were held now, the Republican Party*
> *would not make any show at all in the county. The*
> *reason for this is plain and easy. They promised to*
> *give the people fifteen cents per pound for cotton if*
> *they would vote the Republican ticket. On the strength*
> *of this, hundreds of men voted the Republican ticket.*
> *These men were fooled. They had been promised fifteen*
> *cents for cotton and got only six and one-half cents for*
> *it. You can't fool all the people all the time.*

1955: MOTHERS' MARCH ON POLIO
Porch lights of Piedmont Triad homes were turned on from
7:00 to 8:30 p.m. as the Mothers' March on Polio swung into
operation with hundreds of ladies enrolled to take part in
the march. This was an integral part of the March of Dimes
campaign, seeking contributions to continue the fight against
dreaded polio, a disease that had struck so tragically in the
past years. With new preventatives and cures being developed
and perfected, many authorities felt that the time when polio
could be effectively controlled was fast approaching, but
much more money was needed to continue research and
carry out the preventative and curative methods already
developed and in the process of development.

January 30

1902: THIS DISEASE!

Mrs. W.R. Craig of Walkertown, Davidson County, was operated on for appendicitis at the Twin-City Hospital on this date. The front page of the *Winston Republican* reported the surgery in this way: "The prevalence of the disease is remarkable in point of number. That it can be successfully cured is a matter of gratification, and why it did not exist years ago or if it did by what name is doubtless a question of interest to medical science." The editor offers a possible hope to end this disease: "Perhaps it may run its course and cease to afflict humanity."

1908: FIRE AT NEW YWCA IN WINSTON

On this night, Miss Anna Castle of the National YWCA National Board went to Winston to see and approve the new headquarters, situated above a local hardware store. The women had hung heavy curtains to divide the one big room into more cozy areas and had also installed a small restroom and a kitchenette. Merchants and women of the community had donated furnishings, including a piano. All that good work was destroyed either by fire or water. The women did not let this little trick of fate divert them. With determination and tenacious spirit, they were offered new quarters on South Main Street in Gilmer Brothers' empty second floor.

January 31

1906: A REMINDER OF BYGONE DAYS

In other days, the skillful hands of men and women labored in many ways to supply the demands of their families for both food and clothing. In 1906, many of today's necessities were considered luxuries, and families had to practice the most rigid economy to purchase anything. Pins and needles were bought by weight and were precious articles. If one were, by some unlucky chance, lost, much time was given to hunting for it. Black thorns were often a substitute for pins in everyday clothing. Hooks and eyes had not yet been invented, and when the busy mothers could not take time to work eyelets in frocks so they could be laced, they used nature's pins, the black thorns. Country folks had their own styles, and they were not given to "sudden and mighty changes" with the passing of the seasons.

February 1

1910: "Treed" Officers Confiscate Corn Juice

While Policeman Hepler was "nosing along" the outskirts of a Greensboro thicket in search of "blind tigers" and whiskey repositories, he happened to catch a warm scent and heard a yelp that "would make a pack of hungry rabbit hounds green with every envy." His companion, Policeman McFarland, who was nearby, wondered what had happened to bring forth such an "unnatural" sound, so the two men began an investigation. Snugly hidden in the top branches of a small pine tree was a three-gallon jug of corn juice, while a short distance away, partially covered by dead branches and leaves, was a number of bottles ranging in size from a half pint to a quart. The two officers also found a measuring instrument that "showed signs of frequent and long use." But how would their find be removed from the tree? Hepler began his climb up the tree; however, being a large man, he became tangled in the branches and fell to the ground. Next, McFarland shinned up

Three-gallon jugs of illegal moonshine, or corn juice, and bottles of illegal whiskey were often hidden in trees, with leaves and dead branches partially covering them from investigating police officers. *Wikimedia Commons*.

the old pine tree, reached the jug and took a whiff of its contents. Carefully, this agile officer confiscated the jug and made his descent. Upon further investigation, the two policemen found the jug to contain "as pure an article of corn juice as Nick Williams ever labeled." Mr. Williams and his spouse were duly escorted to police headquarters, where the alleged retailer was languishing in default of a fifty-dollar bond on a charge of larceny that had been issued the night before.

1911: Hege Inn's "Paying Guests"
On February 1, 1911, Lucille Hege, who clerked at W.G. Penry's dry goods store and also taught in her mother's school, married Dr. Charles Meade Clodfelter. When he became ill, she opened her home for "paying guests." This was the beginning of Hege Inn, a well-known boardinghouse in Lexington that ran until Lucille's death on May 8, 1955. The Hege Inn served meals three times a day, seven days a week. All meals were family style. The food, served in big bowls on each table, encouraged the "all-you-can-eat" atmosphere. Sundays found regular boarders and townspeople waiting on the front porch or in the living room for the bell to summon them to their noon meal. After-church family dinners meant fried chicken, ham, fresh vegetables, homemade bread and fruit cobblers served a la mode. Elegant china and silver always graced each table. Lucille also enjoyed teas, showers and civic club meetings held in the inn's gracious parlor. Fresh flowers and starched organdy curtains complemented antique furnishings in each of the parlors. Lucille Clodfelter loved playing hostess to her guests.

February 2

1871: CALVIN WILEY'S CRUSADE FOR WINSTON'S FIRST PUBLIC SCHOOL

Calvin Wiley was not a seasoned salesman. Nonetheless, he embarked on this day on a crusade in his pulpit to start the first public school system in Winston. Wiley was a newcomer to Winston and a good Bible salesman. He understood the benefits of education, and he did not hesitate in advocating free schooling. As he put it, "It is the duty of every citizen in town to aid in the work of the establishment of the schools."

1910: SMALLPOX EPIDEMIC

The February term of Davidson County court was continued due to the prevalence of smallpox. While the disease had not reached any alarming proportions, numerous cases had been reported in Emmons, around Denton and Cid and in Boone, in the Horseshoe Neck at Hannah's Ferry. Thomasville had eleven cases, and there had been some talk of quarantines for Thomasville and High Point. Lexington had not seen a single case of smallpox on or before this date. Mr. Will Freedle and his family, however, had been quarantined because Mrs. Freedle had probably been exposed to smallpox during her recent visit to Thomasville. Some Piedmont Triad citizens had been vaccinated; in fact, schoolchildren received a mandatory vaccine. It was argued that health authorities should require everybody be vaccinated.

February 3

1976: ARRESTS

In Guilford County, fourteen persons were arrested on drug charges resulting from three weeks of diligent undercover work. Included in the fourteen was twenty-one-year-old Anne Karlen Shaw, daughter of Robert Shaw, a Guilford County commissioner and head of the state Republican Party. She was charged with selling and delivering LSD, according to police. A Guilford County grand jury handed down thirty-nine indictments, charging twenty-one persons with selling either marijuana, LSD, PCP or prescription-type drugs. Benjamin Earl Hargrave, twenty-seven, was jailed on AWOL charges after an FBI agent from High Point requested the help of police in taking the man into custody. Hargrave had been listed absent without leave from the U.S. Marine base at Camp Lejeune, North Carolina, since December 1, 1966.

February 4

1980: Welcome Holds Gymnastic Meet

Vogler's Studio of Dance and Baton in Welcome held its first gymnastic meet on this day. North Davidson girls jumped, bent, twisted and performed their difficult floor-exercise routines for the judges. Six-year-old April Jones won a first-place ribbon, as did eleven-year-old Jodi Martin and fourteen-year-old Lisa Hill, each in their individual divisions. A cheerleading team also won awards. An estimated five hundred contestants from several states participated in the big event. Performing was Vogler's award-winning Cheer Team. The contest was sponsored by Drum Majorettes of America and hosted by the East Burke County Bank Boosters.

February 5

1888: Gracious Gift to Yadkin College

Mr. William Thaw donated $500 to Davidson County's Yadkin College. According to Judge H.T. Phillips, the gift came about in this way: A Dr. Clarke, minister in the Methodist Protestant Church, traveled to Yadkin College to deliver the commencement address. Dr. Clarke influenced a friend of his in Pittsburgh, Pennsylvania, to donate a monetary gift to the college. William Thaw sent a check for $500. The Yadkin College community appreciated the generous gift from this kind and liberal man. Fast-forward twenty years. William Thaw's son, Harry K. Thaw, was tried for the murder of Stanford White. This caused local interest and remembrances of more than twenty years.

1913: Three Houses Entered by Very Bold Thieves

Burglars were very busy and extremely bold in west Lexington. They entered the home of Mr. W.R. Gallimore through his bedroom window and, without a peep, stole his watch and chain from his vest. They exited through the front door. They next went to Mr. Solomon Godfrey's home, where they again entered without awakening anyone. They took eight dollars from the pockets of Mr. Godfrey's trousers and also opened a trunk in his bedroom. Things didn't go so smoothly at the third house. The owner, Mr. Bob Disher, heard a noise, arose from his bed and chased the men. They escaped through an opened doorway and then forcefully slammed the door in Mr. Disher's face and shot at him. The ruckus prevented them from stealing anything at this house. Chief Hayworth immediately brought his bloodhound, but no trail was made; however, the dog of another officer followed a man to a tree and "treed" him. Burglars were reportedly becoming more and more frequent in the Piedmont Triad because so many men were out of work and had taken to "thieving to make a living."

February 6

1932: Younce and Brinkley Will Tell Truth
Davidson County sheriff James A. Leonard was accidentally killed by his own pistol while Solicitor George A. Younce of the twelfth judicial district struggled to wrest the gun from him after the sheriff had fired and wounded Neal Wimmer. Walter Foil Brinkley, Lexington lawyer and companion of Sheriff Leonard, and Solicitor Younce were expected to give testimony at a coroner's jury. Mr. Brinkley and Solicitor Younce said they would admit that they "lost their heads and attempted to conceal the sheriff's pistol."

1971: A Good Man Remembered
Mr. H. Cleveland Myers died at "the ripe age of 86." He and his three brothers and one sister had many descendants throughout the Piedmont Triad. All four brothers were farmers, but one, James, made local history by being the first known farmer of Davidson County to raise one

Corn crops in the early days of the Piedmont Triad were valued commodities, and it was not unusual for regional newspapers to report the number of bushels in a measured area. *Wikimedia Commons.*

hundred bushels of corn on a measured area. Cleveland had four children, fifteen grandchildren and eighteen great-grandchildren at the time of his demise. He had been the family historian and knew a great deal about western Davidson County families. For years, he served as a rural mail carrier. Cleve, as he was known, was a good husband and father, neighbor, friend and Baptist.

February 7

1908: REPUBLICAN CONVENTION AT GREENSBORO AND POLL TAX

The announcement came on this day that the Executive Committee of the state Republican Party met. The next state convention in Greensboro was scheduled for April 30 for the purpose of electing a chairman and a committee and for naming delegates to the Republican National Convention. It was further announced that the regular convention to nominate a state ticket would be held sometime during that summer. Interestingly, during the Executive Committee's meeting, members also informally discussed state prohibition issues but decided that they would "keep hands off." Prohibition must have been a hot topic in 1908 because another newspaper article on this same day announced that the election on prohibition had been changed again. The date would be May 26, which would make it necessary for voters to pay their poll tax to vote. If it had been held earlier, "many a man would have voted who will not do so now, on account of the poll tax."

February 8

1910: THE "JUICE" WILL BE TURNED ON

Lexington cotton mills were just about ready to receive the "juice" of the Southern Power Company, as four cotton mills would be operated by electric current. Wenonah No. 1 and No. 2 and Nokomis would be first. The new Dacotah, already connected with power lines, was scheduled to start next. Aldermen were discussing the pros and cons of contracting for the power to operate the town's water and light plant, but a page-one newspaper account indicated that no thorough investigation had yet been made. At the next meeting of the board, a representative of Tucker & Laxton, electrical engineers of Charlotte, would appear before the aldermen with a proposition. In addition, Lexington could buy the "juice" from the SPC at the rate of seven to ten cents per kilowatt, with the rate lowered if more power were needed. On this day, the town paid between four and five cents per kilowatt to make the power it needed, but the demands made were increasing daily. The town sold current to individual consumers at ten cents per kilowatt.

February 9

1976: Adlai E. Stevenson Speaks in High Point

Senator Adlai E. Stevenson III, Democrat from Illinois, spoke at High Point College at 8:00 p.m. in Memorial Auditorium. The public was invited to attend the free event. At that time, Stevenson was a member of the Committee on Banking, Housing and Urban Affairs and the Committee on Labor and Public Welfare. He was also chairman of the sub-committee on Migratory Labor. His political career began when he ran for the Illinois House of Representatives in 1964. Led by Stevenson, the Democrats swept the state election. As a result, all 118 candidates won elected offices. In the Illinois House, Stevenson had a key role in anti-crime legislation and lobby control. He was also active in legislation related to education, credit reform and civil rights. Accolades continued. He served four years as Illinois treasurer and then ran for the U.S. Senate in 1970. Efforts by President Nixon, Vice President Agnew and other Republican leaders failed to defeat Stevenson. According to one report, "his plurality was the second largest in Illinois history, surpassed only by his father's plurality in the 1948 gubernatorial elections."

February 10

1909: "Dixie" Stricken from the Program?

Disturbing gossip reached the Piedmont Triad on this day and made the front page of a regional newspaper. The song "Dixie" had been stricken from the program for Lincoln Day exercises in Chicago. "Somebody away down south in Dixie" wired a stinging telegram and asked if it were treason in Chicago to sing "Dixie" or play it. An answer came back in the form of a denial that the number had been taken from the program. This led to one tale concerning the history of the song. One old Federal soldier said when the news reached Washington that Richmond had fallen, a crowd rushed to the White House, headed by a band, and Lincoln appeared and spoke. In closing, he reportedly said he wanted to hear "Dixie," stating that it was now a national tune and might be regarded as captured property, the Confederacy having fallen. The band played it.

February 11

1902: YADKIN COLLEGE NEWS

Yadkin College (the school) reported a lively crowd of schoolboys on campus. They had done everything including carrying off a boy's wood pile, having "preaching" and dances, raising the town with a peculiar noise loud as thunder and stealing a bell clapper and hiding it under the bushes. Other news from Yadkin College (the town) indicated that the mayor's office and town hall were blown down. The following warning was issued: "When the Mayor fines them, the commissioners of our town will order the resurrection of the building." Looks like boys WILL play pranks!

1960: MARY LOU ANDREWS

Mary Lou Andrews was one of twenty-four students who wanted to do her part to end segregation in High Point. At four o'clock, Reverend Cox and Reverend Shuttleworth led the group on their march to the downtown Woolworth's. They went in the back door of the store, divided into groups and strolled toward various counters. Then the signal came. Reverend Cox doffed his hat, and the group hurried to the segregated lunch counter and took all available seats. The ones that were taken quickly emptied. Students began to do their homework. A waitress asked the group to leave, and then the police arrived. About that time, the lights went out, and an announcement rang out that the store was closing. The students left singing "We Shall Overcome."

Two ministers led a group of young people on their march to the High Point Woolworth's store, where everyone took a seat at the segregated lunch counter. They were asked to leave but stayed there quietly doing their homework. *Courtesy of the author.*

Even though the crowd that followed them pelted them with snowballs, they walked with their heads high back to their black neighborhood on Washington Street.

February 12

1902: BAD BOYS

Professor H.T. McKnight, who was conducting a science school at High Point until it was broken up by a scandal and a suit in 1901, was still living in Greensboro on this day. He was wanted in Ohio and Indiana, and "a man named Norris sent a photograph of him and said that a requisition would follow and that he had served a term in the Ohio penitentiary." On this day in 1902, McKnight continued to live in Greensboro and said that he had secured letters from the officials in the above states disclaiming any knowledge of Norris or of McKnight's imprisonment there.

Just across the Davie County line in Yadkin County, thirteen miles west of Mocksville, Will Kelly, about twenty-five, was found dead in the yard of the widow of Dr. Hunt. The deceased had one bullet hole in the back of his head and two in the shoulders. Will Martin, who fled the county with officers in pursuit, was charged with the killing "on account of family trouble."

February 13

1920: FLU TIDE STILL RISING

There were 864 cases of influenza reported in Davidson County, bringing the total to 2,686. Dr. Long said the influenza tide was still rising in the county and that around Thomasville, the situation was acute. There were some severe cases of pneumonia there. One nurse, Miss Campbell, stated that many of the influenza cases were clearing up but that the pneumonia cases were severe. With limited forces of nurses and volunteer workers, the Red Cross was rendering noble service, but "its hands were almost tied" in the face of the scourge—mostly for lack of proper cooperation. Professional and non-professional nurses, it seemed, could not be hired at any price. The Red Cross was attempting to persuade relatives and neighbors to take care of those near them because it was deemed absolutely necessary that relatives and neighbors assume their "rightful responsibility" for the care of those afflicted. One woman sent her two little children to the home of their grandparents so she could nurse her neighbors.

February 14

1872: WINSTON'S FIRST PERMANENT TOBACCO WAREHOUSE
This small frame structure was on the corner of Church and Third Streets, and on this date the "horn sounded at Winston's first permanent tobacco warehouse." Thomas J. Brown was the proud owner, and he probably agreed with the newspaperman who wrote these words in a comic style: "Any three ol' wimen 'tween the co't house and Nissen's shops kit smoke in their pipes all the 'backer as'd ever be sold in that thar house." Brown's motto was "honest dealing, close attention, and fair treatment to all."

1921: NO VALENTINES FOR THESE FOLKS
Robert C. Sink of Thomasville was sentenced in superior court to serve twelve months on the county roads "following his conviction for receiving imitation leather from the plant of the Thomasville Chair Company." Sink was released on bond by Judge T.B. Finley until the May term of court so that his defense story might be investigated. Judge Finley also heard the case of J. Bryant Gibson of Thomasville "and elsewhere," who had allegedly been involved in some "dramatic whiskey episodes" and had also skipped $1,000 bail. The judge sentenced him to two years on the county roads. The second man was Oscar Weaver, who was "caught red-handed" operating a moonshine still. He was found guilty and sentenced to twelve months on the county roads. No cards or boxes of candy for these folks on this unhappy Valentine's Day.

February 15

1904: THE COST OF SMALLPOX

The smallpox scourge in Davidson County cost $5,000, according to an official. The front page of a regional newspaper reported that the county got off comparatively light, as this was a small amount when compared with the amounts expended by many other afflicted counties. Newspaper reports indicated that everything possible had been done to stamp out and prevent the spread of the disease. Furthermore, the county's money had been handled by capable and efficient officers; every cent paid out had been wisely and judiciously expended. Sheriff T.S.F. Dorsett was also commended for the valuable services rendered to the afflicted and those persons under quarantine. He faithfully looked after their needs, and the public was reminded that his kindness would always be remembered.

February 16

1899: MAYODAN RECEIVES CHARTER

Mayodan, named after the converging Mayo and Dan Rivers, was chartered as an incorporated town with 225 residents. As recognized in *Ripley's Believe It or Not*, Mayodan was the only town in the world with that name. Earlier, when Samuel P. Test arrived at the village, he had found no church. Feeling the need for a place to worship, he held a worship service on the porch and yard of Higgins Boarding House. Later services were held in Ault's Drug Store.

1904: NO HOPE

A correspondent of the *Winston Republican* quoted the following statistics: "In the last election in this State, there were only 5,000 colored voters registered, and 3,000 of them voted the Democratic ticket. The Republicans polled 69,000 votes, 67,000 of which were obliged to have been cast by white men." The article goes on to say that there was a nice nucleus upon which to build a party and that there were many excellent men in the Republican Party in North Carolina—"as good men as there are in any party"—but that there was no hope for an organization that was not above trafficking in offices and quarreling over them and thinking that the chief end of man is to get a political job.

February 17

1904: ALLEGED COUNTERFEITERS

Mr. R.L. Burkhead, cashier of the National Bank of Lexington, learned that one or more $5 bills from the bank had been "raised" to $10. Authorities were at once notified, and as a result of the investigation, Walter Grubb, Joe Wilson and "Son" Burton, all of Yadkin College, were arrested by P.J. Ahern, a secret service officer, and Deputy Marshal B.F. Atkins. The men were charged with counterfeiting. Grubb was charged with raising the $5 bill to $10 and Wilson and Burton with circulating the "raised money." The three men were placed in the Lexington jail, and the next day, the trio was given a hearing before U.S. commissioner J.T. Hedrick. From the evidence, it was shown that Burton was innocent of any wrong intent in circulating one of the raised bills, and the government took a nolle prosequi in his case; consequently, Burton was released from custody. Some of the bills had been found between the leaves of a book in Grubb's house, and another witness testified that Grubb had given him one or more in payment of a debt. Joe Wilson had used one of the altered bills to purchase a gallon of liquor, sending Burton after the liquor and receiving $8.50 in change. Grubb and Wilson were bound over for trial at federal court. Grubb could not pay his $500 bond and was jailed. Wilson gave a $100 bond and was released.

February 18

1891: Normal and Industrial School in Greensboro
On this day, the North Carolina General Assembly passed "An Act to Establish a Normal and Industrial School for White Girls," creating the first public institution in the state to offer higher education to women. This institution of higher learning became North Carolina College for Women in 1919, Woman's College of the University of North Carolina in 1931 and the University of North Carolina at Greensboro in 1963.

1980: 4-H Talent Show at Arcadia
Many events and activities took place on this date. The annual 4-H talent show showcased fifteen members participating in a "Share the Fun" evening. A variety of excellent talent was in evidence, and all who took part were congratulated on their good performances at North Davidson High School. The Arcadia Choral Group, composed of fifteen members ranging in age from nine to fourteen years, performed with their red-white-and-blue motif. The singers gave an enthusiastic rendition of a medley of three patriotic songs, accompanied on the guitar by Bobby Leonard. Each member was awarded a blue ribbon, a treasured prize. Scott Leonard captured a first-place county winner's ribbon for his splendid rendition of a medley of Elvis Presley's favorites. Though Scott had just turned a "tender twelve," he reportedly looked all of fifteen or more with his white pants, blue satin shirt and slick black hair. Applause burst forth.

February 19

1915: AFTER THE TIGERS

Two Greensboro detectives and law-enforcement officers rounded up three notorious blind tigers: Roy Hayes, George Williams and Jule Tesh. This was nothing new for these bootleggers. In fact, Roy Hayes had not been off the chain gang very long. Judge Critcher, who had tried and sentenced him once before, was not inclined to be merciful and gave him two years on the roads—a year in each case. Jule Tesh, another old offender, had served time for selling booze, and he, too, met the same fate. He was given two long years on the gang. George Williams, facing Judge Critcher for the first time, got off lighter. Although he had previously served time for selling liquor long before this case came to court, Judge Critcher gave him six months. Notice of appeal was made in each case. Lawyers for the "sightless beast" planned to spend all their fury on the luckless detectives. Lawyers for the defendants criticized the two detectives for claiming to have evidence against the three, stating that they would "spring it" at court.

Convicted bootleggers were often sentenced by area judges to the "chain gang," where they were required to do manual labor such as building roads and digging ditches. *Library of Congress.*

February 20

1915: HORSE-STEALING CASE

Superior court convened with Judge C.C. Lyon presiding. Seemingly, the most interesting item of business concerned a horse-stealing case. Olin Varnadore and W.R. Young pleaded guilty, and each was sentenced to five years on the road. The circumstances behind the case proved more interesting than the guilty plea and sentences. It seems that Varnadore and Young "hired...the famous spotted pony named Mack" from Mr. W.F. Brendle and took him to the "wilds" of South Carolina, where they kept him for weeks, "awaiting to sell him." In a similar manner with a second attempt, Young, acting alone this time, stole a horse from Mr. J.E. Meredith. He, too, headed toward South Carolina, but he was arrested at the Piedmont Toll Bridge and taken back to Lexington. Sentencing for this horse theft was postponed; however, he did "draw his first five years" for his part in stealing Mack.

February 21

1915: They Read Aloud from Lawbooks

Mid-February proved to be an entertaining time for Piedmont Triad spectators to attend court, as the cases were varied and interesting. The Jennings-Goodwin case was no exception. T.J. Jennings, defeated Republican nominee for clerk of court, sought to oust Judge C.E. Godwin, the successful Democratic nominee, and take for himself the "very lucrative office" of clerk of the superior court of Davidson County. The case drew a big crowd. Jennings appealed from the decision of Commissioner McRae, in which he held that witnesses could not be compelled to give evidence that would tend to incriminate them. Reportedly, this ruling "practically wrecked the investigation" previously conducted because witnesses absolutely refused to answer questions. Attendees in court read aloud from lawbooks for about thirty minutes for the purpose of showing that "witnesses could be forced to testify and that the statute provided a full and general pardon for any wrong-doing admitted by the witness." The argument continued as Mr. E.E. Raper, attorney for Judge Godwin, argued that the statute provided a pardon only for illegal voting and not for illegal registration or perjury in getting his name on the registration books. The case was continued.

February 22

1910: Nip Locker Clubs in the Bud!
The monthly meeting of the Board of Aldermen was the most largely attended session ever held by that body. The room was filled with citizens on business, most of them interested in doing something that would head off a movement to set up a locker club in Lexington. Led by Dr. J.C. Leonard, a number of citizens asked that the aldermen pass some measure that would "nip the club in the bud," then and forever. Lawyers J.R. McCrary and Z.I. Walser discussed the law, which was determined at that time "not what might be called plain on the subject," and finally the board adopted an ordinance placing a tax of $5,000 per annum on locker clubs. Violations were punishable by a term of thirty days in prison. Interestingly, the measure first placed the tax at $3,000, but following a discussion, this amount was increased.

February 23

1913: LOAFERS THOUGHT THEY KNEW IT ALL

A big iron safe was being unloaded from a wagon on Main Street on this day, and half a dozen men strained and tugged at it. Their initial move toward getting it off the wagon "aroused the visibilities" of a dozen loafers, who prophesied disaster—"world without end." Crowding around with advice for the foreman, the loafers told him how foolish and reckless he was. He paid no attention to them, going about his business without a word. He apparently knew what he was doing because the skids did not break, the safe did not tilt over and no one was crushed to death. In fact, the task was completed satisfactorily to everybody except the loafers. They walked away sorrowful, still muttering that although no accident had occurred, the job had not been done correctly.

February 24

1904: DON'T KILL THE BIRDS

A heartfelt plea was sent out to citizens of the Piedmont
Triad from Farmer, North Carolina. The writer notified
the reading audience that wild birds had become scarcer
every year and soon many species of birds would be
exterminated if the "present rate of slaughter" continued.
The plea came from a man who remembered being a boy
forty years earlier, when fields and forests were literally alive
with birds. When the ice and snows of winter had melted
away, the birds came like a "mighty host against the insect
tribes of earth." On this day in 1904, newspaper readers
were informed of damaged cotton crops by the boll weevil
and other insects. How would farmers grow crops without
the birds that were created to destroy and hold in check
those "enemies of the farm"?

February 25

1895: SHARP WORDS WERE SPOKEN BEFORE TROUBLE
OCCURRED

Baxter Shemwell, the son of a prominent Tyro doctor, became involved in a dispute with a local physician, Dr. R.L. Payne. "Sharp words" had been exchanged over the previous weekend between the two men. The next thing the Lexington townspeople saw was Mr. Shemwell walking up and down Main Street with a shotgun on his shoulder. Someone notified Mrs. Shemwell, and she arrived at the scene and "begged and pleaded" with her husband to return to his business. Shemwell obliged, but he then decided to walk to his home, and in doing so, he came up behind Dr. Payne and his son, who were then walking down Main Street. Baxter Shemwell caught up with the father and son, took out a large Colt pistol and fired into Dr. Payne's body. Shemwell was grabbed by officers and taken away. Dr. Payne died from his injuries. After many hours of deliberation, the jury went along with Baxter Shemwell's plea of self-defense and found him not guilty.

1913: ANTI-FLY CAMPAIGN

Mr. J.J. Peacock of Lexington Upholstery Company announced on this day that he was starting an anti-fly campaign. With a fifty-dollar personal investment, he pledged to give fifty cents per 1,000 for all flies delivered to him at his office during the month of March. He further announced that the month of March was when the destruction of one fly meant the diminishing of the total number of flies in the season by more than 200. He elaborated further with statistics: if he got his 100,000 flies in March, there would be 10,000,000 fewer flies than there would have been had his campaign not been started. No, he would not count the flies brought to him; he would weigh the first thousand brought to his office and compute the number of the others brought by the weight so obtained.

February 26

1913: LOWE CROUSE WAS HIRED OUT

Lowe Crouse was considered one of the best blacksmiths but a "chronic troublemaker in his home." He was sent to jail on the charge of quarreling and fighting with his "better half." Judge Justice arranged for a gentleman in the eastern part of the state to give Lowe a job, so the judge "hired him out" for a period of two years on condition that he was to stay away from his family and send his wife half of his wages every two weeks. For a short time, he did fulfill the court conditions. But at this date, he had arrived back home "due to a death in his family," he claimed. The trouble was that he stayed home, not returning to the job arranged for him. Judge Justice would decide later in the week what would transpire next; however, the news report indicated that he might be sent to the roads.

February 27

1905: WEDDING OF KATHARINE SMITH AND R.J. REYNOLDS

On this Monday morning at 7:15, Maxie, Irene and little Ruth, sisters of Katharine, stood in their parents' living room. All three girls were dressed in their best wool dresses, stockings and Sunday school shoes. It was not long before the girls announced their visitor's arrival. R.J. Reynolds's buggy had already reached the end of their road. Inside the Smith home, vases filled with long-stemmed American Beauty roses, sent earlier by the groom, lined the steps. Katharine slowly descended the flight of stairs, holding herself erect as a queen; the sparkle in her blue eyes proclaimed her happiness. She wore a two-piece blue outfit she had designed and sewn. The blouse had long shirred sleeves, and the skirt, which accentuated a waist no larger than twenty-three inches, was adorned with lace, silk and chiffon. A fashionable beaver hat completed her ensemble. When she reached the bottom step, R.J. extended his hand to escort his bride into the living room, where at eight o'clock, they pledged their vows before those gathered.

1980: ALLEGED PROSTITUTION RING

Today marked the second time that a grand jury considered allegations by the FBI that the Trucker's Motel on Interstate 85 was involved in interstate prostitution. FBI Agent Roger Schweickert, who had participated in a search of the motel, appeared before the grand jury at an earlier date to acquaint them with the FBI's investigation.

Persons subpoenaed during the search—both men and women—appeared in Greensboro for questioning by the grand jury. They had allegedly been connected at different times with the motel. Willie Dean Gibson of Winston-Salem owned the motel. A few defendants worked at the motel; they were listed as Willie Dean Gibson of Winston-Salem and Olive Sherman, Kenneth Justice and Donald Whitt, all of Davidson County. Justice rented the motel from Gibson, according to one newspaper account. A sign outside the motel advertised in-room X-rated movies. The women who appeared at the courthouse were alleged to have been prostitutes at the motel.

February 28

1980: HIGH POINT MAN GUILTY OF ARMED ROBBERY
A jury in Davidson County Superior Court found a High Point man guilty of armed robbery of a Thomasville restaurant. Judge Julius A. Rousseau Jr. sentenced Richard Anthony Hoot to forty years in prison for the robbery of the Pizza Hut in Thomasville. Wilson O. Weldon Jr., Hoot's attorney, requested leniency in sentencing Hoots, but Rousseau said, "I tend to take a dim view of anyone convicted of armed robbery." Before Hoots was sentenced, Weldon asked Rousseau if he would hear some comments privately about Hoots from High Point policeman James Bowers. Rousseau agreed, and Bowers was permitted to approach the bench and speak in whispers to Rousseau. Hoots's main defense was that he was sick at home the night that the restaurant was robbed, but restaurant employee Shirley Karen Ruark of Greensboro testified that she saw Hoots commit the robbery. She testified that Hoots held a pistol on her during the robbery.

March 1

1905: One Fell in the Fire, and Another Was Bitten by a Mad Cat

In 1905, front-page news for regional newspapers covered just about every situation. This day was no exception. Mrs. Joe Ellis, who was standing in front of an open fireplace at her home in Silver Hill township, suddenly felt ill and fainted, falling into the fire. She was so badly burned that she was not expected to recover. Her hair, left arm, side and one side of her face were terribly burned. Her husband was asleep in the room at the time of the accident but knew nothing about it until his wife regained consciousness, crawled from the fire and awakened him. Another Piedmont Triad woman met with tragedy on this same day. Mrs. Minnie Layden was bitten by a cat that medical personnel pronounced "mad." Mrs. Layden was in her home when the cat suddenly sprang at her, jumping a distance of several feet, and sank its teeth into the fleshy part of her thumb. The cat was declared "mad" by the Pasteur Institute at Baltimore. Mrs. Layden decided not to travel to the institute for treatment because she said her thumb had almost healed and she had felt no ill effects from her terrible experience.

1981: *Red November, Black November*

The premiere showing of the film *Red November, Black November* was held at a theater in the Greensboro Coliseum complex. The film was about the November 3, 1979 events in which a group of Klansmen and

Nazis opened fire on a Communist-sponsored anti-Klan demonstration in a Greensboro housing project known as Morningside Home. Five were killed and nine wounded. Over two hundred people showed up for the premiere of the film.

March 2

1863: Historic Rockford

On this date in Rockford, a Civil War battle called the Bond School House Shootout occurred. Rockford became a busy little town. Mark York opened and ran the ever-popular York Tavern, providing a place for the gentlemen who came to Rockford to engage in conversation while they enjoyed their evening toddy. The Grant-Burrus Hotel was subsequently built, and the owner liked to tell visitors that the logs used in building the hotel's stable came from the torn-down office of Andrew Jackson. Jackson often rode horseback from Tennessee to attend circuit courts in Rockford and had a law office across the street from the hotel.

1905: H. Clay Grubb Case Moved

After hearing affidavits on this day for and against the contention that the state could not get a fair and impartial trial in Davidson County of H. Clay Grubb for the murder of O.L. Davis, Judge Bryan ordered the case removed to another county. The judge decided that since the homicide, Grubb had not been treated as a person who had been charged with a crime. He had been allowed freedom in the corridor of the jail, where he entertained a number of visitors and friends. Strangely enough, he also had a stenographer and typewriter. Furthermore, he kept quantities of "spirituous liquors" in the jail. He was also allowed to bring in water and coal with the jail door unlocked and without the presence of a jailer, and he was privileged to eat with the jailer's family. In other words, no conveniences or luxuries had been denied him. Through his friends and agents, he had canvassed the county for the purpose of molding public sentiment and hopefully securing a jury that would not convict him, regardless of the evidence against him.

March 3

1904: A DAVIDSON DIVORCE CASE

The *Greensboro Telegram* published an exciting and true story related by Mr. G.S. Bradshaw to a circle of brother lawyers. Mr. Bradshaw said he had instituted a suit for divorce in which his client presented his evidence in a timely manner. On the first day of his hearing, the client appeared with a well-known squire as his witness. All went well until the client showed up when the court bell rang but had obviously taken several drinks of "the ardent" and was told to go to his room to "sober up" before court convened the next morning. When morning came, the client again appeared "loaded for bear." Again his attorney told him he could not go into the courtroom in that drunken state. The attorney told the squire, "For Heaven's sake, Squire, take this man to his room and lock him up until tomorrow morning and get him sober." The next day, the client was so drunk he "could scarcely bat his eyes." The attorney advised the squire to take him home and return the next week. Instead of his return came the following letter:

> *Dear Sir: I drop you these few lines to let you know that I am very poorly and threatened with newmonia* [sic]. *I took deep cold while in Greensboro last week. I drop you these lines to tell you that I won't be there. That woman was buried yesterday. Tell the jedge* [sic] *God has done the work and I won't trouble the court any further. Yrs. Happily.*

March 4

1904: He Recovered Only Thirty-seven Cents

S. Goodman, formerly of Lexington, entered suit against the Western Union Telegraph Company for damages on account of failure of said company to make prompt delivery of a message from Goodman, who was in Baltimore at the time, to his Piedmont Triad attorneys, Walser and Walser in Lexington. The case was heard in Rowan Superior Court. Judge Allen decided that Goodman was entitled to recover only thirty-seven cents, the toll paid the company. As Goodman had sued for $1,000, he undoubtedly was not happy with his recovery.

Suing the Western Union Telegraph Company for failure to make prompt delivery was extremely rare in the Piedmont Triad, but it did happen. *Library of Congress*.

1912: HER CLOTHING WAS IN FLAMES

Mrs. Sallie Thomas of Thomasville was burned on this cold March morning. Her maid had built a fire in Mrs. Thomas's bedroom and then assisted her from her bed to a chair by the fire. The maid left the room, and soon everyone in the household heard Mrs. Thomas's screams. Her son, Charles R. Thomas, his wife and the maid rushed to the elderly Mrs. Thomas's bedroom to find her clothing in flames. Her son grabbed one of her blankets from her bed and wrapped it around her body. With the help of Charles's wife and the maid, they were able to smother the flames that had spread to her bedclothes. But they were too late. Mrs. Sallie, who had heart problems, possibly died from shock before she had time to suffer from the flames. Charles was severely burned with "the flesh on one of his hands roasted to the bone." Both Charles and the maid also suffered burns to their feet.

March 5

1910: COMMISSIONERS TRANSACT IMPORTANT BUSINESS

The Board of Davidson County Commissioners decided to purchase land and erect a new County Home. The call for bids went out to citizens who might have land they would sell for this purpose. Another item of business concerned claims amounting to $434.00 for monthly smallpox expenses in Thomasville. Of these claims, $225.00 was allowed. Dr. Buchanan's claim for vaccinating, quarantining, etc. for the month amounted to $33.75. Dr. Peacock had a similar claim for $22.50 and Dr. Monk for $15.75. In another unrelated item of business, the county did not hold itself responsible for damages caused by crossing the bridge across Abbott's Creek at Feezor's Mill even though said bridge was considered unsafe for heavy traffic.

March 6

1917: TROUBLE AT THOMASVILLE

Archibald Johnson, John Lambeth, W.G. Hinkle and J.A. Morris, four members of the Davidson County School Board, expressed concern and dissatisfaction with the internal management of the Boys Rock School in Thomasville. Professor J.N. Hauss had been the superintendent of the city schools for nearly fourteen years, and he had watched the number of students grow each year from fewer than two hundred to more than seven hundred in the white school. Criticisms had arisen from some of the parents whose children were pupils in the school. This resulted in five boys being called up and questioned by Judge MacRae as to their motive in secreting themselves near the street and throwing rocks where Professor Hauss passed by one night. The boys said they had not intended to injure the professor but wanted only to "scare him and have a little fun." The judge told the boys he would let them go "for this time but that if such a thing occurred again, they would get a jail or road sentence." The young fellows left the courtroom humbled in manner.

March 7

1917: PASSENGER STATION TO BE BUILT

Thanks to the efforts of George W. Mountcastle and H.B. Varner, the Southern Railway Company decided to build an up-to-date passenger station to be located south of the present station, on the site where the baggage room stood. This station would be modern in every respect, and plans were being prepared by the railway company's architect. An inspection of the old station several weeks earlier had indicated the need for a station that would meet the needs of the future and assured the press that people would be delighted with the Southern's handsome new home.

Not all newspaper reporting on this day was centered on business projects. An announcement was made about a spring revival campaign at the Methodist church. The evangelistic party, consisting of Reverend T.P. Jimison, preacher, and Mr. and Mrs. Bassett, soloist and pianist, respectively reported they would like to "find a cottage and do light housekeeping during their stay." Mr. and Mrs. Bassett were reported to be "especially fine" as conductors. They would use the Billy Sunday songbook, *Songs for Service*.

March 8

1917: ELKS' FAIR A SUCCESS
Although the weather conditions proved unfavorable, the first performance of the Elks' Fair was given before a crowd that packed to capacity the grade school auditorium. Mr. Cliff DeLapp and Miss Lois Williams were the country bride and groom. Approximately 150 performers took part during the first evening.

1940: FORECLOSURE NOTICES FOR TAXES
Hundreds of foreclosure notices for Davidson County taxes for the year 1937 were served by deputies. Between six hundred and seven hundred names and amounts for foreclosure were turned over to the office of County Attorney P.V. Critcher for the foreclosure action required under the tax laws of the State of North Carolina, and it was expected that the grand total would amount to about $1,000.

March 9

1910: Daniel Boone Day

Mr. J.R. McCrary, Esquire, of Lexington was untiring in his efforts to perpetuate the memory landmark "for all time" the North Carolina home of Daniel Boone, "the greatest of all trappists and hunters." Mr. McCrary intended to emphasize the importance of preserving not only Daniel Boone's memory but also the history of the area. According to a regional newspaper report, this dedicated chairperson called on the general public to donate any Revolutionary relics such as money, arms or "whatnot." He believed the big celebration, to be held at the old home of the "mighty hunter," should be "the greatest gathering held in this section of North Carolina for many year." Judge Pritchard was scheduled to make the historical address, and other prominent persons were on the agenda as speakers.

Daniel Boone was called the "mighty hunter" and "the greatest of all trappists and hunters." It was important to preserve Boone's memory in connection with Piedmont Triad history. *Library of Congress.*

March 10

1914: Bad Piedmont Triad Roads Cause Unusual Problem
Mr. T.G. Kindley, well-known farmer to Davidsonians and especially to everyone in the Conrad Hill township, related his true story of his having two bushels of fine wheat, for which he was offered $135, delivered to Swing Brother's Mill not far from his home. However, it so happened that the roads were in such condition that hauling was an imposed liability, and he could not deliver the grain. When the roads dried up, he took his two bushels of wheat to Lexington and sold it to Grimes Brothers for $100. Mr. Kindley estimates his "bad roads tax" was $35, plus the cost of hauling his six thousand pounds of wheat considerably farther. He figured that would have paid his road tax for several years; therefore, he admitted he wholeheartedly looked forward to paying the recently voted road tax.

March 11

1914: STRIKE TWO
Mr. Fletcher Cowans, from Denton, was arrested for disturbing public worship during the progress of the Ham revival. Tried before the recorder for disturbing public worship, his "rowdyism" cost him $90. A later warrant was sworn out charging him with selling liquor, and he was subsequently placed under bond of $500 for his appearance at trial. He skipped, and his bond was declared forfeited.

1940: SPICY AND SAUCY
Bill Sharpe, a "shamelessly independent publisher and editor," and his comrades named their new weekly publication Thursday, which made its initial debut at Winston-Salem, and articles were touted as being "spicely [*sic*] and saucily" in tone. Reportedly, the style of the paper was to "cut loose" in any news or feature item with all the editorial flavor the writer might desire to incorporate. Furthermore, readers were advised: "A fellow has to watch his steps or else he will find more tender toes under his brogans than he could imagine might exist in one community of size of North Carolina's second largest city."

March 12

1914: HE KNEW HOW TO KEEP A SECRET

Word reached the regional Piedmont Triad newspaper that Mr. John McCrary was the best man "in that part of the country" to keep a secret. A personal friend, current neighbor and old schoolmate of many, he and Miss Craver of Enterprise married the day before Christmas but "kept quiet about their union until this day in March." In fact, according to reports, Mr. McCrary was so quiet about their marriage that when the news of the issuance of the marriage license reached the newspaper, his initials were not recognizable. Upon the formal announcement, Mr. McCrary reportedly appeared to be "seemingly as glad that he is married as the rest of us are."

March 13

1919: ERLANGER MAN CONVICTED OF RETAILING
Two charges of retailing intoxicating liquor were brought
on this day in Recorder's Court against W.M. McIntosh,
who operated a café and drink stand at Erlanger. Judge
Moyer rendered a verdict of guilty in one case and charged
the defendant $150 and cost and $50 and cost in the other.
Appeal was taken for trial in superior court. The defendant
was placed under bond for his appearance at the next term.

1940: BIG EASTER-EGG HUNT WITH ONE IMPORTANT RULE
Special permission was granted by Lexington city officials
to the Carolina Theatre and Belk's Department Store
for an old-time Easter-egg hunt in the city park near the
swimming pool. One thousand candy Easter eggs were
hidden in every nook and corner by employees of Belk and
the Carolina. Many prizes were offered to the children who
found the most eggs, as well as those who found "golden"
eggs. However, there was one rule: the hunt was for "boys
and girls not over ten years of age."

March 14

1919: Local All-American Football Hero

When he graduated from the local high school in 1915, J.H. Ripple entered A&E College. Having made a splendid record in high school basketball, he entered at once into and made good with college basketball. The most remarkable point about his athletic career, however, was that despite the fact when he entered college he hardly "knew what a football was," he distinguished himself in that branch of athletics. The February 1919 issue of the *State College Alumni News* noted the following: "For the first time in the history of athletics here, we have placed a man on Walter Camp's All-American football team. The Dean of Football bestows the signal honor upon J.H. Ripple by picking him for one of the tackle positions on his All-American second team." Camp further commented, "Ripple is the best tackle in the South and in a class by himself."

March 15

1781: THE BATTLE OF GUILFORD COURTHOUSE

Major General Nathanael Greene gathered his 4,400 Patriots in the early morning hours. The battle that took place that day has since gone down in history as a pivotal event in the Revolutionary War's southern campaign. General Greene knew that an effective strategy would be of utmost importance against the trained and disciplined redcoats, he decided on a plan that consisted of organizing the Patriots into three lines. General Greene ordered all North Carolina militia to the first row and commanded them to "fire two volleys and then fall back to the second line." He continued, "Virginia militia, it will then be your turn to fire at the Red Coats." The final order was extremely important: "After you men on the second line fire, everyone must drop back to the third line where the trained soldiers of the Continental army will then fire the Grasshopper Guns, our four six-pound cannon." The redcoats began their advance. Cornwallis ordered his men to charge and fire. Although many Americans and British were killed, the Patriots halted their advance. General Greene's soldiers left the battlefield. The redcoats won the actual battle for the British, but the price was costly—93 men died on the field and 440 received wounds or were reported missing. The Patriots' tally indicated that 79 men died and 185 sustained wounds.

Major General Nathanael Greene and his Patriots went to battle. With Greene's effective strategy, he ordered his men to charge fire on the redcoats. *Wikimedia Commons*.

March 16

1919: Spruell Plans Reception for Soldiers

At an important meeting held at the courthouse, Mr. J.F. Spruell, chairman of the Lexington chapter of the Red Cross, called for a meeting for the purpose of planning a celebration for the soldiers and sailors who would soon be returning from camps and overseas. At this meeting, the group unanimously decided that some steps should be taken to provide the proper reception and entertainment. In order to get the movement started, Spruell appointed a committee of seven men, himself ex-officio chairman, whose duty it should be to take charge of the celebration, work out plans and possibly call another meeting in which to study plans for assisting men discharged from the service to facilitate readjusting themselves to civilian life. Reverend R.E. White announced that he had already begun working on various plans.

March 17

On its front page, the *Winston-Salem Journal*—which had given prominent publicity to the campaign for a county bond issue of over $37 million but had been careful not to take a side—ran an article stating that the bonds apparently did not have a chance. The *Journal* then rejoiced that a majority of those who went to the polls passed a $24 million bond issue for school building over a period of years and a few more million to provide a water system for the county. It was believed the county had good luck because so many folks stayed at home and did not vote.

March 18

1919: TELEPHONE LINEMAN FALLS THIRTY-FIVE FEET

Mr. Gerald Methvin, telephone lineman, fell from a telephone pole about thirty-five feet to the ground. He struck the pavement below. He had climbed a pole in front of Smith's Drug Store and then "took hold of a live wire." Immediately, he called below for someone to cut off the current. He broke loose from the wire, most likely before the current had been cut off, and fell. His greatest injury appeared to be over his left eye, and he also received a possible skull fracture. At once, Dr. C.R. Sharpe was called to the scene to provide medical attention to Mr. Methvin. Close relatives were notified immediately.

March 19

1919: AMAZING RED CROSS PRODUCTION

Mrs. J.G. Penry announced the "Production Order" of 60 pairs of pajamas for the American Red Cross. Her sincere thanks went out on page one of the *Lexington Dispatch* as she acknowledged with gratitude the following citizens who had worked so diligently to complete this much-needed order: Mesdames W.G. Penry, C.C. Hargrave, W.H. Mendenhall, John Hankins, Sam Finch, Charles Young and E.S. Long. When the group appeared to be behind schedule, Mrs. Charles Young, who was in charge for that day, brought her "workmen" with her: Mesdames Earl Holmes, L.M. Barksdale, Clem Hargrave, W.G. Penry, John Hankins, D.L. Brinkley, Fred Sink, L.F. Weaver, Cliff Pickett, E.S. Long, Dan Philips, Joe Cecil, M.R. Shoaf, John Bower, John B. Wright and Amanda Davis. This crew managed to sew fifteen pairs of pajama pants and ten pajama coats. The next project of these Piedmont Triad women is to complete 120 children's nightgowns in one week.

Women in the Piedmont Triad worked diligently to sew needed garments for the American Red Cross's drive to supply pajamas to soldiers serving their country. *Library of Congress.*

March 20

1919: RED CROSS REQUESTS USED CLOTHING

A front-page newspaper plea called for a weeklong collection of used clothing, shoes and bedding for the "helpless refugees" in Allied countries. This need of clothing in many lands was one of the most serious reconstruction problems, but it was expected that a big step toward solving it would be taken when thousands of Red Cross chapters through the Piedmont Triad began their collection of discarded garments. The Lexington chapter organized for this campaign with Mrs. J.V. Moffit as director. In turn, Mrs. Moffit appointed captains for the four wards of the city. These ladies called on all local citizens, and every type of garment for all ages and both sexes was sought.

March 21

1952: EXECUTION DATE SET FOR JOHN ANDREW ROMAN

John Andrew Roman was found guilty and sentenced to death for the murder of Beulah Mill Hinshaw. Roman had left the ice plant where he worked and gone to Hinshaw's house, according to newspaper accounts. After cutting through a screen door to gain entrance into the house, Roman struggled with sixty-five-year-old Hinshaw, who apparently ran into the backyard. Roman stabbed and raped her and returned to the ice plant about 11:30 p.m. Based on circumstantial evidence, Roman was charged with the murder, but he maintained his innocence. He appealed his conviction to the state supreme court, but the appeal was denied.

1956: ELVIS GYRATES FOR PIEDMONT TRIAD AUDIENCE

He wasn't even supposed to perform for the Lexington Civitan Club. Eddy Arnold had cancelled, so this unknown singer, Elvis Presley, would substitute. And substitute he did. Having just turned twenty-one, the press called him the "whirlwind that blew into Lexington." His appearance at the Lexington YMCA was complete with his intricate motions and caressing and making love to his guitar as he swirled his hips, along with adults' accusations of his "selling sex with cold, deliberate calculation." Mothers in the audience were shocked.

March 22

1898: For Robbing the Mails

From Winston-Salem came the announcement that W.P. Firey, for three years mail agent on the Norfolk and Western Railroad, was before U.S. commissioner Martin on the charge of stealing a registered letter containing $50 in currency from a mail bag. During the hearing, a large number of witnesses were examined. Dr. Fulp, postmaster at a "catcher" mail station, testified that it was his money and that he had put it in the pouch. The defendant testified that the letter was not in the pouch and that it was cut when he received it. Firey admitted that he made good $11 while in the post office service several years earlier. He explained that he had lost a registered letter containing that amount. Firey was bound over to court and his bond set at $500, which he gave.

On this same day, Reed's Academy's closing graduation ceremonies drew students, teachers, parents and well-wishers. The valedictory, by Mr. Albert Evans, was very touching and well delivered.

Author's note: *Research always reveals unknown family facts. Albert Evans was my paternal grandfather.*

March 23

1824: LEXINGTON BECAME THE PERMANENT COUNTY SEAT
Twenty-five or thirty lots in Lexington were sold on March 23, 1824. Three founders and first builders deeded for the benefit of the county twenty-five acres in Lexington, the consideration being fifty cents. From the sale of this land, a fund was raised to build a courthouse and a jail.

1906: NO HARM WOULD FOLLOW
Anderson Moyer, an old man who drove a hack in Winston, was waiting at the depot for a train. He happened to doze off with a fifty-cent piece in his mouth. When someone ran up shouting the train was coming, it awoke Moyer suddenly and frightened him into swallowing the money. He became extremely anxious about the effects until a medical doctor assured him that no harm would follow.

March 24

1906: THE SOUTHBOUND RAILWAY WILL BE BUILT

A front-page article assured Piedmont Triad citizens that the Southbound Railway would be built. Mr. O.H.P. Cornell, the chief engineer of the Southbound Railway, and Colonel Charles H. Blair, a New York attorney, visited Lexington. Mr. Cornell said positively that the railroad would be built and that work would begin immediately. The contracts for $80,000 of work at the Winston end of the road had been issued. If "foreign capitalists" could not be interested, the road would be built by "home folks." In Winston, a $500,000 construction company was organized. Mr. George W. Montcastle, president of the Bank of Lexington, was one of the directors. With the $875,000 of bonds voted by the people "along the road," it appeared that the railroad would definitely be constructed. These bonds would not expire, so hope was high for the project.

1914: ERLANGER COTTON MILLS COMPANY OPENS

The production of cloth began for the BVD Company. Officers and superintendents arrived to fill various advertised jobs, obligations and responsibilities. Laborers came from all over the Piedmont Triad to work on the production. While houses sprang up for married men and their families, single males also needed a place to live. Mill officials opened a boardinghouse at 38 Mill Street. The men (and, later, women) stayed for extended periods for a nominal weekly fee, which provided a place to sleep, a shared bathroom and hearty family-style breakfasts and supper five days a week in the large dining room. In addition, boarders received a brown-bagged dinner (noon meal in the South) of sandwiches to take to the mill to enjoy when the whistle blew for their lunch break.

March 25

1786: LITTLE RED MAN

A shoemaker, Andreas Kresmer, was killed while digging a new foundation for an addition to the Brothers' House in Old Salem Village, Winston-Salem. Late one night, a huge chunk of dirt toppled on Brother Kresmer and smothered him. Years after this horrible accident, the building became a home for Moravian widows. The story goes that one day, a deaf child went to visit her grandmother, who lived at the widows' home. Although Little Betsy could not hear, she could speak. She apparently did not know the story of the resident ghost. Little Betsy rushed inside from the garden and told her grandmother about a little man in a red cap who had motioned for her to join him in play.

The early Moravian village in Old Salem had a building called the Brothers' House, and it was here in 1786 that Brother Andreas Kresmer was killed when a huge chunk of dirt toppled onto him.

March 26

1906: Bridge Breaks Down Under Team

Mr. A.D. Kinney, a Confederate soldier and a well-known farmer, had quite a dangerous experience, but he luckily escaped with his life. He was crossing the Flat Swamp Creek bridge when some timbers gave way and "precipitated horses, wagon and driver" into the creek fifteen feet below. The water was about four feet deep. Mr. Kinney was thrown clear of the wagon and timbers but escaped unhurt. Nearby people went to Mr. Kinney's assistance. The team was also removed from the water. It was deemed "nothing short of a miracle that the driver and horses were not killed."

1956: Blue Laws Amended

This new ordinance pertained to service stations only and permitted them to stay open at all times except for five specified hours on Sundays. Under the new law, all service stations must be closed on Sundays from 9:30 a.m. until 12:30 p.m. and from 7:00 p.m. until 9:00 p.m. The stations were allowed to remain open at all other hours, while the previous ordinance had permitted them to be open from 12:30 p.m. until 7:00 p.m.

March 27

1906: Free If It Fails

Mr. Welborn of the Lexington Drug Company was asked by a regional newspaper reporter how he could back his claim that Vinol was proven to bring satisfactory results. The pharmacist backed his claim with the following guarantee: "If Vinol were a patent or a secret preparation, it would be another thing, but it is not. Everything it contains is named on the label." Mr. Welborn went on to explain that Vinol was the up-to-date version of cod liver oil, which had been touted for centuries as the "grandest of all bodybuilding agents for wasted body strength and vitality." This claim was backed by Lexington Drug Company to refund consumers' cost if the product did not provide satisfactory results. Vinol was guaranteed to tone up the digestive organs, make rich red blood and create strength.

March 28

1906: THIS AND THAT FROM WINSTON-SALEM AND BEYOND
A twenty-two-year-old hen died in Winston-Salem, and although it is said she refused to lay eggs on Sundays, she had managed to produce in her twenty-two years more than seven thousand eggs.

George Richmond was locked up in Winston for a supposed attempt to poison his better half. He sprinkled some sort of powder over her food at a meal. When it was analyzed, it was found to be harmless, so Mr. Richard was released.

Not all the news from the Piedmont Triad on this day was quirky and whimsical. An announcement was made that the Kennedy Public School House closing would be followed by another closing at Enterprise Academy. Both institutions of learning planned public entertainment, addresses, band music and exhibitions on various occasions to commemorate the schools.

1956: TROUBLE, TROUBLE, TROUBLE!
Ray Wright Jr., a High Point man who pretended to be a doctor after he was picked up with a physician's bag stolen from a doctor's car parked at Lexington Memorial Hospital, had recently pleaded guilty to a larceny charge in county court. Since the bag represented a value of over $200, Wright was bound over to superior court for trial. Judge L.A. Martin set his bond at $500. In an unrelated incident, two-year-old Jackie Dale Coleman decided to go for a spin in his father's car. The little fellow got in the car and started

the motor, and the car shot forward. It ran down a grade and plowed into the front of his parents' home, knocking down some steps and knocking the foundation out from under one end. Damage to the house was estimated at about $675, while the car's damage was negligible. The "driver" was not injured.

March 29

1898: THE MEETING CLOSED

The "little colored girl evangelist" who conducted revival in the courthouse closed the meeting Sunday night. Quite a number of professions of religion were made during the week, and several additions to the "colored churches" were reported. Collections were taken up on different occasions, and a liberal amount was presented the evangelist for her work. Great interest was manifested by both white and colored during the entire meeting, and not a night passed when more applied for admission than could be seated in the large five-hundred-seat courthouse. The article went on to sing the praises of the child evangelist, who was thought to have great powers "whether attained by careful training or otherwise."

March 30

1902: PAY UP

The Town of Winston was told to pay $901.13 to settle with the R.J. Reynolds Tobacco Company for 1900 taxes. This edict was in reference to the tobacco company storing tobacco in the town of Salem, although the company had its official office and place of business in Winston. A legal opinion rendered by Watson, Buxton and Watson stated, "It seems that Salem has the right to collect the tax on such property as if stored in that town."

The Little Red Factory was R.J. Reynolds's first tobacco factory in Winston. *Forsyth County Public Library.*

March 31

1906: New Manufacturing Concern

At the close of March 1906, the big news on the front page of a regional newspaper was the assurance that a new manufacturing industry would be coming to Lexington. This new concern would manufacture desks for the foreign and domestic trade and would have capital of $40,000. Within just a few days, the work of organizing the company was expected to be completed, factory buildings erected and machinery installed. Apparently, this venture had been talked about for quite a while, and now Lexington was considered "the richer by one more important manufactory."

April 1

1771: GUILFORD COUNTY'S ADMINISTRATION
The law creating Guilford had passed in 1770, and the county started administration of its territory on this day. The Guilford County Court met every February, May, August and November on the third Monday of the month. When Guilford County was formed in 1771, a temporary courthouse in western Guilford County, along the Deep River on the property of Robert Lindsay, was used for three years. The house was made of white clapboard and had blue-green wooden shutters. Stone steps led to the three front doors, called "witches' doors." The Great Hall in the central portion of the house became the place where court was held. A still was conveniently situated on Still House Creek, about one mile southwest of the house. Robert Lindsay also operated a store on his two thousand acres. A road went to the store, while a private drive bordered by cedars, large English boxwoods and mulberry trees led to the house. The Lindsays had goods hauled by wagon from New York and Wilmington. They sold "Irish Linnings, Cambricks, Lawns, Silks, and Gauzes, Caligoes Chints, men's and women's Worstsed Hoes, Syths, Hats, Books, & Many Other Articles."

1865: GENERAL GEORGE STONEMAN INVADES WINSTON AND SALEM
According to Carolyn Fries Shaffner's diary entry on April 1, 1865, the Union cavalry was nearby. She wrote, "We

immediately commenced packing, as we were certain that they would burn the factories and we feared the house would go also." The townspeople of Salem hid their silver, gold and valuable jewelry in holes they dug near Home Moravian Church. In addition, "two fine black stallions were spirited away to the basement of the Female Academy's Main Hall." Colonel W. J. Palmer, who was with General George Stoneman's brigade, was met "with a most cordial reception, very different from the usual greetings. The ladies cheered and brought out bread, pies, and cakes." Consequently, Salem residents' fears of destruction were unfounded.

April 2

1936: FUNNEL-SHAPED WITH TIP GLOWING

The *Greensboro Record* reported Greensboro's first tornado in this way:

> *Funnel-shaped, with tip glowing like fire in light reflected, it came swirling and rushing, dipping to earth here and there as it swept on an east-northeast course, leaving a trail of wreckage, fire, injury, and death in its wake. It was gone in the span of a few minutes—almost before anyone realized it was happening.*

Within just a few minutes, the tornado had left twelve dead and over one hundred wounded and had caused property damages estimated at $1,500. In addition, the city was plunged into darkness, for Duke Power Company had found it necessary to cut off the current to prevent the outbreak of additional fires.

April 3

1896: JUVENILE LYCEUM AT KÖRNER'S FOLLY

Alice Körner, wife of Jule Körner, established the Juvenile Lyceum in "Cupid's Park" on the top floor of Körner's Folly in Kernersville. This was a drama society that encouraged individual recitals. Programs were performed in the early afternoon every two weeks. Children from seven to thirteen years of age throughout the town were invited to participate. Forty-two children attended this first meeting. Performances consisted of plays, recitals, pantomimes, readings and both vocal and instrumental music. Soon, dancing and entertainment followed the programs. There was no expense to the children; however, their parents were expected to assist with the performances. "Cupid's Park" was a name derived from the multitude of Caesar Milch paintings of cupids adorning the theater's walls and ceiling.

April 4

1906: THE R.J. REYNOLDS FAMILY GROWS

Richard Joshua Reynolds Jr. was born on this day to Katharine and R.J. Reynolds. A year and four months later, a daughter, Mary Katharine, joined the family. Then, less than a year after that, Nancy Susan arrived. Finally, Zachary Smith was born in 1911. Katharine had given birth to four children in less than six years. The family hired a full-time nurse, Henrietta van den Berg, a graduate of the Johns Hopkins University School of Nursing. A bevy of servants worked at 666 West Fifth Street: Lizzie, a nurse; Jessie, Katharine's maid; and Eliza, a housekeeper.

1921: PERSONAL EMANCIPATION

Dick Reynolds turned twenty-one years old on this day. This was known legally as "the day of emancipation," and Dick took it literally. According to one family member, Dick "formally discharged Will Reynolds and Ed Johnston as guardians. Now he had a greater, though still limited, right to draw his dividends directly from the RJR legacy. His income from the trust rose to $100,000 a year."

1944: NO RETURN TO THOMASVILLE

Hoke Barnett had found work in Thomasville. At Easter, he decided to go to Charlotte for a short vacation. However, according to a newspaper report, "he would have been much better off had he not decided to take an Easter holiday and go home." Following was the reason why:

> *His wife shot him five times in the presence of the seven children in the home, and also in the presence of one Barnes Cauthen, father of twelve children, whose presence in the home started the fatal argument. Barnett reportedly pulled a revolver and shot Cauthen in the arm while another bullet went wild and wounded his daughter, Florence, 16. Then his wife, Blanche, opened up at close range and finished Hoke off completely with five shots.*

April 5

1920: Saws Steel Bars

A desperate attempt was made by several of the prisoners at the Davidson County jail to gain their freedom. When Mrs. Michael, the jailer's wife, was awakened by the noise of a hacksaw rasping against steel, she reacted in time to prevent any escapes. Since the jailer was out at the time, Mrs. Michael summoned police, who arrived on the scene in minutes. On investigation, they discovered the lock had been sawed from the cell occupied by two prisoners, Leo Lenz and Charlie Bailey. Also, one bar had been sawed through and then removed and another sawed part of the way through in one of the windows on the south side of the building. Vestie Matthews, a seventeen-year-old woman convicted and sentenced to three years at Sararcand, was the ringleader and "brains of the attempt." The young woman, who was allowed the freedom of the corridor, admitted having the saws and giving them to the two men. She said she found the saws in an old stove in the jail and kept them concealed in her corset. The two men did the actual work. They had started sawing at about eleven o'clock the night before, and the alarm was given between two and three o'clock the next morning.

April 6

1964: HE DEFENDED HIS MOTHER
Jerry Wayne Huntley, a fourteen-year-old Thomasville boy, used an axe to bludgeon his mother's attacker. Jerry appeared in juvenile court and told his side of the story. He reportedly used the axe to inflict a death-dealing blow to the ear of Rowsell Clinton Baker, forty-two. The incident occurred at the home of Jerry's mother, Mrs. Roxanne Huntley. Police said Baker had brandished a knife and had slashed Mrs. Huntley's arm, although not seriously. Baker then forced her to the ground, and her cries for help brought the young son, who hit Baker in the back of the head with the blunt end of the axe. Baker died in the Moses Cone Hospital at Greensboro.

April 7

1907: WOMAN'S TRADUCER ARRESTED
D.J. Trotter, a young man twenty-four years of age, was arrested in High Point on a warrant from Randolph County. He was charged with writing abusive and indecent letters to Miss Agnes Burrow, of Asheboro, and having "indecent and libelous talk" with others concerning her character. The letter that got him arrested had been written on Christmas Day.

1914: INNOVATIVE BUSINESS ANNOUNCEMENTS
The Lexington House Furnishing Company sold eight of its Hoosier Club memberships. This club was open to only twenty-five persons who were tired of the "old way" and wanted to try the "Hoosier Way." The McCrary Furniture Company called attention to its great sanitary refrigerator, the "Automatic." The reading public was instructed that they might "lessen their chances of typhoid by having an Automatic" in their homes. Everyone was invited to view the new window display.

April 8

1916: Carnivals Still Forbidden

When carnivals and tent shows tried to show inside the corporate limits of Lexington, they were "still named mud." An effort was made to have the ordinance forbidding these shows within a certain distance of any residence repealed, but the aldermen disagreed. At their monthly meeting, Mr. D.C. Hayes appeared on behalf of the firemen and asked that the ordinance be shelved so that a carnival could come in and donate a percentage that would enable the fire company to rid itself of a debt of $100 incurred by the recent purchase of a horse. The city fathers came to the relief of the "fire daddies" and appropriated the money from the town exchequer. The firemen were happy—after all, it was the hundred they wanted "and not the carnival," according to Hayes.

April 9

1914: Snazzy New Cars

F.L. Hedrick and C.U.G. Biesecker purchased handsome five-passenger Studebaker cars, 1911 models, equipped with electric lights, electric starters and other "up-to-the-minute" features. Mr. I.A. Beck purchased a Maxwell touring car, Dr. E.J. Buchanan purchased a new Ford runabout and Mr. H.E. Hedrick bought a Ford touring car. All were delivered by Mr. F.J. Cox, local agent for Ford and Studebaker. The previous week, Mr. Cox had also sold his Ford limousine to Mr. R.E. Kinzer.

April 10

1916: FLAGS SOLD TO AID BELGIUM

Mrs. Samuel W. Finch, regent of the General William Davidson Chapter of the American Revolution, the previous week received the following telegram from John Beaver White, of New York, director of the work in America of the Commission for Relief in Belgium: "Let us justify Queen Elizabeth's message. We must not fail Belgium now. Only foreign country where our flag reverenced. Think of their need. Giving day's labor is so little. Your help vital for success."

April 11

1916: ERLANGER BASEBALL OPENS

On this day, Piedmont Triad fans were promised the opportunity of seeing good baseball this particular season. The Erlanger team had been practicing and getting into "good form." The first game was planned for them to meet the Mount Pleasant Collegiate Institute team on Erlanger Field. Barnes, one of Erlanger's best twirlers the previous season, was predicted very likely to be on the "firing line," while Honeycutt would do the "receiving act." The newly completed grandstand, seating three hundred fans, had been completed, and the diamond had been leveled and scraped until it merited first-class accolades. Erlanger was ready to play serious baseball.

April 12

1903: DAVIDSON COUNTY SUPERIOR COURT
The complaint read:

> *Henry C. Kennard, Trustee and Executor of the estate of James E. Clayton, deceased, Plaintiff Against the Conrad Hill Gold and Copper Company, of Davidson County, North Carolina. The Conrad Hill Gold and Copper Company, of Baltimore City, and the Conrad Hill Gold and Copper Company, of Baltimore, Defendants.*
>
> *Two of the above dependants will each take notice that an action entitled as above has been commenced in the Superior Court of Davidson County to perfect the title of plaintiff to a certain tract or parcel of land situated in Conrad Hill township known as the Conrad Hill Gold and Copper Company and to remove a cloud from plaintiffs title set up by the defendants, and the said defendants will further at the August Term of the Superior Court of said county to be held on the 2nd Monday before the 1st Monday in September 1903... and answer or demur to the complaint in said action, or the plaintiff will apply to the Court for the relief prayed for in said complaint.*

April 13

1914: SHOOTING AT THE ERLANGER COTTON MILL

In the office of Superintendent J.M. Gamewell at the Erlanger Cotton Mills, W.T. Childers shot three times at C.L. Rose and then dropped dead, supposedly from heart failure. According to front-page newspaper accounts, the two men had had an altercation the previous Saturday night, and Mr. Gamewell had summoned them to his office for an investigation. Mr. Gamewell was seated at his desk, directly between Childers, who was standing next to the window, and Rowe, who was near the door. The men began to quarrel about the past Saturday night's trouble. Then Childers whipped out a Colt .38 and began to shoot. Two shots were fired over Mr. Gamewell's head, one going wild and the other striking Rowe in the hand. Rowe started to run. Childers shot again as Rowe went through the door into the main office. He followed Rowe to the outer door but did not get another chance to shoot at him. He went down the office steps and started walking to his boardinghouse when he fell dead on the sidewalk.

April 14

1914: OLD BOOZE

The announcement came on this day that *Everybody's Magazine* was running a contest and offering cash prizes for the best letters on "What I Know About Rum." This raised the curiosity of Piedmont Triad folks, so Judge Critcher of Recorder's Court reviewed the records to see just what "Old Booze had done in Lexington." He said he found the facts startling. The Recorder's Court was established on March 15, 1913. Up to March 15, 1914, exactly one hundred criminal cases had been tried. Cases included "blind tigers," assault with a deadly weapon, simple assault and battery, affray carrying a concealed weapon, forcible trespass, false pretense, abandonment, resisting an officer, larceny, embezzlement, perjury, murder, disposing of mortgaged property, keeping a disorderly house, beating a board bill, vagrancy, injury to real property, selling cigarettes to minors, cruelty to animals and gambling.

April 15

1911: BOYS' CORN CONTEST
Making front-page news in a regional newspaper, an article entitled "Nearly Fifty Progressive Lads Already In—Others Are Coming in Rapidly" touted a Davidson County boys' corn contest that promised to be the "best ever, with a predicted total of over one hundred entries." Mr. I.O. Schaub, special agent of the U.S. Bureau of Plant Industry, wrote P.S. Vann, county superintendent, urging him to offer county prizes. The rules and regulations were not given in the article—hopefully they were printed elsewhere.

1918: WHAT HAPPENED TO THE CHIEF?
Speculation continued concerning the disappearance of Chief of Police J.H. Mingus, who was said to have left Lexington and hired a transfer owner to take him to Rowan County, his old home. Later, a doctor in Winston-Salem sent a message indicating that he was treating Mr. Mingus, who was ill. Word around town indicated that Mr. Mingus hosted a "party" in his office, as "a great lot of bread crumbs and other remnants were found on the floor and a glass sitting in the room smelled very strong of whiskey."

April 16

1916: EASTER FESTIVITIES

A Sunday school picnic and egg hunt on the grove at Liberty Church was announced to take place Easter Monday. All were invited to come and bring baskets. In addition, in connection with Reverend P.L. Shore's regular appointment, the Arcadia Sunday school planned an Easter "entertainment" for Easter Sunday night. This was the first "entertainment" in the congregation's new church.

1921: MURDER ON SALEM STREET

On Salem Street in downtown Thomasville, shoppers attended to their Saturday morning chores. Twenty-nine-year-old Police Chief John E. (Edgar) Taylor was reportedly pacing up and down the sidewalk when he met an acquaintance, A. Hodge Varner. During their conversation, "Salem Street was rocked by a gunshot explosion that could have been heard well above any fast-moving freight train." A second shot followed. Both hit Chief Taylor, but he was able to escape into a store. Varner ran across Salem Street. Pedestrians then saw Dr. J.W. Peacock, their town's respected physician, with his head bandaged and his hand holding a .45-caliber German Luger pistol. Peacock ran into the same store that Taylor had entered; from the doorway, he fired two more times directly at the chief. Moving close to the now-dying man, Peacock fired two more shots, which proved fatal. One shot passed through Taylor and hit Henry Shaver, a customer in the store. Speculation continued concerning this "mild, law-abiding, compassionate" medical doctor who turned killer.

April 17

1916: Auction of Young Ladies

On this evening at "the school building," Miss Penny and the members of the Newsom Canning Club gave a party for the benefit of the club. Mr. Dave Leonard of Lexington sold seven girls and young ladies at auction. The bidding was lively, and no Lexington man brought a "purchase" back. A supper was served after the sale. Mr. Leonard said that he had sold quite a lot of different property but had never been called on to sell young ladies. Dave said he had "sold just about everything under the sun" at auction but that this was the most valuable property he had ever cried to the public. He added that he rather liked the job.

April 18

1911: Big Time at Daniel

Easter Monday was a big day for High Rock (aka Daniel), and nearly one thousand people went there to "make merry." Daniel had recently changed its name to High Rock, and natives believed this was fitting because there was another town named Daniel in the state of North Carolina. So in order for the folks in this Daniel to have a post office, the old name had to be discarded. The big crowd gathered early and listened to speeches on a variety of subjects.

1914: Swiss Bell Ringers to Entertain

An announcement on this day to Piedmont Triad citizens invited one and all to the Friday night Swiss Bell Ringers program at the Graded School Auditorium. A matinee would be held at three o'clock on Friday afternoon for the schoolchildren, and admission would be ten cents. Prices for the evening performance varied from twenty-five to fifty cents. All proceeds were designated to go to the school library fund.

April 19

1914: A LARGER OUTLOOK FOR THE MODERN WOMAN

During this period, it was not unusual for readers of regional newspapers to send in essays. Ella Wheeler Wilcox submitted her thoughts concerning the "Modern Woman." She began her treatise by stating, "Every day, new doors are flung open for women whose homes are disappointing and whose hearts are unsatisfied; doors which lead to agreeable occupation, to earnest endeavor, and to the happiness which comes from busy days well employed." Wilcox contended that this larger outlook for women made her a better mate for her husband and other men and also lessened the chances of her occupying the unenviable position of a neglected wife as the years passed. Her argument was this: "No absolutely lovable woman ever goes unloved through life."

April 20

1916: BIG STILL TAKEN IN FORSYTH

Deputy Collector C.H. Haynes and Deputy Sheriff O.W. Hanner of Forsyth captured a 285-gallon still in Little Yadkin township, about sixteen miles from Winston-Salem. The still was in full blast when the officers arrived. Whiskey was pouring from it into a galvanized iron tub. There were about 20 gallons of booze when the officers found it. Nearby were about 2,300 gallons of malt and bootlegged beer. The operators got away. It was thought they heard or saw the officers and left quickly. A dinner bucket with a fork and spoon was found along with a pair of overalls and a coat. Just above the captured still was a place where another still had been in operation but had since been removed. On an adjacent tree was carved "No. 1." Sheriff Hanner said he guessed the captured still was number two. This captured still was one of the largest found by the revenue officers.

April 21

1916: The Gypsies Are with Us

A large group of gypsies had been camping for several days north of Lexington. The front page of a regional newspaper elaborated by printing, "They are of the modern variety and do their traveling in automobiles, principally Fords. Some of this crowd claim to be of Indian blood." Much interest was created by the gypsies' appearance because of a report that a gypsy band had stolen little Jimmy Glass, a lad who had been taken from his home six months earlier and had not been found. This Piedmont Triad "sighting" produced folks who thought they had seen a small boy with these gypsies who looked somewhat like the Glass child because both had light hair and blue eyes.

Residents of Piedmont Triad towns often distrusted bands of gypsies that camped on the outskirts of their respected neighborhoods. *Wikimedia Commons.*

April 22

1909: A COLORED WOMAN'S GIFT

Unusual interest was attached to the placing of a brass railing and a beautiful plush curtain in the choir space at the Presbyterian church. The railing, which was costly, was paid for by money bequeathed to the church by Aunt Jessie Payne, a colored woman, who died at an advanced age. She had been a slave of the Payne family in Davidson County and had been a member of the Presbyterian church all her life, dating back to the time when blacks attended the "white folks' church" in antebellum days. When she died, she gave one-third of her small estate to the colored Presbyterian church, one-third to the Presbyterian church and one-third to her daughter.

April 23

1912: ONE WIFE TOO MANY

W.O. Coble, a native of Guilford County, was arrested at High Point on a warrant from Alabama charging him with bigamy. Coble had a wife and children in Guilford County, and on August 7, 1911, he married Miss Essie Sparks of Birmingham and later deserted her. Consequently, Mr. Coble was tracked to his old home in High Point. Reportedly, he had been in trouble even before going to Alabama. The *Greensboro Record* explained that in 1894, while an employee of the Singer Sewing Machine Company, he was convicted of forgery and served time on the roads.

1916: BIG REVIVAL PLANS ANNOUNCED

Lexington was in the midst of a number of religious meetings at different churches. The big revival at the Methodist church had already been in progress for two weeks and would continue for another seven days. Much interest was being manifested by the quality of the preaching. Special services involved "fraternal night," "textile workers' night" and "furniture makers' night." At the conclusion of the revival, converts were received into the church. The Presbyterian church welcomed Dr. William Black, "syndical evangelist," as speaker for both morning and evening services. Assisting Dr. Black was Mr. Burr, a renowned singer of religious songs. At the Reformed church, a series of special services was being held with Dr. J.C. Leonard and Reverend Mr. Welker. Special Easter services lasting a week were also in progress at the Lutheran church.

April 24

1826: FOUNDING DATE OF THE *GREENSBOROUGH PATRIOT* DISPUTED
When the weekly periodical the *Greensborough Patriot* debuted, publisher T. Early Strange announced that he had purchased an earlier paper, the *Carolina Patriot*, thought to be published in the year 1821. He printed the following evidence:

> *Joseph Reece, first editor of the* Daily Record, *wrote that he once encountered a very old farmer who peddled eggs in Greensboro. "See here," said the old man, "the* [founding] *date on that* Patriot *is wrong. It's 1821, and I'll tell you how I come to know. In the year 1821, there was a big murder case on trial at the courthouse here and I had come up to hear it. I was standing on the corner where the* Patriot *office is when along come one of them journey-man printers. He was drunk...and when he got to the corner he fell sprawling into a page of the* Patriot *type put out in the sun to dry. And that's why I know the* Patriot *was published that year."* *Reece looked up the date of the mentioned murder case and found it was in the year 1821.*

1916: DANGERS OF A MOVIE STAR

This day marked the arrival of the long-awaited Broadway Universal Feature *A Soul Enslaved*, a five-act emotion drama, at the Lyric Theatre. Cleo Madison, star of the feature, met with an accident during the production of the photoplay. The picture was delayed ten days and nearly cost the beautiful star the sight of her right eye. According to the report:

> *A fisherman had occasion playfully to chide a young girl. She ran from him and was about to leave the house when Abbott threw a stick after her. It was Abbott's intention, of course, to have the stick fall short of the fleeing girl, but he threw it with more force than was planned, and just as Miss Madison was about to make her escape, it struck her under the eye, cutting quite a gash. The wound bled profusely, and Miss Madison, at sight of the blood, became hysterical.*

Miss Madison was not able to resume her work in the picture for a week. Abbott vowed that he would never throw another stick at a woman.

April 25

1909: PEOPLE WILL PETITION FOR GOOD ROADS

In order to bring about good roads, businessmen from town and country met in the Davidson County Courthouse, where they heard a number of interesting addresses on the subject of roads. Captain Frank C. Robbins, a "grand old soldier and citizen," presided over the meeting and delivered a speech favoring good roads. He used horses and mules to support his plea. He further stated, "If broken names and wagons and bad words and bad tempers were set down in dollars and cents, the sum that is annually lost in Davidson County on account of mud would astonish us." He continued his speech by advocating the issuance of bonds, which he called a "blessing."

April 26

1912: BREACH OF PROMISE
Surprisingly, this front-page article needed to be read very carefully. The first three paragraphs gave background concerning the case; however, the language, though vague, would have made Piedmont Triad newspaper readers wonder what was going on with a "prominent Lexington citizen charged with trilling with a widow's affections." As it turned out, this was a mock court trial. Sponsored by the Woman's Betterment Association of Lexington Graded School, all benefits would go to that organization for its work. A brief scenario pointed to the gentleman's claims that although the widow had become attached to him, he had not been serious in his intentions and was not attached to the lady. Nevertheless, she had become attached to his property.

1918: CHARLIE CHAPLIN DISAPPOINTED PIEDMONT TRIAD AUDIENCE
An excited crowd gathered to meet the famous silent movie comedian at the Davidson County Courthouse steps. The audience expected comedy, but Chaplin's fifteen-minute speech was extremely serious. He urged his audience to buy war bonds during World War I's Third Liberty Loan. The lack of comic gestures or antics from the famed Chaplin disappointed the crowd. The newspaper reported, "There was no hint of the funny walk, the funny mustache, and the fancy little tricks that endeared him to everybody's heart. He favored them only by a funny toss of the hat. When the press asked him to do some funny stunts, he replied, 'It is serious business we are now engaged upon.'"

April 27

1912: In Superior Court
The April term of superior court closed. Judge O.H. Allen had presided with general satisfaction throughout the term. Most cases were reported as long and tedious. Of extraordinary interest was the case of the *Healing Springs Company vs. T.W., J.M and W.T. Daniels.* Several months earlier, this company had purchased an interest in the famous Healing Springs property and some time earlier had brought suit before the clerk to have the land sold for partition. The clerk sent the case to superior court on the grounds that there were a number of timber rights involved that would have to be settled before he could act on it. The property had now been designated for sale, and the Healing Springs Company intended to undertake extensive improvements around the property.

1947: The Union and R.J. Reynolds Tobacco Company
By this date, the Local 22 Union and the R.J. Reynolds Tobacco Company had been "haggling over a new contract for almost nine weeks." Union leader Glenn Jones convinced the crowd of thousands of blacks that they should call a strike against the tobacco company. Everyone present begin singing an old black spiritual, "I Shall Not Be Moved."

April 28

1912: FIDDLERS' CONVENTION
The Fiddlers' Convention, which was held in the auditorium of the graded school building, was a success "in every particular." Miss Zula Hedrick, secretary of the Woman's Betterment Association of the graded school, who was in charge of the gathering, handled everything "admirably," and the entire success of the convention was a tribute to her ability as manager. A big crowd attended, and everybody got "his money's worth." Superintendent Jarratt, stage manager, assembled his musicians—fiddlers, banjoists and guitarists—and started the convention with the "Old Ship of Zion." Mr. Jarratt announced it as "Be Robbed and Ready," but that was because, according to the report, "he did not know any better." Nevertheless, the audience caught the grand swing of the melody, and every foot tapped in time to the music. It brought a "tremendous yell" from the house. After the opening piece, the musicians got busy, and there were competing string bands, duets, fiddle solos, banjo solos and all sorts of "delightful music." The fiddlers "fairly lifted the roof" with "Mississippi Sawyer," "Arkansaw [*sic*] Traveler," "Sugar in a Gourd" and "Pop Goes the Weasel."

1964: NORTH CAROLINA SCHOOL OF THE ARTS
Governor Terry Sanford's advisory committee visited Winston-Salem. Its mission was to thoroughly investigate the possibility of establishing North Carolina School of the Arts in that city. The final contenders were Winston-Salem,

Raleigh, Durham, Greensboro and Hillsborough. Earlier in the morning, Smith Bagley and other campaigners from Winston-Salem had solicited pledges to raise $900,000 for dormitories. By five o'clock on this same day, they had raised $214,729. Their goal was achieved the following day.

April 29

1909: PROTOCOL SIGNED
Announcement was made that complete peace reigned between F.S. Tuttle and Huge Fulp in Germanton. The forty-five-year-old Tuttle had married Fulp's fourteen-year-old-child. When the pair came from the "runaway," Fulp "beat the skin off of Tuttle's countenance." Consequently, the bridal couple left again. It was then agreed that Tuttle could live on his farm and that his child wife would live with her parents. Tuttle had visiting privileges to see her as often as he pleased.

1945: ROUND DOZEN CLUB
This was a social club in the Piedmont Triad. Membership was limited to twelve women who engaged in their individual needlework projects for an hour in the hostess's living room, always decorated with fresh flowers. Refreshments of Coca-Colas, "a delicious ice course" and salted nuts followed the work-chat hour and were often served by the designated hostess's daughters and granddaughters. Each lady in attendance was named in the newspaper article. Interestingly, they were all referred to as "Mesdames" followed by their husbands' names, not their given first names.

April 30

1920: PARKER MAKES ADDRESS

J.J. Parker, Republican candidate for governor of
North Carolina, delivered a beautiful and inspiring
address to the graduating class of Tyro High School
at the commencement exercises. Mr. Parker reportedly
"departed from the beaten paths of commencement
oratory and flavored his address with originality." He
addressed both young women and young men. However,
the following address, printed in the newspaper, refers
specifically to men:

> *If there is one person in the world who appeals to me
> it is the young man who stands upon the threshold of
> life, with feet unaccustomed to the ways of the world,
> with eyes not trained to distinguish between that which
> is and that only seems to be: but who in his youth and
> his inexperience is required to make the greatest decision
> that man is ever called on to make, what he shall do
> with the life which God has given him.*

Interestingly, only at the end of his address did Parker
refer to both genders, urging them to pay the highest debt
of gratitude to the fathers and mothers who had made their
education possible.

1962: HIS MOTORCYCLE DISTURBED AILING WOMAN

Kenneth Eugene Murray of Thomasville was charged with
shooting Jerry Cody in the shoulder after a dispute between

the two that allegedly began by Cody riding a motorcycle by Murray's house and disturbing his ailing mother. State's evidence contended that Murray went to Cody's house and asked him to apologize for some words he had allegedly spoken. Later, Murray shot Cody and then took the injured man to the hospital. Sentencing by Judge Eugene G. Shaw took an unexpected turn when Murray was sentenced to four to six years in the state prison.

May 1

1959: MAN FOUND GUILTY OF RAPE CHARGE
An all-male jury returned the verdict of guilty as charged in
the bill of indictment against Matthew Lindsey, a resident
of Midway. Lindsey was accused of entering the house of
George O'Farrell on Midway School Road and attacking
Mrs. O'Farrell and attempting to rape her. At the time of
the attack, O'Farrell was returning home from a nearby
store. Hearing his wife screaming, the middle-aged farmer
rushed into the house and saw Lindsay bending over Mrs.
O'Farrell, choking her. Lindsay then lunged at O'Farrell,
and the two men grappled with each other before O'Farrell
"got hold of" a stick of wood and hit Lindsay in the head,
forcing him from the home. Lindsay refuted that testimony,
stating that he had entered the O'Farrell house to use the
telephone and that when Mr. O'Farrell came home and saw
him talking on the phone, he hit him in the head, creating
a wound that required ten stitches.

May 2

1906: FORSYTH MAN IN LUCK
While walking along the railroad east of Winston, Caleb Thomas, a one-armed man, discovered a broken rail. Knowing that a passenger train would be due in a moment or two, he ran down the track and flagged the train, preventing what might have been a serious and costly wreck. Some days afterward, he received a letter from the railroad company, thanking him and telling him to write to the division superintendent's office whenever he wanted to travel and passes would be furnished him and his wife.

1942: BANDITS ROB MIDWAY GROCERY/SERVICE STATION
Wade Loflin of Thomasville and two other convicts at Anson County State Prison Camp overpowered a guard, escaped and held up a Midway grocery store/service station. After taking sixty dollars in cash and "a batch of cigarettes," the three made their getaway in a green 1942 Mercury. Reportedly, the bandits had driven by the station several times before making their entrance. Two of the bandits, one being Loflin, went in the station armed with a sawed-off shotgun and a .32-caliber pistol. After leaving the station, they drove off in the direction of Winston-Salem.

May 3

1903: Struck by the Train

Anthony Hargrave had a narrow escape from death. No. 30, a fast northbound passenger train, struck Hargrave, an aged man, near the depot at Lexington, inflicting serious wounds on him. Hargrave was "said to have been drinking." A few minutes before the arrival of No. 30, Hargrave had walked up the railroad tracks and sat down on the end of the crossties of the main track. He buried his face in his hands and did not move when the train came in sight. The engineer said he repeatedly sounded the danger signal by blowing the whistle, and parties nearby hollered to the man to get off the track. He paid no attention to the warning and "set still" until the stops of the cab hit him on the head, knocking him unconscious alongside the track. The train stopped, and a physician was summoned. He found that the man was badly hurt by the blow to the head, a "great hole being made" where the stops struck him. Hargrave was removed to his home, where he was given "a fair chance to recover."

May 4

1903: Mr. Moyer Is Elected

The election in Lexington for mayor and town commissioners was hotly contested, but there were no serious outbreaks. The "adherents" of the opposing candidates were on the grounds early to look after the interests of their favorites. Throughout the entire day, their work went on with marked energy. On the front page of the local newspaper, it was reported that the contest was extremely interesting from start to finish. There were no issues as to what policy either candidate would "persue" on any question pertaining to the management of municipal affairs. It was only a question as to who should be mayor of Lexington. It took the official count to determine the result. When the polls closed, a great crowd hung "round the court house" to get the result. The counting was watched with much interest and resulted in Mr. Moyer's reelection for the eighth consecutive term by a majority of 8 votes—Moyer with 104, and Mendenhall with 96. The town commissioners were now W. McCrary, James Smith, Captain C.W. Trice, E.E. Raper and Z.I. Walser. When the result was announced, there was good-natured cheering and "hurrahing" on the part of the friends of the successful candidate.

May 5

1925: FLAMBOYANT EVANGELIST BILLY SUNDAY'S BOOZE SERMON
Billy Sunday preached at Thomasville's Community
Church. Following is an excerpt from his famous "wicked
booze sermon":

*The saloon is the sum of all villainies. It is worse
than war or pestilence. It is the crime of crimes. It is
the parent of crimes and the mother of sins. It is the
appalling source of misery and crime in the land. And
to license such an incarnate fiend of hell is the dirtiest,
low-down, damnable business on top of this old earth.
There is nothing to be compared to
it. I go to a family that is broken
up, and I say, "What caused this?"
Drink! I step up to a young man on
the scaffold and say, "What brought
you here?" Drink! Whence all the
misery and sorrow and corruption?
Invariably it is drink.*

Billy Sunday's anti-
booze sermons drew
big crowds. *Wikimedia
Commons.*

That Sunday afternoon, before
leaving Thomasville, Billy Sunday
climbed the town's original Big Chair
and posed for the camera in his famous
flamboyant pose—knees spread and
arms uplifted. His photograph atop the
Big Chair eventually appeared on the
cover of the *New York Times Magazine*.

May 6

1901: Pay Up

The following serious notice was sent out via the regional newspaper concerning taxes: "Those who have not paid their taxes for 1900 had better see Sheriff Dorsett at once and save trouble and expense, as he is compelled by law to collect immediately."

1901: Here's Your Chance

On a lighter note, the announcement was made on this day that another buggy would be given away. The *Dispatch* had purchased another fifty-dollar buggy to be given away on the same conditions as the one won by Mr. M.W. Tysinger of Silver Hill in 1899 and the one won by Mr. Lee Rush of Bringles in 1900. The buggy was manufactured by the Continental Carriage Company of Cincinnati, Ohio. It was sold and warranted by the Lexington Hardware Company, which always had on hand a complete line of buggies, surreys, phaetons, etc.

May 7

1865: HISTORICAL NOTICE SENT TO CHIEF OF POLICE IN
GREENSBORO
Union army captain Henry Brown sent the following notice
to Greensboro:

> *Sir: On the 4ᵗʰ of May, 1865, companies B & K
> of the Tenth Ohio Volunteer Cavalry, at the railroad
> company's shops of the North Carolina Railroad,
> between Hillsborough and Greensborough, N.C., found
> between $80,000 and $100,000 in gold buried in
> boxes and sacks and marked Commercial Bank of
> New Bern, N.C. The money had been divided amongst
> the finders and officers of the command. I understand
> some of the officers concerned are about resigning with
> their booty in their pockets. If any action is taken in the
> matter, it should be at once.*

Of course, no one knew the exact amount buried, as no
actual accounting existed.

1930: SHE WENT BERSERK WHILE BEING JAILED
In jail, she was known only as Reverend C.O. Roughmays,
and she had been incarcerated for some days when the
preacher-prisoner was told she was going to be bathed.
For some unknown reason, that request did not please her,
so she "saw red," produced a razor from her clothes and
slashed the two female prisoners who had been directed
to see that she was bathed. One of the women received a

four-inch cut on her lower leg that "laid the flesh open to the bone." The other was slashed to the bone across the top of the forearm. When the reverend was taken to the state asylum, guards there discovered bags containing roots and herbs, powders of some kind, old teeth and "other materials sometimes regarded as charms" in her corset.

AUTHOR'S NOTE: *My uncle, Dr. G.C. Gambrell, was the county health officer called to treat the two injured women and examine the reverend.*

May 8

1941: ANNOUNCEMENTS FOR GASOLINE RATIONING

The announcement was made that 1942 would be a time of strict gasoline rationing. A total of sixty-one thousand forms would be used for gas registration in Davidson County. These would be divided proportionately between Thomasville and Lexington. Principals of separate grammar schools would serve as administrators. Teachers and town citizens would act as assistants. Each vehicle owner would present his motor vehicle registration card and would then answer necessary questions on the number of "essential" miles he would cover in going to and from work. Five different types of rationing cards would be issued.

May 9

1913: THE GOLDEN HYPHEN

Today was the official date of the consolidation of Winston and Salem. Reportedly, Winston was almost twice as big as Salem, but Salem was still more influential. Earlier, the *Union Republican* newspaper of Winston had "pushed for the merger," stating, "Were we consolidated under one charter, we would be a city fifth in population, third in wealth, and second in business and enterprise to no other place in the State." The *People's Press* of Salem had opposed consolidation, stating, "We can see no real benefits for Salem in the proposed union at present. We may be shortsighted, but judging from past experience, we cannot endorse the movement." The people of Winston voted 800 to 260 for consolidation; Salem voted 385 to 224. The vote was in, and the new name was declared: Winston-Salem.

1940: MINISTERS VOTE PRISONER AID TO HELP REESTABLISH MEN

Reverend Louis S. Gaines, pastor of the First Baptist Church and chairman of the Lexington Red Cross and the Davidson County division of the North Carolina Rehabilitation Bureau, organized a meeting of local and county ministers and several invited citizens. The bureau proposed to arouse interest in the work of returning former prisoners to useful places in the community. State prison chaplain Reverend Lawrence A. Watts, who spoke at a union service at First Methodist Church, led the conference on this day.

May 10

1901: HIGH POINT MINSTRELS
The High Point Minstrels gave a performance in Lexington. The event was called a "real treat," and congratulations were in order because the "boys" gave a splendid performance and everyone was extremely pleased. A number of High Point residents went to Lexington to see the performance.

1940: INTERCESSION FOR PEACE SERVICES IN WAR-TORN WORLD
Reverend Dan W. Allen, rector of Grace Episcopal Church, announced regular Thursday morning services at his church for intercession for peace and individual needs. This service was planned to give Christians an opportunity to reaffirm their faith in God while asking His intervention in a war-torn world.

May 11

1811: Bunker Siamese Twins Born

The Bunker brothers were born on this day in Siam (now Thailand) to a fisherman and his wife. Because of their Chinese heritage, they were known as the "Chinese Twins" in Siam. They were joined at the sternum by a small piece of cartilage. In 1839, they moved to Mount Airy and married two sisters—Chang married Adelaide Yates, and Eng married Sarah Anne Yates. Chang and Eng fathered a total of 21 children, and today their descendants—including several sets of non-conjoined twins—number more than 1,500. The twins died on the same day in 1874.

1940: Poppies Sold

The announcement was made that Poppy Day would be observed throughout the entire Piedmont Triad on the Saturday before Memorial Day. Mrs. Joe McCrary, president of the Jim Leonard unit of the American Legion Auxiliary, proclaimed that on that day, all Americans would be asked to wear memorial poppies in tribute to the World War dead and to aid the victims of the war. Under the direction of Mrs. A.L. Disher, chairman of the Poppy Day committee, the little red memorial flower would be distributed by women and girls from the Lexington unit and Girl Scouts.

May 12

1903: RURAL FREE DELIVERY
The government of the United States had been exceedingly
wise in its policy of increasing and improving the facilities
for delivering mail in the rural districts of the Piedmont
Triad. Rural Free Delivery, which some people in the Triad
thought was great "humbug when it was first announced,"
proved to be a wonderful blessing to many neighborhoods,
affording people remote "from the centers of thought and
life" services that were never dreamed of a few years earlier.
As of this day, daily papers were now going into many homes
that heretofore had a hard time getting a paper once a week.
Consequently, children in the "back-country districts" were
now learning more of the world. The government was
praised for providing the means for finding and bringing to
its service those "strong country boys" who, having learned
how to manage stubborn "critters on the farm," learned to
control the more "stubborn elements in public life."

Rural Free Delivery
afforded rural
Piedmont Triad
citizens various
services they found
advantageous and
interesting. *Library
of Congress*.

May 13

1940: THE GREATEST RENDEZVOUS
Approximately two hundred Sea Scouts attended the third annual Sea Scout rendezvous held at the Greensboro Sea Scout base on High Rock Lake. This outing was sponsored jointly by the Uwharrie and Greensboro councils of Boy Scouts of America. In that group were thirteen representatives of the Lexington Sea Scout ship *Bluenose*. "It was the greatest rendezvous we have had yet," said Director Charles T. Hagan, skipper of the national Sea Scout ship *Davey Jones*.

1958: DAVIE YOUTH KILLED MOTHER
Jimmy Cline of Mocksville, who fatally wounded his mother with a shotgun, was sent to Jackson Training School for examination and perhaps a short stay. Davie sheriff Ben Boyles said he would take Jimmy to the school on this day. Jimmy maintained that the shooting of his mother, Mrs. Walter Cline, Route 2, Advance, was accidental. He said he got the shotgun to scare away Charlie Mason, who had been drinking liquor in his mother's kitchen.

May 14

1902: New Hospital and a Nursing School
In Winston, Slater Hospital's "nurse training department"
opened during Slater School's ninth commencement
exercises. The purpose of Slater was to emphasize
education and the need for black medical professionals.
Prior to the opening of Slater, "blacks were either cared for
at home or not at all," wrote Robert Prichard, MD, of the
Bowman Gray School of Medicine at Slater. In its first year
of operation, the hospital treated ninety patients, fifteen of
them emergency cases; performed twenty-one operations;
and saw ten patients die. Two nurses and the Ladies
Auxiliary, composed of women in the black community,
cared for the patients who filled the hospital's seven beds.
Slater Hospital ceased operations ten years later, at which
time the previously all-white Twin-City Hospital recorded
the admission of its first black patients.

1940: Excellent Piedmont Triad Photographer
In his "About Town" newspaper column, Dave Sink
informed readers of the talents of a local photographer. He
wrote, "Have you seen those children's portraits displayed
in the Ideal Dress Shop windows? These are the excellent
work of Paul Knepper, who had made several photographs
of Kirksey and Page" (Mr. Sink's two daughters). Sink
praised these as splendid examples of camera work and
issued an invitation to readers to take advantage of Mr.
Knepper's specialty in home portraitures.

May 15

1903: BRANCH WATER CONTAMINATED

The report went out that there was something wrong with the water in the small branch a short distance below the railroad depot. Nineteen dead eels were counted along the course of the stream within a distance of less than half a mile. Then, a valuable cow belonging to Mr. D.F. Conrad of the Elk Furniture Company died. It was supposed that her death was caused by drinking water from this same stream, as she had been pastured along its banks.

On this day, a front-page newspaper article reminded citizens to list their taxes, according to the law. Persons exempted from poll tax permanently for the year 1903 were required to present a certificate of release when they went to list; the list taker would make an entry as to the fact that he was released. Those who may have lost their certificates of exemption must have them renewed at the June meeting of the Board of County Commissioners.

May 16

1771: THE REGULATOR WAR
Strangers, called "Regulators," appeared in Salem with the
intent of "bringing down the royal government." Moravians
became upset because they had done no wrong. They had
"paid their rent without complaint and remained on good
terms with the royal government." After the Brethren were
sometimes threatened with whippings, they suggested the
Regulators take their complaints to court. They chose
not to do so but instead gathered on the western bank of
Alamance Creek on this day and were "crushed by eastern
militia under Governor William Tryon." Thus, the tyranny
of the Regulators ended once and for all.

1966: SALVATION ARMY GIRL GUARD TROOP
Organized by Mrs. Lieutenant Fred Craver, wife of the
commanding officer of the Lexington Salvation Army
Corps, a Girl Guard Troop helped celebrate the fiftieth
anniversary of the organization. The troop, under the
leadership of corps assistant Lieutenant Peggy Lovette,
observed weekly meetings. Roxanne Everhart and Susan
Everhart were patrol leaders. These girls, ages eleven
through eighteen, enjoyed singing, handcrafts and
swimming. This program was inaugurated in New York
by Evangeline Booth, the national commander of the
Salvation Army. On this date, there were over fifty thousand
Girl Guards representing almost every free nation of the
world. The four-fold purpose of the Girl Guard program
was "the guarding of the soul, mind, body, and others."

May 17

1903: Mrs. Bailey Is Found Dead in Well

The regional newspaper reported the death of Mrs. B.R. Bailey of Advance, Davie County. She was found dead in a well at her home on this day. No particulars were ascertainable, aside from that the lady had been of "feeble mind" for several weeks and that it is supposed she jumped in the well during a fit of "mental aberration." Mrs. Bailey was the wife of Mr. Brack R. Bailey, brother of C.G. Bailey, who was treasurer of the Republican State Executive Committee. She was a sister of ex-sheriff E.E. Vogler of Davie County and also had many known relatives. The deceased was about forty-five years old.

May 18

1903: THOMASVILLE, POPULATION 2,224
Professor Hauss of the Thomasville Graded Schools had his
pupils take a complete census of Thomasville. They found
a population of 2,229, divided as follows: white, 1,681;
colored, 548. This enumeration placed the number of
children at the Thomasville Baptist Orphanage at 248, with
teachers and others accounting for 24, making a total at the
orphanage of 272. The editor of the *Lexington Dispatch* sent
his congratulations to his "sister town" and also hoped she
would soon have 10,000 happy and prosperous souls.

1948: RUBBING DOCTORS ROB AGED CITIZEN AT WELCOME
Lewis Thomason, seventy-nine, who resided near
Welcome, reported that he had been robbed about
ten o'clock by two women and a man traveling in an
automobile who took from his person a pocketbook
containing four dollars and then drove away. Sheriff W.G.
Fritts said the description given indicated the group might
be gypsies. Thomason was quoted as telling officers that
the trio called him to their car and told him they were
"rubbing doctors." When they drove away, he discovered
his overalls were unfastened and that his pocketbook had
been removed. This was found some distance away, torn
in pieces and the contents gone. Sheriff Fritts said that the
description of the car was rather indefinite.

May 19

1966: FOLLOW SCOUT MOTTO

The Boy Scouts of Troop 239 stuck by their scout motto—"Be Prepared"—when they reported for an emergency rescue mission practice near Paul's Chapel Church. They took foul-weather gear with them and found it very handy when heavy rains struck the area. They marched back to the assembly area following completion of their mission.

1966: NO MATTER WHO MAKES IT, A&P GUARANTEES IT!

An A&P full-page advertisement bragged, "No matter who makes it, if A&P sells it, A&P guarantees it!" Groceries on "special" on this day included three cans of Ann Page tomato soup for thirty-five cents; freshly ground beef, forty-nine cents a pound; sliced beef liver, forty-five cents a pound; Clorox bleach, thirty-seven cents for a half gallon; Sunshine Hydrox cookies, forty-three cents for a one-pound package; Heinz hot tomato ketchup, twenty-five cents for a twelve-ounce bottle; and Stokely cut green beans, two cans for forty-three cents.

May 20

1940: COMMENCEMENT AT CHILDREN'S HOME
Commencement exercises at Lexington Children's
Home would begin with the annual class day, and the
commencement sermon would be preached at the Vance
Auditorium by Reverend H.C. Allen, pastor of First
Methodist Church of Lexington. Twelve seniors had
earned diplomas of graduation. The closing exercises
at the home were scheduled about a week earlier on
this year; however, a "complete nine-months term" was
completed in the classrooms. Since the enrollment at the
home had been recently expanded through change from
national to state Junior Order operation of the institution,
future graduating classes were expected to be larger. An
interesting program was prepared, and the people of the
Piedmont Triad were invited to all exercises.

1955: "JOLLY BLACK WIDOW" SERIAL KILLER
On this day, Nannie Doss pleaded guilty to killing four of
her husbands (one of them Arlie Lanning), as well as her
mother, her sister Dovie, her grandson Robert and her
mother-in-law. The prosecution found her mentally fit
for trial. Eight years earlier, in 1945, Nannie had arrived
in Lexington and married laborer Arlie Lanning, who
reportedly "loved his alcohol and females." At times,
when she was most upset, Nannie would leave for an
extended period of time; however, she always went back
home to Arlie. When Arlie died suddenly, the doctor
found no reason for suspicion. He thought most likely

it had been the dangerous flu virus that had swept the area. Arlie had had all the symptoms, including sweating, vomiting and dizziness. Nannie played right into the doctors' diagnosis as she talked with her neighbors. "Poor, poor Arlie," she said. "You know what he said to me before he breathed his last? 'Nannie, it must have been the coffee.'"

May 21

1907: HELL HATH NO FURY LIKE THE WOMAN WHO
HATED LITTER
While complaints were addressed to Lexington's street
superintendent, the new Board of Aldermen and the
Street Committee, ladies from the town, usually slow to
wrath, were rapidly "reaching a frame of mind that bodes
no good for the powers that be." One such concerned
lady approached a reporter, and the following reportedly
transpired between the two:

> *She held him with her glittering eye. "Why don't
> you put a piece in the paper about the streets!" she
> demanded. "They are a disgrace to the town. I think it
> is per-fect-ly scan'lous!"*
>
> *"But soon, dear madam, they will be macadamized,"
> quivered the newspaperman.*
>
> *"I'm not speaking of mud!" she snapped. "I am
> talking about the litter, the paper and the trash and the
> rubbish all over this town! I have reference to the weeds
> that almost lap across the costly granolithic walk in
> places. It is a shame, and I want authorities to have a
> spring cleaning up and get this stuff off." "And I want
> to say something else, too," she added, as she started
> off. "No gentleman will expectorate on these granolithic
> sidewalks."*

May 22

1907: Various Local Items

A representative of the Gibraltar Paint and Roofing Company of Norfolk, Virginia, after having had a small house built in front of the Lexington Hardware Company's store and having painted it inside and out with the new Gibraltar paint, set it on fire to demonstrate the protection Gibraltar paint afforded against fire. About eight hundred gathered, the interesting event having been advertised well, and everybody was impressed with the wonderful exhibition. The representative made a short talk about his paint and proceeded to apply the match. The house, with its windows and chimney all complete, was filled with combustibles and saturated with oil. When the combustibles were nearly all consumed, the firemen turned on the hose and put out the embers. Only "here and there" was the house affected by the fire, so the paint was declared to be a wonderful protection.

May 23

1903: ANNOUNCEMENT OF SUNDAY SCHOOL EXCURSION

The front-page article of the regional newspaper announced, well in advance, the date of the Sunday school trip to Raleigh under the personal management of the members of the Baptist and Reformed Church. Members were urged to "save the date" of June 20, 1903. The train was scheduled to leave Lexington at 6:30 a.m. and was due to arrive at Raleigh about 10:00 a.m. Returning, it would leave Raleigh at 7:00 p.m. and would hopefully arrive back in Lexington about 10:00 p.m. The round-trip fare would be only $1.50. Folks were reminded that the trip would be a "delightful one." It was hoped a large crowd would take advantage of the splendid opportunity to visit the capital city of the state of North Carolina.

Church and civic groups found excursion trains convenient and economical at the beginning of the twentieth century. Day trips were popular at a minimal cost. *Wikimedia Commons.*

1966: Man Accused as "Paddler" Will Face Kidnapping Charge

Twenty-five-year-old George Ken Wallace, a Winston-Salem man identified as the "mystery paddler" who assaulted five boys, waived preliminary hearing in Recorder's Court at Thomasville. He pleaded guilty to a charge of impersonating an officer and was given eighteen months on the roads for that offense. Wallace also faced two charges of kidnapping and two charges of impersonating an officer in Guilford County. He was taken to the Thomasville court from High Point, where he was being held in jail. The paddlings, occurring over a two-month period, involved boys at Thomasville, Greensboro and High Point. The Thomasville boy, fourteen, was the most painfully assaulted. He was picked up by a man posing as an officer and was driven to near Wallburg, where his beating occurred.

May 24

1903: Broadnax Hanged Friday

From Reidsville came news that John Broadnax, sixteen years old, was hanged at Wentworth. On March 19, he had murdered Sidney Blair, a farmer, and wounded Miss Sallie Walker. The murderer made a statement on the scaffold, saying he planned and executed the murder himself and exonerated Nat Fuller, whom he at one time claimed was implicated with him.

1928: Winston-Salem Couple Held for Poisoning Girls

Herbert E. Hall and his wife, Laura Grace Hall, were placed in jail in Winston-Salem on the charge of first-degree murder "growing out of the death of two small daughters of Hall and stepdaughters of Mrs. Hall." It first appeared that the girls had died of ptomaine poisoning following a dinner of sardines. After his daughters' deaths, Mr. Hall asked Forsyth County to pay their burial expenses.

May 25

1903: MADMAN TERRIFIES NEIGHBORS

Mr. Charles Atkins, a reputable citizen whose home was between Waughtown and Kernersville, became violently insane "on the subject of religion." Mr. Atkins ran his family from their home. He then went to St. Delight Church and smashed all the windows of the building. From there, he went to the home of Mr. Bunyan Linville. There he saw a horse belonging to Mr. Adolphus Sink and struck the animal a terrible blow, sinking an axe into the horse's body and inflicting a dangerous wound. The horse jumped and jerked the axe out of the "madman's hand." Mr. Sink and others then caught and bound Mr. Atkins. He was taken to Winston and confined in the county jail. People felt great relief when Mr. Atkins was "secured and placed where he could do no harm."

May 26

1903: Bride Almost Fourteen

At the residence of the bride's father, Mr. Robert Rodgers, his daughter, Miss Carrie, was united in marriage to Mr. Wood Gilliland. Both parents were "of well-to-do" families. The bride lacked a few days of being fourteen years of age. The front-page wedding announcement concluded with this editorial comment: "There seems no necessity for Mr. Gilliland choosing a child for a bride when the country is full of women between the age of 20 and 50 who are willing and anxious to marry."

Piedmont Triad history saw many young "child" brides married to older men. While this practice was often the rule rather than the exception, newspaper editors often commented on these weddings in uncomplimentary language. *Library of Congress.*

May 27

1907: BRIDE SEVENTY, GROOM FIFTY-EIGHT

One of the most interesting weddings that ever occurred in Davidson County took place at Silver Hill on this day. Mr. David Pahl, of Nebraska, age fifty-eight, was married to Miss Hannah Pruitt, seventy. Squire Charlie Hedrick officiated in the presence of a large family and interested friends. The wedding was the result of advertising. Mr. Pahl made it known in a newspaper that he desired to wed some good lady, as he was "all aweary of living by his lonesome." The advertisement "came under the eyes of Mr. F. Wachter, of Silver Hill," to whom the "wild joys of living appealed with peculiar force" and "wit and humor exuded from his every pore." So he showed the paper to Miss Pruitt, and she desired him to take the matter up with Mr. Pahl. So successful were Mr. Wachter's negations that after only four letters had passed, Mr. Pahl announced that so far as he was concerned, it was "eureka." Consequently, Miss Pruitt returned a true bill, and the deal was closed. Mr. Pahl got his "papers," and that night the two were "made one—two souls with but a single thought, two hearts that beat as one."

May 28

1907: Wants to "Corry Spond"

A charming young lady of Davidson County received the following letter from a "gay young gent," and she turned it over to the regional newspaper, saying, "Pass it on and let all young men learn to write letters." It seems that the long-distance lover had seen her name in some voting contest in the Piedmont Triad, and that was all he knew about her. Here "followeth the espistle, just as it was written on cheap tablet paper":

Dear Miss I Wold Bea Glad to Corry Spond With you I have found your name in the Contest Papers & Picked you for My Better half So I Want Worry you long So as I ame looking for Some Girl that Wants to Marry & I Will Chang forter Grafts you So I Can describe My Self I am 26 years of age 6 ft. tall Weigh 165 lbs dark Complection Was Rased in Mississipapa & iff you Would lik to Corry Spond With Mea I Wold be glad So Please answer Buy Return Mail & yor Postage Returned Pleas Send yer picter in first better 'iff Convenient So I Will Clos hoping to hear Soon address Mea at Lesflin P.O. Stat Ala. R.f.D. No. 6. Pleas exCus Bad Riting So Good Buy

May 29

1910: COTTON FIRE ON HOLT FARM

The entire previous year's crop of cotton on the "famous Holt farm at Linwood" was set on fire by two small sons of the superintendent of the farm, Mr. W.J. Whitener. The young boys were "essaying to smoke a cigarette stub" found by them in the yard. The value of the cotton was about $16,000; there was no insurance. At first, it was thought that perhaps four or five bales could be saved, but "as in cotton fires," it was difficult to subdue the insidious flames. The two little boys, one five and the other seven years of age, found the cigarette stump in their yard, secured matches from their kitchen and hid behind the cotton house, proceeding to "negotiate their first smoke." Upon the alarm being given, the entire community turned out and, with the poor facilities at hand, fought valiantly. Also destroyed were the cotton shed and a great quantity of corn—so "fierce and stubborn was the fire" that even the residence on the farm caught fire several times. The crop had been held for higher prices, and only the day before prices of fifteen cents had been quoted by a firm to which samples had been sent.

May 30

1903: INCIDENTS OF THE EXCURSION
A part of the Lexington contingent that went on the excursion to Charlotte "ran up against it" all along the line. One or more young men spent part of the day in the Charlotte Police Station trying to sober up. A large number left by the train in the evening, and three were taken in charge by the Concord police while trying "to beat their way home" on the regular passenger train. They were heavily fined and remained in jail until friends secured their release. Aside "from these pleasantries," a party of some ten or fifteen engaged in a "knock-down and drag-out fight" on the excursion train while returning home and when they arrived were adorned with black eyes, bruised scalps, etc. and "looking very much as though they had just escaped from a slaughter pen."

May 31

1865: Major General Judson Kilpatrick

Union general H. Judson Kilpatrick and the Ninth
Pennsylvania Cavalry patrolled the Piedmont Triad area
in order to establish order as Reconstruction began. Dr.
and Mrs. William R. Holt, owners of the Homestead on
North Main Street in Lexington, felt that they needed to
safeguard their home from possible destruction, so they
did an unheard-of thing: they offered the Homestead to
Kilpatrick as his headquarters. His staff officers "placed a
United States flag at the gate and posted sentries around the
house." The house remained undamaged, and the family
was treated with consideration. Even so, iron brackets
remain today on the door of the girls' bedroom, evidence
of Mrs. Holt's determination to safeguard them during the
two months Kilpatrick's men occupied the house.

June 1

1908: A Defective System

In earlier days, the *Lexington Dispatch* was known to speak some blunt truths—not palatable, it was true, but truths nevertheless:

> *It is true that North Carolina's system of valuing property, if it may be dignified by calling the methods of getting at the value of property a system, is the veriest humburgery. We recall that several years ago when the Southern Railway Company resisted the effort to assess its interest to North Carolina at what it claimed was an excessive figure, the railroad recurred affidavits from taxlisters in various sections of the state. Some of them deposed that it was customary to assess property at one half its cash value; others operated upon a basis of 66 to 20 percent, while some others used from 75 to 20 percent of the true value of the property as a basis. The injustice to those counties which are taxed upon a high valuation is obvious, to say nothing of the false light in which North Carolina in the matter of wealth is placed before the world.*

The article concludes by calling for a sensible and fair system of assessing property in North Carolina.

June 2

1900: No Cigarettes on the Sabbath!

The City of Winston's city ordinances had read in part: "Drugstores may be kept open at all times, but no cigars, tobacco, soda water, mineral water, or any goods except for medical purposes shall be sold on the Sabbath at any place within the corporation of the City." On this day, the ordinance was changed at a Town of Winston Direction Board meeting. A motion was made to amend this section by striking the words "cigars and tobacco" after the words "but no" and inserting the word "cigarettes." Five aldermen voted for the amendment, while three others voted against the change.

June 3

1967: PIEDMONT TRIAD CONCERN OVER FIGHTING BETWEEN ISRAEL AND SYRIAN FORCES

When it appeared that the war in the Middle East had about ended, and when Egypt and Jordan had "thrown in towels," fighting erupted between Israeli and Syrian forces along the wide border between these two countries. Syria had at first declined to accept a ceasefire order from the United Nations Security Council but then changed its mind and agreed to stop fighting. The ceasefire order had been passed after a prolonged debate. After Syria accepted the ceasefire order, Israel was reported to have followed suit. Then Israel reported that Syrian forces had begun shelling a series of Israeli villages and had continued this through a long night. It was agreed that Israeli forces had replied, contending that they had attacked in self-defense.

June 4

1909: PROHIBITION AND LAW ENFORCEMENT

Good citizens were urged to lend their aid in the proper enforcement of all laws "writ on this statute, whether such laws are exactly to his liking or not." In some localities, it had been violated more than in others. In some localities, public sentiment was more emphatic on the issue than in others. Although prohibition had been in force in North Carolina for nearly five months, there was a marked improvement. The revenue officers were locating and catching the moonshiners on a daily basis, and the state and federal courts made it "mighty warm" for the man who violated the law, but "the tiger was declared hard to get at."

Temperance was an important subject in the Piedmont Triad at the turn of the twentieth century. The prohibition law, it seemed, was being violated on a daily basis. *Library of Congress.*

1906: For a Town Clock

On this day in history, Davidson County commissioners considered the matter of purchasing a town clock and having it placed in the courthouse tower. To consider the matter further, a committee of one was appointed to confer with a like committee from the town commissioners. The county offered to pay half of the cost, provided the entire bill be no more than $800. Citizens believed the entire cost should be borne by the county; however, money might be raised by private subscription. Several had already indicated their willingness to donate liberally. This obviously would be a good time to purchase and install a town clock because the courthouse at this time was being "made over."

June 5

The night was warm. Drinks consisted of corn liquor, home-brewed beer and White Rock soda water. Eleven people gathered on the concrete patio of the boathouse on the bank of Lake Katharine. Host and hostess were Smith Reynolds and his wife, Libby Holman. After the party ended, the later-reported events were contradictory and fuzzy. One thing was certain: Smith Reynolds died from a fatal gunshot wound. Whether it was suicide or murder, we will probably never know.

Lake Katharine was located on the Reynolda estate of R.J. and Katharine Smith Reynolds in Winston. The patio of the boathouse was the scene of many gatherings. *Forsyth County Public Library*.

June 6

1963: JESSE JACKSON ARRESTED IN GREENSBORO

At first, Jesse Jackson and his followers began their demonstrations outside a Greensboro cafeteria one hot day in May 1963. They knelt and started saying the Lord's Prayer; the police reportedly stopped in their tracks and put their hands over their hearts. Later, the Greensboro police—having run out of jail space—took approximately 400 students to the dilapidated wards of the abandoned polio hospital on Summit and Bessemer Avenue. The deserted barracks-like building, meant to hold only 124 occupants, had demonstrators struggling for fresh air. When Jackson arrived at the old polio hospital, police, dogs and troopers guarded the structure. Tears and sweat from the bright sun ran down his face, and he then began delivering an impromptu speech, poignantly focusing on all the suffering involved with the civil rights movement. On this day, Jesse Jackson was arrested in Greensboro for "inciting to riot and disturbing the peace and dignity of the state."

June 7

1908: MULE LUNCHED ON A $24 CHECK
A businessman at Mints wrote the following letter to the
National Bank of Greensboro:

> *Dear Sir: In regard to your check of even date*
> *herewith for the amount of $24.27, which was for*
> *credit of your account, I regret to advise that I put it*
> *in a letter and sent it to the post office to be mailed to*
> *the National Bank for deposit, and my driver, on the*
> *tram road, laid all my letters down while he stopped*
> *for something, and one of the mules took this letter in*
> *his mouth and ate it up, letter, check, and all. I know*
> *this is the way the check was lost because my father*
> *happened to be present and looked in time enough to*
> *see the letter in the mule's mouth, but too late to rescue*
> *it from the mule. I had made check on my bank on*
> *account of this deposit which I though I had made,*
> *and now it is too late for me to call back my checks,*
> *therefore, I have asked my bank to honor my checks*
> *until I can get a duplicate for you.*

June 8

1904: TRAIN RAN INTO OPEN SWITCH

Engineer Tyler D. Haynes and his fireman, Jim Watkins, were instantly killed by the wreck of a Southern passenger train, the wreck having been caused by an open switch. The disaster caused a delay of over two hours. No. 40, one of the Southern's fast passenger trains between Atlanta and Washington, was the train that "came to grief." The train had been running at a good rate of speed with a clear track, but then, without warning, the locomotive plunged into a siding known as "the ice factory switch." The locomotive "turned turtle," and the postal car followed suit, instantly killing the engineer and fireman, who "stuck to their posts." The coaches remained on the track, and aside from being generally shaken up, none of the passengers was injured.

June 9

1950: HUGE LIQUOR STILL DESTROYED

One of the largest liquor stills to be found in Davidson County was broken up by members of the sheriff's department. Located in the Petersville section of Tyro township, the still included four upright furnaces, four seventy-five-gallon boilers, one seven-hundred-gallon upright wooden steam still, one two-hundred-gallon double filter, two fifty-gallon filter boxes and two radiator condensers. Also found were six thousand gallons of mash, eleven four-hundred-gallon boxes and two five-hundred-gallon boxes. Twenty-seven gallons of distilled whiskey were found at the site in five-gallon cans. Officers salvaged valuable parts of the still and destroyed the rest with dynamite. Ownership was unknown.

June 10

1908: MAPLE TREE ONE HUNDRED YEARS OLD

Francis Shore, of Winston-Salem RFD No. 4, shared a well-preserved copy of the first deed made to his grandfather for the old Shore homeplace, on which he now lives. A maple tree designated the southwest corner of the tract, and this corner was designated in the first deed, dated 1815. The deed was written "so many poles to a crooked maple tree in a great thicket." In 1908, this same tree was still standing and had marked the corner of said tract of land for more than one hundred years. The tree stood in a fine piece of meadowland, the dense thicket having been cleared up years previously, but the "crooked maple" continued to do the same service as was designated in the deed of 1815.

June 11

1904: Democratic Primaries in the Piedmont Triad
Democratic primaries for several townships in Davidson County were held. From every precinct heard from, the report came that the primaries were largely attended. The consensus was that "Mr. Glenn is nearly the universal favorite." Chairman Moyer called the Lexington township primary to order. Mr. O.F. Hankins was then called to the chair, and Mr. Charles E. McCrary was elected secretary. A township executive committee was elected as follows: S.L. Owens, W.H. Phillips, W.F. Thomason, C.D. Sink and A.C. Harris.

1921: Katharine Smith Reynolds and Edward Johnston Exchange Marriage Vows
Katharine Smith Reynolds and Edward Johnston exchanged their marriage vows in front of the huge fireplace at Reynolda in Winston-Salem. Wisteria hung from the balcony, and baskets of flowers filled the reception hall. The organist played Mendelssohn's wedding march on the pipe organ as Katharine walked down the stairs. Under a thirteen-light Edward F. Caldwell chandelier decorated with amethysts and amber prisms and a large gilt-metal tassel, the couple was united in marriage by D. Clay Lilly, Katharine's friend and former minister. The bride was forty-one years old, while the groom was twenty-eight. Mary, Nancy and Smith served as their mother's attendants.

June 12

1793: County Seat of Randolph County

Asheboro had become the new county seat of Randolph County. On land owned by Jesse Henley, the new court held its first session on this date. The court sessions produced many people and varied activities. Among the pastimes, horse swapping and drinking grog produced a great deal of party-like noises outside, which often caused the presiding judge to send his high sheriff to the square and demand that the ruckus stop—pronto!

1904: A Narrow Escape

Mr. J.W. Gregory of Lexington was in Winston on business. His little son was with him, and they drove to the depot. While attempting to cross the railway tracks in front of a moving train engine, the horse became frightened and ran backward. Mr. Gregory jumped from the buggy and ran to his horse's head. A gentleman who was in the vehicle also jumped and rescued Mr. Gregory's little son. The horse lurched against Mr. Gregory, knocking him against the moving engine. He was knocked down and rendered unconscious for some time. Physicians were summoned and found it necessary to take nine stitches in Mr. Gregory's back. He was also bruised about the head and shoulders. The horse ran away but was captured before doing any further damage. Mr. Gregory was expected to recover from his narrow escape.

June 13

1904: A Murderer Caught

Thomas Broadway, from Fairmont, Davidson County, was captured in North Dakota. Seven years previously, Broadway had shot and killed Miles Reid of Rowan County. Immediately after the shooting, Broadway escaped, and for seven years his whereabouts had been unknown to officers. The crime for which Broadway was wanted was a particularly atrocious one. On December 30, 1897, Reid and his brother were accompanying Broadway and his wife in a wagon to a neighbor's house. The men became involved "in a row" and left their wagons. After a few minutes, Broadway shot Reid from behind, killing him instantly. The cause of the shooting, according to Broadway, was Reid's addressing an insulting remark to his wife. The slayer then left for "parts unknown" but was later discovered near his old home in Davidson County. For several weeks, armed posses searched for him, but he eluded the officers. Some time later, a friend who knew his whereabouts "partook too freely of corn juice" and while in that condition "let fall a clue," whereby the officers learned the fugitive's location.

1966: New Radio Station to Reach More Than One Million

A new "all country music" radio station—WLXN—went on the air in Lexington. Omar G. Hilton was manager and co-owner of the station, an FM broadcast outlet located at 94.1 on the dial. It was operated with a power output of 4,320 watts, and engineering surveys showed that it would reach more than one million people in the Piedmont Triad. The staff at the station included well-known Lexington, Winston-Salem, King and Thomasville citizens, including Ralph C. Smith, who had eight years' experience in the country and western music field and had appeared with such personalities as Bill Anderson of the Grand Ole Opry, Mike Landon ("Little Joe" on the *Bonanza* TV program) and George Hamilton IV.

June 14

1904: Greensboro's Benbow Hotel

Mr. Z.I. Walser, of Lexington, and Miss Grace Daniels, of Yadkin College, were married in the parlors of the Benbow Hotel in Greensboro. Harlee MacCall acted as best man and Miss Lucy Holt as maid of honor. The wedding announcement was a "pleasant surprise" by the many friends of Mr. and Mrs. Walser in Lexington and over the entire Piedmont Triad. The affair was "not a runaway, but was known only to the parties directly involved." Mr. Walser was a well-known young attorney of Lexington. His bride was a daughter of Mrs. W.T. Totten of Yadkin College and was held in "the highest esteem by all who knew her."

1905: 666 West Fifth Street, Winston

R.J. and Katharine Reynolds set sail as first-class passengers on the SS *Celtic* from Liverpool to New York. When they docked in New York, they traveled by train, arriving in Winston in mid-June. It wasn't long before their children began arriving. The Reynoldses' children adored their easy-going father. When his children asked him how he got those little red spots on his skin, R.J. made up a tale: "A big red rooster pecked me while I was in the hen yard. And every place he tapped me, one of those red dots appeared. I suppose I will have them the rest of my life, and they will eventually spread until I am nothing but one giant red ball."

June 15

1897: STATE NORMAL AND INDUSTRIAL SCHOOL IN GREENSBORO
The June 15, 1897 issue of *State Normal Magazine* published the following mission statement for graduates:

> *It is the duty of each one to go forth into the State and endeavor to improve the condition of the people and uplift the lower classes by creating in them a desire for higher education and by aiding them to obtain it.*

1914: A LOCKSMITH SAVED THE DAY
A drugstore in Winston-Salem was searched for liquor, but none was found until the safe was opened. The proprietor said he had lost the combination, but a locksmith opened it under directions of the chief of police and found seventy-six half-pint bottles and two quart bottles full of whiskey.

June 16

1954: Thomasville Ministers Protest Show of Scantily Clad Negro Women

A special biracial meeting was called on this day by the Thomasville Ministerial Association to consider what a spokesman said was the question of public morals affecting both races. The show, advertised as "Sugar Ray Robinson's Own Great Acts in Person," among other things, had come under protest at Thomasville. The entertainment, "Stars over Harlem," was scheduled to begin in a three-thousand-seat tent. Police Chief Frank N. Littlejohn said he would try to prevent the scheduled performance of a road show that advertised scantily clad Negro women. He further objected to the show on the grounds that it would include performances of "lewd and lascivious dances." He added that he would attempt to have the show banned under a section of the city code that prohibited "indecent exhibitions, publications, pictures, plays, dancing and sacrilegious songs."

June 17

1861: FORSYTH COUNTY FANFARE SENT CONFEDERATE SOLDIERS
OFF TO WAR
These were the first men in the county to join the army.
They gathered on this solemn day at Salem Academy for a
send-off that included parades and brass bands. Alfred H.
Belo, son of prominent Salem merchant Edward Belo, had
formed a company called the Forsyth Rifles. The women of
the village had made a flag for Belo and presented it to his
company. Rufus Wharton and his Forsyth Grays and Frank
P. Miller's group followed as Reverend George F. Bahnson
prayed for the men's safety and also "warned them about
the temptations of a soldier's life."

1965: HOWARD JOHNSON RESTAURANT PERSECUTED BY SANITARIAN
Charges that the Lexington Howard Johnson Restaurant
had been persecuted by a sanitarian of the Davidson
County Health Department were made by B.F. Lowery,
manager of the restaurant. Lowery, convicted in Davidson
County Superior Court for failure to post a sanitation
grade card, told the local newspaper reporter, "The
particular health man involved has persecuted the place
for eight years since it was built." The sanitarian he spoke
of was O.W. Strickland. Lowery said, "He even went so far
in his persecution as to suggest I get another job." Lowery
claimed that Strickland found most of the faults in his
grading with the construction of the restaurant, even
though it was built along the lines of all other Howard
Johnson establishments.

June 18

1905: Unusual News of the Day

Mr. D.F. Andrews, who was employed at the Elk Furniture Co. factory, went on a big coon hunt on Muddy Creek in Arcadia township. He captured four coons and one opossum and said it wasn't a good night for coons either. Mr. Andrews, the owner of five "as good dogs as ever hunted," took his catch home with him and planned to make pets of the coons. From Linwood came another unusual notice. Clarence Spaugh, an industrious young man, sent the following letter of explanation with a cotton blossom: "I send you a cotton blossom, plucked from a patch which father gave me for my task last year. This patch consists of four-fifths of an acre and it produced 763 pounds of lint. Cotton is blooming earlier, but is not looking as well as it did last year at this time."

June 19

1944: FLYBOY

Tom Warth, a fighter pilot from Greensboro who flew eighty-two missions to prevent German fighters from attacking American bombers flying to Germany, France and Russia, kept meticulous flight records. Following is an excerpt from one his entries:

June 19, 1944: We escorted the bombers on a raid on Bordeaux. I led the squadron, and the mission went off better than any I have been on in a long time, and they were solid…up to 35,000 feet. I started to climb up through it and came back but someone called and said they were at 33,000 feet and still hadn't broken through it. So, I decided to let down through it and try to find a layer to fly between. I told the other three flights to stay at 18,000 feet, and I would let down and try to find a break. Everything was going fine until I got to about 13,000 feet and started getting iced up. So, I started to climb back up. About this time, my instruments went out, and I lost control of my plane. I must have rolled it over and went into a steep dive because before I knew it, I was doing 560 mph and had no idea of which end was up. I finally, by the grace of God, saw the ground up above me (I was upside down) and rolled out just in time to keep from cracking up.

1963: BESSEMER HIGH WHIPPETS WON THE STATE 3-A
BASEBALL CHAMPIONSHIP

Greensboro Bessemer won its first high school baseball championship since 1925 by defeating Chapel Hill. The victory, achieved before an estimated seven hundred fans, closed out the Bessemer High School era in athletics on a glorious note. The next fall, Bessemer would be converted into a junior high. Richard Straughn, whose steal of third base set up the winning run, shared his laurels with lefty Wally Pegram, Wayne "Bubba" Bryant and Wayne Nunn.

June 20

1900: THE AMENDED AMENDMENT
The legislature did an important day's work on this date in amending the election law and making the constitutional amendment stronger than it was before. The part of the amendment that was changed is as follows:

> *Section 4: Every person presenting himself for registration shall be able to read and write any section of the constitution in the English language. Before he shall be entitled to vote, he shall have paid on or before the first day of May of the year in which he proposed to vote, his poll tax.*

1914: REPORT REVEALS STATISTICS SURROUNDING DEATHS OF TEXTILE WORKERS
This was the first attempt to report vital statistics in North Carolina concerning deaths in mills. These statistics indicated that the death rate for Negroes was much higher than the death rate for whites and that there were three great causes for the death of persons between the ages of five and fifty: typhoid, tuberculosis and pneumonia. This vital statistics report was submitted by W.H. Swift in the eleventh Biennial Report of the North Carolina State Board of Health.

June 21

1943: HE PATTED HER ON HER BACKSIDE, SO SHE LEFT
John Ayers, a sixty-four-year-old Thomasville furniture
worker, killed his neighbor, William Jordan Mitchell,
thirty-nine, at the end of a homebrew drinking spree with
six shots from a .22 pistol. He was committed to Dix Hill
in Raleigh for a thirty-day mental examination by state
psychiatrists. Ayers was taken to Raleigh after examinations
by Dr. M.E. Block, county coroner; Dr. Dermont Lohr,
county health officer; and another physician. He was
very distraught and made no statement in regard to the
shooting. Mrs. Mitchell recounted the following events
leading up to her husband's death:

> *Mrs. Mitchell said her husband went to the Ayers'
> home for a visit about 9 p.m. A couple of hours later,
> she said she went to the home to remind her husband
> that it was getting late. She said Ayers came to the door
> to let her in and that he patted her on her backside.
> She said she slapped him and left immediately. Her
> husband followed her, and when she told him what had
> happened, he said, "Oh, he was just drinking a little,
> but I'll talk to him." He went back to the Ayers' house,
> she said, and a few minutes later, she heard the shots.*

June 22

1906: PLETHORA OF PEACHES

The peach market in Lexington was glutted with several loads of Georgia peaches. Everybody had peaches. From one end of town to the other, the products of Georgia peach orchards were scattered. The peaches came at a time when the homegrown fruit was just beginning to come on the market, and they were seized upon rather eagerly. What caused this windfall? The train carrying the peaches hit a defective track. The wheels on one car left the track at the Nokomis Cotton

Peaches were a summer favorite of many family members. Pies, cobblers, homemade ice cream and cakes were made with peaches shipped from Georgia. *Wikimedia Commons.*

Mill switch and ran several hundred yards until a high hill was reached just beyond the mill. Here nine cars tumbled down the embankment, and nearly all were reduced "to tooth pick timber." A tenth car remained on the hill but partly off the rails. This was next to the caboose, which also held to the track. The forward part of the train was not damaged. The track was torn up and damaged, but it was only a short time until it was repaired. In the meantime, the folks about Lexington had free peaches.

June 23

1906: FIRST TRAIN TO DENTON

The Thomasville & Glen Anna Railroad had been completed to Denton, and on this day, a big celebration was held in honor of the event. The citizens gave a dinner to the officials and employees of the road and to all who were present. After dinner, Professor H.W. Rinehart and the Honorable A.F. Sams addressed the people on the importance of the railroad in developing the resources of the section and advised the people of Denton on preparing a formulation for the newer and bigger town that must now spring up since the railroad had come. It was assumed that Denton would build up very rapidly at this point, as it was centrally located in a rich section and was in easy reach of Lexington, Asheboro, Troy, Albemarle and Salisbury, all flourishing county seats.

June 24

1914: DAVIDSON'S BOOZE

Page one of the regional newspaper ran an article on this day that touted Davidson County as one of the places in North Carolina where booze still flowed and, every now and then, where a raid was made, with the discovery "something frightful to behold." A man "whose name makes no difference" was called upon to show the booze he had, and in the raid that followed, a wagonload of empty whiskey kegs was discovered, along with all kinds of empty bottles—and some not so empty. The remainder of the account urges the courts "to do their duty" so there would be no whiskey sold. Road sentences were advocated for offenders because "five years on the roads in stripes" may seem like an "awful price to pay, but one blind tiger can debauch a hundred young men." Enforcement of the law would stop it!

June 25

1918: Those Funny French Costumes

Corporal J.C. Hoffman, who had been in France for some time, reported to Piedmont Triad civilians. He related that soldiers in France did not get much war news and that the war was not discussed among the boys. The men were allowed out of camp every night until 9:00 p.m., and lights out was at 9:30. Corporal Hoffman admitted that he had met with some strange experiences in France but that he was restricted from discussing those. He then wrote about the "French lasses" and admitted that some of them are "knockouts." The French had been very sociable, and if some "mademoiselle should ask you to her home for dinner," it was important to study the French customs. The first thing offered when you entered her home was a kiss from her and then a kiss from her mother. After that, the monsieur stepped over, pulled down your face and "whanged it a couple." Thinking this was the "latest dope," he sprang it on his buddy in the barracks, who then proceeded to toss him into a corner, saying, "Are you going bugs in your old age?"

June 26

1906: THOMASVILLE BAPTIST ORPHANAGE

Owning to circumstances over which the Board of Trustees had no control, the annual meeting of the Thomasville Baptist Orphanage was changed from this date to July 4–5. Heretofore, the Board of Trustees met for its regular meeting to transact such business as might come before it, and the annual sermon was preached on the night the board met. Also announced were details concerning the public exercises held by the children at Thomasville Baptist Orphanage.

This day also marked the close of the second week of the *Dispatch*'s "Great Popular Voting Contest to Send Six Ministers to New York City." Votes, which came in daily, indicated that the people in Yadkin, Montgomery, Davie and Randolph Counties had been thoroughly informed about the contest and were now "bestirring themselves" in the interests of their favorite preachers. This was the perfect opportunity to get your favorite preacher away from work for ten days, during which he would be sent to the "greatest city in the world" and be royally entertained. Furthermore, he would find the trip a welcome rest and a delightful change and would also draw "much profit and knowledge."

June 27

1906: How the Famous Davidson Congressman Got Out of a Tight Place

In the late 1860s or early 1870s, members of one Congress voted themselves additional salaries, which they convinced themselves were due them from the preceding session. Among those voting for this measure was the late General James Madison Leach of North Carolina, then a representative. The next was a candidate for reelection, and when he was "thundering away on the stump one day," a man in the audience interrupted him: "But what did you do with your part of the back salary grab?" he asked. "I used it to pay a security debt for your daddy, damn you— that's what I did with it."

June 28

1907: NOT DEAD BUT SLEEPING
The report reached Thomasville on this day that a man
was lying dead by the tracks two miles south of town,
having been mangled by the train. Hurriedly ordering his
two white horses, the coroner summoned a company of
"grave and reverend citizens" and rushed to the scene. He
approached the remains and laid his hand on the body when
the man, who was simply taking a nap, roused himself and
remarked, "How is you all today?" The coroner and his
company, as they slowly returned home, drove "in a walk
by a back street."

1950: ONE-LEGGED MAN ROBBED AT ERLANGER
Approximately $6,000   in   building-and-loan   stock
certificates, around $130 in cash and a tool chest with
some tools were taken from the home of James Biesecker.
Deputy Leonard stated the robbery occurred at Biesecker's
home and that Biesecker, a one-legged man, said that
only a few days earlier he had seen his chest containing
the stocks, money and tools, which he kept under his bed.
The building-and-loan stock certificate robbery was the
second reported in Davidson County recently. Two weeks
earlier, the home of Marshall E. Wilson of Midway was
entered, and some $25,000 in such certificates were taken.
Three men were later arrested on charges of breaking and
entering and larceny and receiving. Some of these bonds
were reportedly recovered.

June 29

1921: Tobacco Crop Forecasted as Smallest in Ten Years
The tobacco crop was reportedly the smallest in 1921 since that of 1911. The 1921 production was valued at 933 million pounds, which was more than a third less than the former year's record crop. The condition of the crop, which was 71.9 percent of normal, was lower than it had been on that date in twenty-one years. It was 10.2 points below the ten-year average condition on July 1 and 12.4 points below the previous year's July 1 average. An average acre yield of 697.3 pounds was forecasted to be almost 100 pounds less per acre than was harvested the previous year.

1950: No Consolidation!
Linwood school patrons spoke against the proposed consolidation of their high school with the high school at Junior Children's Home by rather convincing majority. One newspaper editor explored possible reasons for rejecting the consolidation:

> *Some reflections upon children at the Junior Home, and upon other students in orphanage schools generally, have been rather assiduously circulated in Linwood and other districts interested in high school consolidation proposals. We believe that officials of the Junior Home, of Mills Home at Thomasville, at Methodist Children's Home at Winston-Salem, and others would overwhelmingly refute any aspersions against*

the children who are trained in these institutions. The record of their graduates for fine citizenship can perhaps be equaled by hardly any public high school in all North Carolina.

June 30

1921: J.A. WALSER'S STOLEN CAR RECOVERED NEAR LINWOOD
Sheriff Fred C. Sink went to the home of Jim Smith near
Spain's Old Mill site not far from Linwood and brought
back the Ford automobile that had been stolen from J.A.
Walser at about one o'clock one recent morning. The car
had been standing in Smith's yard since about three o'clock
on the morning of the theft. One rear tire was missing, and
the radius rod was bent, accounting for the abandonment
of the machine. Smith said that a man drove up there with
the car and asked to leave it until the next day, when he
would come back and pay for accommodation. He told
Smith about attending a party in Lexington and that he
had "got into a little trouble and somebody shot at him."

July 1

1887: O. HENRY
William Sidney Porter of Greensboro eloped on this
day with seventeen-year-old Athol Ester, who was from
a wealthy family. Ester's mother objected to the match
because her daughter was ill, suffering from tuberculosis.
The couple continued to participate in musical and theater
groups, and Athol encouraged her husband to pursue his
writing. He began developing characters and plots for such
stories as "Georgia's Ruling" and "Buried Treasure."

1954: DESTRUCTIVE GRINDLE CAUGHT AT HIGH ROCK
A castoff of the fish world identified as a grindle or bowfin
was caught in High Rock Lake by John Turner of Route
6. It weighed three and a half pounds and was lured by
worms. The odd fish looked like a cross between a catfish
and a bass and was considered a destructive enemy of game
fish. The grindle is a freshwater fish not often found in the
Piedmont Triad area. Fishermen at High Rock Lake were
warned to destroy these fish when they were caught—they
were not good to eat!

July 2

1903: DEATH UNDER CAR WHEELS

W.E. Shargreen, a Greensboro resident and collector for *Collier's Weekly*, was run over by a "making-up train" on the shifting yard at eleven o'clock on this morning; he was killed instantly. He stepped from one track to escape an approaching shifting engine and was knocked down by a boxcar on another track, the wheels completely "disemboweling but not otherwise mutilating him."

1954: HOUSE TRAILER DUMPED BY WIND

An empty house trailer went for a brief but wild ride during heavy wind and rain. The trailer, property of Mock Yarbrough, was not extensively damaged, although it was carried about thirty-five feet and dumped over on its side. Parked beside Yarbrough Hosiery Mills, the trailer experienced strong gusts of wind that shoved it out into the street and turned it over. A wrecker was summoned, and the trailer was quickly pulled back to the mill lot.

July 3

1903: SHE DEMANDED MORPHINE
In Winston, a young married woman applied at a drugstore for morphine, stating candidly that she wanted the drug to kill herself. She was refused, and she was so violent that she was placed in jail to prevent her from harming herself. Reportedly, the poor woman was driven to distraction by the infidelity of her husband.

1921: AT HEALING SPRINGS
Quite a number of Piedmont Triad people were enjoying the "fine waters of Healing Springs." Among those occupying cottages there were Mr. and Mrs. John T. Lowe and children, Mr. H.W. Dorsett and family, Mr. C.C. Hargrave and family and Mr. E.E. Raper and family. Mr. and Mrs. Bailey were camping there. Large numbers had visited the springs recently, and they compared High Rock to Atlanta City. The "bathing" was enjoyed by "a large patronage."

July 4

1783: PERHAPS THE FIRST FOURTH OF JULY PARADE IN NORTH CAROLINA

The Treaty of Paris ended the Revolutionary War, so the first Fourth of July celebration in Salem was a significant event. There was an early morning band recital, prayer service, love feast and procession through the streets. Holding candles, Salem residents formed a circle and sang the following song:

Peace is with us! Peace is with us! People of the Lord!
Peace is with us! Peace is with us! Hear the joyful word!
Let it sound from shore to shore! Let it echo evermore!
Peace is with us! Peace is with us! Peace, the gift of God.

1903: HOLINESS PREACHER AND ERRING WIFE

Mrs. Jennie Harrill was enticed away from her husband by a holiness preacher who used his Bible to prove to Mrs. Harrill that she would be justified in leaving her husband and in going with him. Mr. Harrill followed his erring wife and the preacher to Chattanooga, Tennessee, and had the preacher arrested. Mrs. Harrill begged her husband to forgive her and let her return home with him, but he would not grant her request. Some years earlier, a holiness preacher had tried to entice a wife away from her husband by telling her that the Lord had given him a revelation that she should leave her husband and go with him. The lady told her husband what the "so-called holiness fellow" had proposed, and when the enraged husband saw the preacher, he said, "Look here, you blankety-blanked, jingle-jawd limb of Satan...when did the Lord make that revelation you were telling my wife about?" "Last Monday," replied the preacher. "Well, now," said the husband. "I've seen the Lord about that matter and I've got a later revelation and that is to beat the very devil out of you." And then and there, the more "holier than thou" preacher "got the medicine he needed."

July 5

1903: NEW LUMBER COMPANY
The Finger Lumber Company of Lexington was
incorporated by the secretary of state. The company
had an authorized capital stock of $10,000 that could be
increased to $50,000. The incorporators were Messrs. H.K.
Finger, W.A. Anthony, E.J. Buchanan and D.F. Conrad
of Lexington. This was the second company of this kind
organized in Lexington. The new company purchased
seven thousand acres of un-cleared timberland near Old
Fort and planned to establish sawmills by which to "cut and
market this timber."

1917: SPLENDID COUNTRY ESTATE
Katharine Smith Reynolds and her assistants gave a
demonstration in dairying at her modern dairy barns.
Attending were prominent farmers and dairymen of
the county. The demonstration also included methods
of utilizing the dairy equipment, particularly the steam
sterilizing machine, in canning. A number of ladies
attended. These demonstrations were given in an effort
to stimulate food production and conservation. The
containers were secured through the government and were
put up under government regulations and according to
government specifications.

July 6

1921: First Services Held in New Beulah Church
The first service was held in the new church at Beulah with a record-breaking attendance, there being 290 present at Sunday school. The church was complete except for the pews and furniture. The pews and the pulpit from the old church were being used. About two hundred new chairs were expected to be placed to accommodate the congregation. The special revival meeting was scheduled to take place on the fourth Sabbath of the month, and the preaching in the meeting would be done by Reverend J.A. Koons. The people of the community were very proud of their new church and wished to thank all the friends who contributed labor, lumber and money toward its building. Mr. John Ham Leonard desired to express special thanks to his friends who contributed through him. An invitation was extended to all friends to worship in the new church. Mothers were especially invited to bring their babies. "Babies never disturbed the pastor of this church, and he believed they ought to be taken to church from infancy," the paper reported.

1932: Torch Singer Accused of Murdering Millionaire Husband
Although Libby Holman, one of the first torch singers on Broadway, was accused of murdering her husband, Smith Reynolds, at Reynolda in Winston-Salem, no conclusion was ever reached. The grand jury did issue a presentment charging that Libby Reynolds and Abe Walkers "on or

about the sixth day of July, 1932, with force and arms, did unlawfully, willfully, feloniously, premeditatedly, of their malice aforethought murder Z. Smith Reynolds." Later, the indictments were dropped "to obviate the baring of Libby's and Smith's private lives before a jury." Judge A.M. Stack hammered his gavel and announced, "Let the defendants be discharged and their bonds be released."

One of the first torch singers on Broadway, Libby Holman married Smith Reynolds and resided for a while—until her husband's mysterious death—at Reynolda in Winston-Salem. *Wikimedia Commons*.

July 7

1934: THE PAUSE THAT DID NOT REFRESH
Johnny Copeland of Thomasville was taken into custody.
His arrest was based on the fact that his fingerprints
were found at the Thomasville Coca-Cola Bottling
Company, where $1,000 was missing from the company's
safe. Thomasville officers became suspicious when they
learned that Copeland had been spending a great deal of
money—money that officers believed he could not have
secured legally. One of the indications, police asserted, was
that he had hired a taxi to take him to South Carolina.
Thomasville officers attempted to pick the man up but were
unsuccessful, learning that
Copeland had then taken
a taxi to High Point. High
Point police, acting upon
information   furnished
them by officers of the
neighboring city, raided
the   Edmondson   Street
home where Copeland
was attending a party. He
offered no resistance.

Coca-Cola bottling companies
sprang up in many Piedmont Triad
towns, and bottled Cokes appeared
in most homes and cafés. This was
a big business, so perhaps the
Thomasville thief who broke into the
Coca-Cola Bottling Company safe
knew there would be "big bucks"
inside. *Wikimedia Commons.*

July 8

1903: A Romantic Courtship

Boarding No. 39, the southbound passenger train, at Lexington on this day were Squire William A. Heitman, who resided about two miles north of Lexington, and Reverend D.P. Tate, a Methodist minister. These gentlemen were en route to Spartanburg, South Carolina, where Squire Heitman would be joined together in holy wedlock with Miss Mary Harty, "an estimable lady of that city." Reverend Tate, as a mutual friend of the "contracting parties," went to perform the ceremony. Squire Heitman was a widower, his wife having been dead for a number of years. His acquaintance with Miss Harty had been made only a short time earlier, Reverend Tate "being the medium" through which the introduction was secured. The parties to the marriage had not, up to this date, seen each other but one time, and this was during the month of May, when Squire Heitman went on an excursion to Charlotte to meet the lady with whom he had been conducting a correspondence. The meeting, though of brief duration, was "sufficiently long to cause mutual admiration" and was "followed by love and a proposal which was accepted and culminated in marriage at the home of the bride's brother."

July 9

1905: Fifteen-Year-Old Boy Allegedly Poisons Water Supply

Marcellus Daniel was seen by neighbors going from the direction of the house owned by Mock Proctor. The residence had been entered after a staple was removed from a door. The family was away. Because nothing was missing, officers surmised that the burglar had become frightened and left. When Mr. Proctor's family members went to the spring near the house for a bucket of water, they noticed that the water didn't look right; an investigation revealed the fact that Paris Green had been placed in the spring. An empty can bearing the label of this deadly poison was found in nearby bushes, where it had evidently been thrown.

1917: Possible Draft This Week

The local Draft Board completed the preliminary work preparatory to the draft that was expected to take place soon. All the registration cards had been given new serial numbers beginning with the number one and going through all the cards that were within the jurisdiction of Davidson County, about 2,600. This serial number was the number that would be used in the actual draft of the first 687,000 called for by the War Department. Every man who registered was urged to know his serial number, posted on the courthouse door.

July 10

1917: Those Who May Be Exempt from the Draft

The following persons were to be exempt by the local board upon their filing and writing the proper claims: United States and state officers, preachers, divinity students, persons in military service, German subjects and resident aliens, county and municipal officers whose terms of office are elective and cannot be filled by appointment for the unexpired term, postal employees, pilots and mariners. Those who claimed exemption on account of their occupation, such as agriculture, manufacturing and other pursuits useful in time of war, had to present their claims for exemption not to the local board but to the Federal District Board.

July 11

1917: CITIZENS RESPOND TO RED CROSS

The Lexington Red Cross committee in charge of the special campaign to raise $3,000 in Davidson County announced that the full amount had been secured. On this date, only about $500 needed to be secured. A progress report from Thomasville was not yet available, but $2,000 had been assigned to that district. In the Piedmont Triad, High Point had already closed its campaign with some $500. Women of the Lexington Red Cross chapter met and called for items for "the soldier boys who would go to France," and these ambitious women, "with thimble and needles," were busy with sewing much-needed items.

July 12

1921: ANOTHER BONEHEAD PLAY

Lexington baseball fans who had watched W.E. Marlette in action during the season and who had cause to appreciate his gentlemanly qualities—both on the baseball diamond and off—could not help but laugh at the following uncalled-for item that appeared in the *Thomasville Times*:

> *The Lexington team has been greatly strengthened. The only weak spot of that team at the present time is at first base. Marlette does not seem to be popular with the fans, as he pulls off some mighty bad bonehead plays when they will do the most damage. Of course, Marlette is only hitting about 10, which is calculated to increase his popularity with some of the "fans" in other towns where they have ball clubs.*

July 13

1942: COAT-HANGER ABORTION

Cornelia Moore, a seventy-three-year-old woman, was placed under a $1,000 bond for her appearance at superior court on a charge of attempting to produce an abortion. Also bound were Mr. and Mrs. Wesley Stoneman of Thomasville and Charles Stoneman, Wesley's brother. The following incidents had transpired earlier:

> *Lula Belle Jones, a 36-year-old woman of Thomasville, lodged the charges against the four accused after she had previously preferred a formal charge of non-support of an unborn illegitimate child against Charles Stoneman, 19 years old. The Jones woman testified that she had been living with a family at Thomasville and serving as a nursemaid when she became expectant. Charles Stoneman was the father, she said. She quoted Charles as saying Mr. and Mrs. Wesley Stoneman would help her be rid of her embarrassment. She said Charlie and Mr. and Mrs. Wesley Stoneman took her to see Cornelia Moore, who prescribed that she take separate doses of quinine, camphor, and lemon extract. The Moore woman was paid $5. The next day, the doses were repeated—without any effect. She testified Charles then procured tablets for her and that Mrs. Stoneman advised another form of treatment, but all in vain. Then, Mrs. Stoneman contrived a crude surgical instrument from a coat hanger and advised her as to its use.*

Lula Belle Jones testified that her physician had told her she would never be able to carry a child full term.

July 14

1905: PIEDMONT TRIAD LADIES ENJOY SEASHORE

Misses Sallie Zimmerman, Ollie Hege and Carrie Hege sent a note of thanks, through the regional newspaper, to their friends who so kindly aided them in winning an outing to Wrightsville Beach. They stayed at the Seashore Hotel, which had broad verandas on either side. Toward the west was the sound, and beyond that was an expanse of seaweed, a family of grand oaks festooned with hanging moss and summer cottages of the wealthy. In addition, these three ladies commented on "breaking into the scenery" where large streams from the upper mountain region had tumbled down "from their birth place and been caught and tamed by human cunning." They were also impressed with a fishing party on the *Virgie Male*.

July 15

1910: THE SABBATH

All pastors in Thomasville had agreed to preach on the proper observance of the Sabbath. This brought the following editorial comments from the editor of the regional newspaper:

> *It ought to do good, and we believe the example of these pastors ought to be generally followed. The change in the estimate of the Sabbath that has come over the minds of men within the past two decades reveals the danger to which we are exposed. How is it with you? Do you feel the same way about keeping the Sabbath holly* [sic] *now that you did twenty years ago? The Southern railway trains make more fuss on Sunday than on any other day because there are more of them. Sunday is the big day for the fruit trains that go crashing through the town at a high rate of speed. Men who own automobiles having nothing else to do, sleep too late to go to church, but go out for a ride Sunday afternoon, and return too late to attend the evening service.*

July 16

1921: MASS MEETING OF BASEBALL FANS HELD

A mass meeting of the baseball fans of Lexington was held at the courthouse for the purpose of discussing "ways and means" for the balance of the year. It was estimated that besides the amount that had already been underwritten by certain guarantors in the city, it would be necessary to raise about $1,200 more. The sentiment of the meeting seemed to be that whatever amount was needed must be raised. Many matters were discussed by those interested in the "great national pastime."

July 17

1907: Mrs. Carry Nation's "Hell Hole on Earth"

Mrs. Carry Nation was circulating in North Carolina, visiting High Point and Greensboro. When she left, she went to Durham, "where she cussed out everybody on account of the tobacco and cigarette business." Reportedly, she proceeded to "vent her spleen" on the cigarette when introduced to a young man. The following conversation was printed:

> *"I small cigarettes," said the woman of hatchet fame.*
> *"Yes, madam, I smoke cigarettes," said the young man.*
> *"I thought so," said Mrs. Nation. "I can always*
> *tell when there is a skunk near by the smell."*

An argument followed, during which the young man told her that obviously she was a lady and that it was the custom for a gentleman not to slap the face of a lady. Later, on a streetcar, Mrs. Nation pointed to a tobacco sign in a drugstore window. "See that, see that!" she exclaimed. "It is worse than a bar room sign. That place is a hell hole on earth."

1988: Killing Spree Along Old Salisbury Road

People in the Piedmont Triad were privy to the chain of events preceding Michael Hayes's killing spree. Ronald Hull, thirty-two, and his wife, Darlene, twenty-nine—wounded but survivors—pieced together the events of the evening. They had been at a family celebration with their son, Ronald Adam Hull, eight. After the Hulls left the gathering, they started home in their truck, driving along Old Salisbury Road. Someone in the road waved the vehicle to a stop. The second that Hull applied brakes, the assailant, Michael Hayes, smashed the driver's window. Hayes put a gun to Hull's head and pulled the trigger. When Darlene started screaming, Hayes shot her, but not before she yelled for their son to get on the floorboard. Next, Hayes shot Melinda Yvonne Hayes (no relation), age twenty-one, as she returned from driving her boyfriend to his house on Jonestown Road. Hayes's next target was Crystal Suzanne Cantrell, sixteen. He stopped her black Camaro and killed her. In his old Dodge pickup, Bobbie Jo Eddleman was headed home to his parents' house. Tragedy struck him in the form of Michael Hayes standing on the centerline of the darkened road in front of his parents' moped shop. Hayes received a "not guilty by reason of insanity" verdict and was sent to Dorothea Dix State Mental Hospital.

July 18

1921: Dr. Peacock Is Tired of the Pen
Dr. J.W. Peacock, Thomasville physician and murderer of Chief of Police Taylor, reportedly intended on making an effort through his attorneys and friends to secure a transfer from the state penitentiary to one of the hospitals for the insane. Friends of Dr. Peacock hoped to find some way to make the transfer possible, although none of them at that particular time were able to say just how it could be done. It was emphasized in the regional newspapers that Dr. Peacock's skill and ability would be valuable if some way could be found to use his medical talents. Superintendent Anderson at the hospital for the insane at Dix's Hill in Raleigh was quoted as saying that Dr. Peacock would be "gladly received at his institution, if the law would permit."

1989: Blanche Taylor Moore
Blanche Taylor Moore, nicknamed the "Black Widow," was charged with the first-degree murder of her boyfriend, Raymond Reid. She had slowly but deliberately poisoned him with arsenic, afterward assuming the persona of a wholesome, grieving woman. She enlisted Reverend Dwight Moore, a local United Congregational Church minister, for comfort. Four years later, they married. One of their first meals as husband and wife included waffles, bacon and arsenic. Moore became ill, recovered, regressed and recovered again. Finally, toxic tests proved that Moore had ingested a great

deal of the poison in the banana pudding that Moore made and spoon-fed him while he lay in the hospital. Reverend Moore lived through the ordeal. After this incident, the bodies of Robert Reid and Moore's first husband, James Taylor, were exhumed. They, too, had lethal doses of arsenic poisoning; however, they were not the first. Moore had poisoned her father, Parker Kiser, by doctoring his beer stein with poison.

July 19

1907: Fight Near Pomona in Greensboro

Passengers arriving in Greensboro on the Winston train related a few facts relative to a somewhat "lively scrap" up near Pomona. When the train stopped at a junction just beyond Pomona, a man under the influence of liquor began cursing at a "furious rate" at some of the train crews. A revenue officer on board named Shepard, who "withstood the volley of oaths as long as he deemed it proper within the bounds of justice," leaped from the train and dealt the cursing man some blows to the face, which floored him and incidentally brought blood gushing from his mouth. The train moved off and left the two combatants on the scene of battle, but reportedly peace had already been restored.

July 20

1921: FORMER SURGEON IN CONFEDERATE ARMY

The Piedmont Triad prided itself on grand old citizens and heroes who had been followers of Lee and Jackson, realizing these men were a "Thin Grey Line," with the line growing thinner each year as certain files dropped out to join their comrades and beloved leaders "in another land where their tired frames would find peace that knows no pain." One great man was still among the living on this date. He was Dr. B.F. Carey, eighty-four years of age, slightly lame from a stroke of paralysis and a fluent talker rich in war reminiscences. He had served under Hunter Maguire as assistant surgeon through the war until he was captured a few days before the surrender while foraging for food at Fredericksburg. He was attached to the Thirtieth Virginia Field Brigade and saw action in several battles.

July 21

1921: PUBLIC OFFICE HURTS MANY MEN

A newspaper article on this day explored one example of how politics nibbled away a public servant's monetary worth. Franklin K. Lane, after fifteen years in public service, died, leaving his family only $10,000. He was well-to-do when he went into office, but "politics nibbled away his accumulations" until at his death, after valuable service to his country, his estate yielded his widow and children a "bare $40" a month. The question was asked: "How many men who seek and find a political job, enjoy it for four, eight, or twelve years, return to private life only to find themselves unfitted for the task of earning a living against competition?" The answer: "There was no competition in office. The salary was regular, and the people paid the freight. But the aftermath!"

July 22

1907: HER LIFE WAS SAVED

Thomas Gildings, the aged man charged with incest, was bound over to court in Winston for the sum of $500. His daughter shed no disposition to free her father from the "terrible charge, although approached by two men who tried to get her to swear that there was nothing to the charge." The two men, Lester Sanders and J.E. Cline, were fined $25 and costs for trying to influence her. Gildings tried to bribe witnesses but, upon failing, drew a pistol on his daughter. Her life was saved by the pistol failing to fire. Gildings then drank carbolic acid and was "in a precarious condition."

July 23

1917: MR. BASEBALL

Ernest Grady Shore, who was born in Yadkin County in 1891 and starred as a pitcher at Guilford College, went on to pitch for the New York Giants. He pitched a perfect game on July 23, 1917, after relieving his roommate, Babe Ruth, who had been thrown out of the game for "walking the first batter and arguing with the umpire." For many years, the game was listed in record books as a "perfect game," but it was eventually ruled a no-hitter shared (albeit unequally) by two pitchers. Following the game, Ruth paid a $100 fine, was suspended for ten games and issued a public apology for his behavior. In an interesting aside, Shore retired to Winston-Salem, where he served as sheriff and led the effort to build a minor-league baseball park.

1918: R.J. REYNOLDS INCLUDES SLATER HOSPITAL IN HIS WILL

Even as he lay dying, R.J. Reynolds summoned his attorney and amended his will, leaving $120,000 to Winston-Salem's Slater Hospital for Coloreds. According to research on Slater Hospital, R.J. Reynolds had told a legislative committee years earlier that he wanted a place for his sick employees to get treatment from black medical professionals. His thought was that his workers would miss less work if they had proper nursing. The translation of his thoughts into action was recorded, albeit incompletely, in the minutes of the institution he was instrumental in founding, the Slater Hospital.

July 24

1917: ERLANGER WINS IN WALK

The strengthened Erlanger baseball team had an easy time walking away with the heavy end of the score in the game with White Oak. The count ended 10–1 in favor of Erlanger. They opened up on Lambeth huskily in the first inning when Loman singled, McQuaig sacrificed and Miller and Kirk followed with triples. Kirk cracked the first ball thrown to him, which was "quite a nice introduction." In one inning, he stole both second and third, and all the White Oak boys could do was to hit him in the back with the ball. The Erlanger boys looked more like a real ball team than they had at any other time that season.

July 25

1960: First Meal at Greensboro's Newly Integrated Woolworth's Lunch Counter

Irony played an important role on this day. The Greensboro Four, as they were called, did not have the honor of eating the first meal at the newly integrated lunch counter. Geneva Tisdale and two other female kitchen workers, all wearing their best clothes, were the first African Americans served at Woolworth's sit-down lunch counter. Tisdale had an egg-salad sandwich and soda. "It was a good sandwich," Tisdale told the press. "I know because I made it myself! They never knew that it was Woolworth girls that was the first to sit at the counter to be served after they opened it up."

After all the newsworthy Greensboro Woolworth lunch counter sit-ins had ended, three African American kitchen workers and servers were the first people served at the sit-down lunch counter. *Wikimedia Commons.*

July 26

1913: Finis and Hopefully Forgotten

Brothers Charles and Frank Snipes were arrested following a fight with two members of the Winston-Salem Twins baseball club. Charlie allegedly had a baseball bat under his coat and after the game scuffled with two members of the Twins. Snipes then went home, got a Winchester rifle and went with several others to the Webster Hotel on Trade Street, where the team was staying. Snipes and a member of the Twins, Tiny Stuart, "went at it again." Officers responded and took Snipes outside, charged him and sent him home. Snipes and his friends again returned to the hotel later that evening and started another fight. Sergeant Thompson put Snipes under a $500 appearance bond and again sent him home. Thompson was suspended for five days without pay. The Snipes brothers received "time on the road gang," and the baseball players were fined.

1917: Save the Date

Announcement was made concerning the second annual Davidson County Fair, which would be held for three days in October. The agenda was planned to assist the U.S. Navy in advertising for recruits. The Navy Department promised to provide attractive posters and to draw recruits and officers.

Right: Fair week was an appropriate time for the U.S. Navy Department to post and distribute posters advertising for recruits and officers. *Wikimedia Commons*.

Below: The Davidson County Fairgrounds drew hundreds of men, women and children. The merry-go-round was a popular ride for both children and adults. *Wikimedia Commons*.

July 27

1917: PROPHESY OF GREAT CHANGES TO COME

The August 1917 issue of *American Magazine* presented a brief review of big events that had happened in the last thirty-five years and then "took a dip into the future." Following was what the writer foresaw:

There will be a king, emperor, czar, or Kaiser in Europe. Ireland will be an independent republic; so will Poland. Liquor will be taboo the world over—barred at its source. Women will have full suffrage everywhere. Socialism will not have displaced republican government. There will be an aerial route across the Atlantic and Pacific Oceans with stations or controls at intervals. There will be telephone connections without wires across both oceans. All principalities will have double-decked streets, the lower strata for traffic by vehicles exclusively. Emigration from one country to another will be rare. Firearms of all kinds will be obsolete, forbidden everywhere.

July 28

1910: Mr. and Mrs. W.N. Reynolds Donate to Jackson Training School

Mr. and Mrs. W.N. Reynolds of Winston donated $1,000 to the Jackson Training School, near Concord, North Carolina. The money was designated to be used to erect a stable, and the balance, if any, would be applied to the purchase of white spreads for the boys' beds, as well as sheets and towels for the boys. This school, a state institution, was reportedly doing a good work in "saving the wayward youth."

All was not joyous news on this day, however, as a terrible accident occurred. After falling thirty feet from the bridge over the South Fork Creek on the Southbound Railway, Edward Brewer regained consciousness two hours later and talked with his brother for a few moments. Thirty minutes later, however, he was dead. The young man was at work on a cross brace near the top of the bridge endeavoring to get it in place so that he could bolt it. He had some trouble in getting the brace in place, and he struck it with his hammer. The other end was dislodged, and he was precipitated downward, head first. His head came in contact with another brace, or lug, thirty feet below and was split open.

Jackson Training School, a state institution known for "saving the wayward youth," appreciated any and all donations for erecting buildings and buying needed supplies. *Wikimedia Commons*.

July 29

1917: Superior Court in Session

In his charge to the grand jury, Judge W.F. Harding, who was presiding over superior court, took occasion to remark that Davidson's courthouse badly needed a good coat or so of paint. He suggested the installation of a heating system, which he said would be cheaper to operate than the numerous stoves and would be much more comfortable. The building, he said, was much better ventilated than some new and costly courthouses in the area, but it certainly didn't look like progress when one noted how badly some paint was needed.

1917: New Special Taxes

At a special meeting of the city commissioners, a number of new ordinances were adopted and ordered printed. Special taxes would be issued to the following: peddlers of merchandise, $25 per day or $50 per year; vaudeville circuses, $50 per day and $10 for each side show; peddlers of meat or beef (except persons who raised

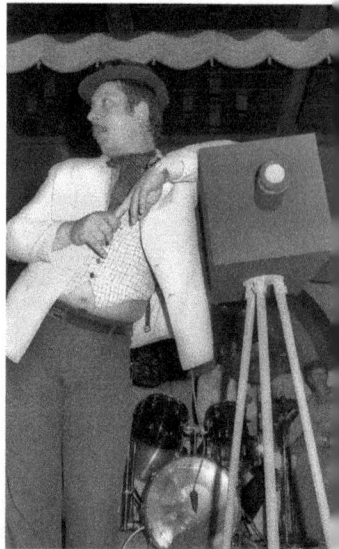

Special taxes were always being issued by city commissioners, and the year 1917 was no exception. Many of the taxes were levied on peddlers selling various merchandise or services. *Wikimedia Commons.*

same), $15 per year; solicitors of photos, portraits, etc., $5 per day; dance schools, $5 each; sleight-of-hand performers and wire dancers, $20 per performance; automobile garages, $25 per year; transfers, $8 per year; barbers, $5 for first chair and $2 for each additional chair; bottling companies (in or out of town), $25; bootblacks, $1; bill posters, $25; cold-drink stands, $10 per year; fortunetelling by gypsies or others, $100 per day; fireworks dealers, $5; feather renovators, $50; horse traders (on streets or public squares), $25 per day or $50 per year; ice dealers, $1.50 for each horse wagon; junk dealers, $5; and portable peanut roasters, $3.

1918: DEATH OF R.J. REYNOLDS
At one o'clock in the morning, while lying in his hospital bed at Reynolda and surrounded by family, R.J. Reynolds died at the age of sixty-eight. Outside the bungalow on the grand estate that had been his home for only a few

Above: R.J. Reynolds's family at Fifth Street House in Winston. *Front*: Mary, Nancy, nephew, R.J., Dick. Standing is Katharine holding Smith. *Forsyth County Public Library*.

Previous page: Nancy and Mary Reynolds on a pony with Nurse Lizzie, groom and Henrietta Van der Berg nearby. R.J. Reynolds is holding Smith. *Forsyth County Public Library*.

short months, the formal gardens were in bloom, and the model farm attracted visitors from around the countryside. After estate taxes of $370,000, "the largest ever in North Carolina—and last-minute bequests to two hospitals for another $240,000, the vast bulk of R.J.'s holdings was divided between Katharine and a trust for his four children."

July 30

1759: THE FOUNDING OF BETHANIA
On this day, twenty-four town lots, two tracts of meadows and several acres for gardens and orchards, "2,000 acres in all," were laid out. A new settlement in a small valley, Black Walnut Bottom, was begun and became what church officials in Europe had termed a "Unity farm." This was the beginning for Gottfried Grabs, his wife and their son William, who, desiring to live with Moravians, moved into the first cabin in Bethania. Other residents soon followed.

1917: WAR EFFORTS IN THE PIEDMONT TRIAD
Ladies of the Red Cross who had been engaged in the task of sewing for the soldier boys needed reinforcements. They called for volunteers, proclaiming that "there was no money involved" but that it was an excellent opportunity to serve one's country. The women had already completed making seventy-five surgical shirts; they planned to begin on surgical dressings.

A number of merchants contributed toward the purchase of a quantity of lemons and sugar to make lemonade to refresh the men of Captain Leonard's company after their hard marches every morning. Contributions needed included cash, bags of apples, peaches, cantaloupes or watermelons.

July 31

1910: A MONSTER RAT OR A GOOD LIE

Mr. G.W. Stevens of 386 North Main Street in Lexington probably held the record of having caught one of the largest rats in the community (and possibly in the entire Piedmont Triad). Mr. Stevens had been bothered by the rat for some time, having lost several chickens and a number of eggs. After moving the chickens from the coop to the barn, he finally caught a glimpse of the giant rat. When he tore the planks from the barn floor, he discovered the rat in its hiding place and killed it. When he measured it, he found it to be exactly nineteen and a quarter inches from the tip of its nose to the end of its tail.

August 1

1917: Examinations Begin Monday

On this date, all drafted Davidson County men were notified that they would be expected to appear, in specific order and on certain days, before the exemption committee of the Davidson County for examination. All 316 men who sought exemptions from the draft would be examined in the Biesecker Building over the Conrad Hardware Company in Lexington. Claims for exemptions had been running very heavily, and a word of caution was issued: the Draft Board planned to be careful about exempting anyone who was not justly entitled.

August 2

1910: FAMOUS BBB MEDICINE REMEMBERED

Dr. L.M. Gilliam, the formulator of Botanic Blood Balm (BBB), first began to manufacture and use this medicine when quite a young man at his old home at Pilot Mountain. He gathered many of the botanical ingredients used in the manufacture of his blood medicine along the sides of the mountain. He prepared and used this blood medicine in his practice for many years before it was placed on the market as a proprietary medicine. He afterward moved to High Point, where he continued practicing, using the same formula that proved so successful in curing all skin and blood troubles such as eczema, rheumatism, scrofula and catarrh and bone pain.

The Big Pinnacle of Pilot Mountain has been an interesting and exciting visitors' spot. Pilot Mountain was the home of Dr. L.M. Gilliam, the formulator of a medicine called Botanic Blood Balm. *Wikimedia Commons*.

August 3

1956: A LOOK AT ELVIS PRESLEY

On this date, Elvis was perhaps more renowned for his hip wriggles than his vocal cords, and these had reportedly brought him denunciation from ministers and parents who said his wriggles "are too suggestive." Published in a Piedmont Triad newspaper, an article referred to Elvis as a "sex-bomb entertainer." Consequently, sex had become a travesty because the public believed a man could win the girl of his choice if only he used the right kind of hair tonic or deodorant. Public opinion stressed that the way to a man's heart could be won by any girl if she used the right kind of lipstick or dentifrice or went to the right charm school. In other words, "this was the public that thought beauty was a quality that could be measured."

Who in the Piedmont Triad has not heard of Elvis Presley? Public opinion, of course, differed over his "suggestive wriggles" and "sex bomb" actions.
Wikimedia Commons.

August 4

1956: OLD MAN'S NIGHT OF COMEDY

An hour and a half of laughter was in store for ticket buyers who saw the production *The Old Maids' Convention*. The ladies of Reeds community and members of the school PTA joined forces to create the performance, which was held in the Reeds school auditorium. The plot wove around a group of old maids who had formed a matrimonial club with the sole intent of finding lovers and winning husbands. Their problems in so doing presented an evening of comedy for playgoers.

August 5

1900: Lillie Meyers's Diary Entry
Lillie's diary entry for this day reveals the following details of her visit to the jail for prayer meeting:

> *Tonight I am 78 miles away from home. As soon as we started up stairs, I began to wish that I hadn't come. There were seventeen prisoners, four white men, two Negro girls and the rest Negro men—it was a very sad sight and* [they] *closed us up in that out-of-the-way place where we couldn't see anything of the bright world around us.*

1956: Mills Home Homecoming Reunion in Thomasville
Signs read "Welcome Home, Alumni" as final preparations were made. A number of out-of-state alumni attended. The program began at 10:00 a.m. with the invocation by the Reverend Roger E. Williams Jr., new pastor of the church. Bringing the main address was the Reverend Horace "Bones" McKinney, assistant basketball coach of Wake Forest College. Another highlight was a memorial tribute to the late C.M. Howell by Dr. E. Norfleet Gardner, pastor of the First Baptist Church in Laurinburg. Mr. Howell was for many years the driving force behind the alumni association. Lunch was served at noon by the Mills Home staff.

August 6

1917: SURPRISE PACKAGE

Mr. Walter E. Conrad received delivery of a typewriter box, which came by express. The box had markings, but neither Mr. Conrad nor the express man had noticed the nature of the contents from the description outside. Thinking the box contained the cabbage plants that he had ordered, Mr. Conrad went to work, telling his wife to open the box and sprinkle water on the plants. However, when she opened the box, Mrs. Conrad smelled medicine very strongly, and her suspicions were aroused. She called in neighbors, and to their horror, the box contained an embalmed human arm. There was no mark on the box indicating to whom the arm belonged. The mystery was solved when Mr. Conrad received a letter from his son, Raymond, that had been dictated in a Pennsylvania hospital. Conrad related that he had lost an arm when he was "struck by an obstacle while hanging on to the train on which he was brakeman." A telegraph followed from Raymond, requesting that the arm be buried beside his mother at Pilgrim.

1944: GEORGE PREDDY

Born in Greensboro in 1919, George Preddy learned to fly before World War II. On this day, he shot down, within five minutes, a total of six German fighters. He returned on leave to his hometown, but on Christmas Day, Preddy was back in the skies over Belgium, chasing German planes in his P-51 Mustang. An American team on the ground missed its target, the Germans, and hit him by mistake. George Preddy earned the reputation of being one of the best American aces in the European theater. U.S. Air Force records credit him with twenty-six victories.

August 7

1905: GAMBLING CHARGES

A number of Reidsville society people who had been giving prizes at euchre parties were summoned to appear at Rockingham Superior Court at Wentworth to answer charges of gambling. However, it was discovered that under a decision of the supreme court, playing cards for prizes was not gambling. To the great joy of the society people aforesaid, the cases were not processed.

1910: D.H. BLAIR NAMED REPUBLICAN CANDIDATE FROM THE FIFTH

D.H. Blair, a lawyer from Winston-Salem, was named as the Republican candidate from the Fifth District to oppose Major C.M. Stedman of Greensboro. While some had made the contention that Chairman Morehead would "be the man," he "flatly refused" to accept the nomination. The Fifth District Democratic executive committee that met in Greensboro on the same day of the Republican Congressional Convention stated that a challenge for a joint canvas with the Republicans would be requested.

August 8

1905: MORE FEDERAL PRISONERS MOVED
Deputy United States Marshal Carroll arrived this evening
from Winston-Salem, taking with him five federal prisoners
to Greensboro. These men had been confined in the county
jail of Forsyth but were ordered removed by Marshal
Millikan. The reason for the removal of the prisoners, said
Marshal Millikan, was that the prisoners had been allowed
too much liberty by the sheriff and jailer of Forsyth County.
The marshal had been reliably informed that the jailer had
allowed Mott Richardson to go away from the jail at will
to see his family and "any one else he might choose." He
also was informed that Allen White was allowed to leave,
unaccompanied by an officer, "to see his girl."

August 9

John Motley Morehead, governor of North Carolina from 1841 to 1845, strove for internal improvements throughout the state. He earned the title "Father of Modern North Carolina." *Wikimedia Commons.*

1821: JOHN MOTLEY MOREHEAD

On this day, at the age of twenty-five, John Motley Morehead began his illustrious political career when he was elected by the voters of Rockingham County to serve in the North Carolina House of Commons. He would eventually be elected to serve consecutive two-year terms as North Carolina's governor from 1841 to 1845. He supported an ambitious program of internal improvement, including a statewide rail and water transportation system, free public school and more humane treatment of deaf and blind children, prisoners and the mentally ill. These policies were very progressive for the Old North State, earning him the nickname "Father of Modern North Carolina." The Morehead family, which consisted of eight children, lived in the six-room farmhouse called Blandwood.

1905: Neighboring State Would Not Take Piedmont Triad Crazy Man

Sheriff T.S.F. Dorsett of Davidson County went to Anderson, South Carolina, on this day with John A. Leonard, "a lunatic in his charge." He said Leonard had been in the North Carolina Hospital in Morganton for a few months until it was discovered that he was a citizen of South Carolina, at which point North Carolina officials had ordered him sent to the sheriff of Anderson County because the man had lived there in the past. South Carolina sheriff Green refused to accept the man into custody because he had no authority to do so. Dorsett left him anyway and started for the depot. Leonard collected enough travel money from folks in the courthouse, followed Dorsett to the train station, boarded a train and got off at Pelzer. Although Sheriff Dorsett had carried out the instructions of the Davidson County commissioners to take Leonard to South Carolina and leave him there, it was reported that the "insane man was roaming around over the country."

August 10

1905: Winston and Forsyth News

After the Board of Aldermen of Winston had been in session for an hour and a half and had listened to speeches from a number of prominent citizens, the motion to grant license for a distillery was withdrawn, the status of the whiskey business in Winston thereby "remaining the same." "Ade [*sic*] Walker," who shot and killed Eugene Lamar at Kernersville, was arrested near his home, half a mile from Kernersville, two or three hours after the tragedy. He was given a preliminary hearing before Squire Guyer and Mayor Linville, who bound the defendant over to the next term of Forsyth Superior Court, ordering him committed to jail without bail. At the preliminary hearing, Granville Manuels, in whose blacksmith shop the crime was committed, testified that Walker and Lamar came into his shop and began discussing a game of cards that they had played earlier. The witness gathered from the conversation that Lamar had won $1.10 from Walker. The latter suggested they play another game—"shoot it out." He pulled his pistol and began firing upon Lamar. He died in about forty minutes. Walker received a wound in his left leg, inflicted by one of the shots fired by Lamar.

August 11

1905: He Took a Drink of Whiskey from the Jug

Mr. J.C. Kimel, a prosperous farmer who lived one mile southwest of Friedburg, died suddenly about 8:00 a.m. He arose as usual in the morning and took a drink of whiskey from the jug and then went to the stables to feed the stock. Returning in a short time, he remarked that he believed the liquor was going to kill him. He grew worse rapidly and seemed to be in a great deal of pain. Dr. Lee Hill was summoned, but Mr. Kimel died before he arrived. He was forty-six years old and a bachelor.

1936: Suspect in Berrier Murder Rushed to Jail

Dudley Moore, an eighteen-year-old Negro who lived at the Berrier home in Welcome, was arrested and rushed to a jail outside the county for safekeeping during further investigation. Mrs. Jacob G. Berrier had been beaten and shot to death in her home. She was found in a clump of honeysuckle vines about two hundred yards southwest of the home. Fred Wilson and Ham Berrier, neighbors, found the gun. The weapon was in four pieces, having been taken apart, but still contained the empty shell. Some blood was on the weapon, and the stock was splintered. One piece of the stock was believed to hold fingerprints. There was also a small piece of Mrs. Berrier's dress sticking to a portion of the gun.

August 12

1905: NAT CRUMP FOUND GUILTY

The trial of Nat Crump, the outlaw charged with the attempted assassination of H. Clay Grubb and Clarence Thompson, began on this date. Both Grubb and Thompson took the stand and swore positively as to the identification of Crump and that he had fired one or more of the shots. Crump testified on his own behalf and denied the shooting, swearing that he was in Davie County at the time. Crump said he did not remember making any confession to Sheriff Dorsett and others, claiming that he had been in great pain and was partially unconscious from the time he was shot until the next day. The drama exploded when Crump heard someone say there was a crowd going to lynch him. He asked Sheriff Dorsett to take care of him, and the sheriff agreed.

1951: HE SHOT HER THROUGH THE KITCHEN WINDOW

Alexander C. Clodfelter, a foreman at the Amazon Cotton Mill in Thomasville, shot his estranged girlfriend, Mrs. Christobel Sharpe. When Clodfelter confessed to police, he said he had started making the rounds of beer joints at about five o'clock that evening. Later, he went to the home of Mrs. Sharpe, walked up the driveway and saw her sitting in the kitchen. He shot her through the kitchen window with a pistol and then turned and ran, throwing the pistol away after he had traveled several blocks. Police arrested Clodfelter after they learned he had threatened Mrs. Sharpe's life because she had begun "courting someone else, spurning Clodfelter."

August 13

1907: SHUT UP IN COLD STORAGE

For nearly two hours, two tinners, Ed and Amos Hege, were accidentally imprisoned in a cold storage room in Winston. The temperature was down to thirty-six degrees. As soon as they found themselves shut in, they attacked the door with their cold chisels and had cut through five inches when released. Both were exhausted, and Amos Hege fell to the floor.

A cold-storage room was probably one of the worst places where someone could be imprisoned. With the temperature down to thirty-six degrees, immediate rescue was essential. *Wikimedia Commons.*

August 14

1907: CAPTURED AFTER SEVEN YEARS

Police in Winston-Salem received notice that Pink Fulton had been caught in Columbus, Ohio, where Winston authorities ordered him held. He was wanted in Forsyth County for murder. A reward of $200 had "been standing for him." Fulton, seven years earlier, had been a guard on the chain gang and had unmercifully whipped a boy named Rand Hart, who refused to work. Hart died, and Fulton left before a warrant could be issued.

August 15

1905: KING SNAKE AND RAT FIGHT TO THE DEATH

On this August afternoon, a crowd watched a battle between a king snake and a rat in one of the display windows at Mr. C.E. Pugh's Greensboro grocery store. After a fierce fight of about an hour, the snake killed the rat. But the little rodent gave the serpent the "best he had in his shop." Those who saw the conflict said it was hard fought. The snake would strike at the rat and elicit a squeak of pain. Then the rat would bite at the snake furiously, "though it did not seem to make much impression on the snake's hide." The snake finally got the best of the rat by coiling itself around him and squeezing him to death. Spectators noted that it took a long time for the snake to kill the rat because the nimble rodent kept slipping from the snake's coil.

August 16

1905: ROOSEVELT'S SHORT STOP IN GREENSBORO

Officials in Washington, D.C., announced on this day that President Theodore Roosevelt would stop in Greensboro on his southern tour in October. Because of a busy schedule, the president would be able to spend only five minutes in the Piedmont Triad. Citizens of Greensboro were "desirous that he make a longer stop there" because they were eager for him to visit the Guilford Battleground. Senator Simmons said he hoped the program could be changed to lengthen the stop.

President Theodore Roosevelt's short stop in Greensboro was scheduled so that Piedmont Triad citizens could meet his train and greet him. *Wikimedia Commons*.

August 17

1916: CONTESTANTS SOUGHT TO BREAK THE WILL
An interesting case from Davidson County argued before the supreme court was that of J.A. Clodfelter and others of Winston-Salem versus Isaac Clodfelter. The contestants sought to break the will of the late Isaac Clodfelter, and the fight was waged around the proof of the will, which was of the holograph variety. After the death of Mr. Clodfelter, this will, written with a lead pencil, was found among his valuable papers and made Isaac Clodfelter his heir. Other relatives contested the will but failed to break it in superior court and then appealed. Nearly two hundred acres of land were at stake.

1920: THIS ONE MADE IT TO THE *NEW YORK TIMES*
The *New York Times* published the following headline: "ACCUSES WIFE AND NEGRO: North Carolina Editor Asks Divorce and $100,000 Damages." Following is an excerpt from the story:

> *Henry B. Varner, former President of the National Editorial Association, ex–Commissioner of Labor and Printing, now Chairman of the State Prison Board, has brought suit for $100,000 against R. Baxter McRary of Lexington, Grand Master of the North Carolina negro Masons and perhaps the best-known negro in the State, for alleged alienation of Mrs. Varner's affections. When Varner was in New York, citizens saw McRary enter the Varner home. They*

surrounded it. When they threw flashlights on the
cellar, he tried to escape but was caught under the floor.
He was arrested and warned by Mayor Hedrick to flee.
Immediately Varner attached all the McRary property
and entered the suit. Mrs. Varner returned to her old
home in Kentucky.

Interestingly, Robert Baxter McRary served as a trustee of Lincoln University from 1931 to 1946 and was known for "his grace of manner and dress, his elegance, and the effectiveness of his public and private speaking in the Methodist Episcopal Church."

August 18

1919: Liquor Men Have Narrow Escape

The Davis brothers, two policemen on duty, had a hard race with Boots Miller and Edgar Williams. Early in the morning, Miller, who drove the Southern Express Company truck, and Williams, who was rapidly gaining the reputation of being an "old hand in the liquor game," came into Lexington driving the express truck, the property of the local express agent. Approaching Main Street from a back thoroughfare, these two "tigers" were seen by the policemen. Immediately, a race began, and jugs and bottles flew. From Main Street to the depot, the race extended. Two one-gallon jugs and one quart bottle full of the fluid were broken, but a two-gallon jug was captured. The truck was seized.

August 19

1919: WINS DOUBLE-HEADER

The double-header between Erlanger and White Oak Cotton Mill resulted in two victories for the home team, Erlanger taking the first game by the score of 3–6 and the second, 6–0. This was deemed one of the "prettiest exhibitions of the nation's pastime" of the season. White Oak found it impossible to connect with pitcher Holt's "hot-shots." The home team gave Holt excellent support, and "therein lay the secret of the success." With the goose egg behind them as a result of the first game, the White Oak team was unable to exhibit enough strength to make the second game interesting. Sorrell, who pitched both games for White Oak, was weakened a great deal in the second inning and consequently gave up five runs to Erlanger.

White Oak Cotton Mill in Greensboro reportedly lost this double-header to the Erlanger Mill baseball team. *Wikimedia Commons.*

1936: CHILDREN MUST HAVE WORK PERMITS

Welfare officer Curry F. Lopp stated that a report had come to him that a number of business houses in Lexington were employing children under sixteen years of age who did not have work card permits. All children under sixteen who engaged in any kind of work must, under the law, have one of the cards, which would be issued after they had gone to the welfare office, secured blanks and properly filled those out. Lopp further stated, "The law provides a fine and penalty for employers working children without cards."

August 20

1919: JUVENILE MATTERS

Sam J. Smith, as judge of the Juvenile Court, and County Superintendent of Public Welfare P.L. Freezor, as probation officer of the county, disposed of two cases against youthful delinquents, boys ages fifteen and nine, charged with stealing cement sacks from the Harbin Construction Company. Ernest Price, the fifteen-year-old, was required to attend Sunday school and church regularly, be off the streets by 9:30 p.m., work eight hours a day every day he could, report to the probation officer every Monday and pay the cost at the rate of $0.50 a week until the total of $5.05 was paid. Pete Hargrave, the nine-year-old who was charged with aiding Page in the theft, was required to do all of the things required of Page, except work and paying the cost, "his tender years preventing him from working."

Another August 20, 1919 report focused on L.O. Spease, a Winston-Salem businessman who was fined $250 in city court for having too much whiskey in his possession. Officers found nine gallons in his home; however, there was no evidence that Mr. Spease had offered any of it for sale. Interestingly, Mr. Spease's twelve-year-old son was responsible for his indictment. It seemed the boy had been threatened with punishment by his father for disobedience, and he soon proceeded to put some of the officers "wise to the fact that dad had a lot of whiskey in his home."

August 21

1910: CONVICTED OF MANSLAUGHTER

Bud Harrell, who had shot and killed Clarence Craven at Fairmont on August 7, was tried today in superior court and sentenced to fifteen years in the penitentiary. The jury, after being out a short while, returned a verdict of guilty of manslaughter. On the day of the murder, Harrell and Craven, both employed at McKinney's Southbound Railroad camp at Fairmont, had engaged in a drunken row over a woman and were both told to leave the shanty. Harrell started out, with Craven following, threatening

A straight razor was sometimes the weapon of choice at the beginning of the twentieth century in the Piedmont Triad. Threatening someone with a drawn straight razor meant serious business. *Wikimedia Commons.*

him with a drawn razor. Harrell retreated some distance and then drew his gun and fired two shots, one striking Craven in the abdomen and the other going wild, hitting the door facing and glancing through the trousers of a third man who was "said to have moved about lively."

August 22

1910: Report Largely Magnified
An Advance correspondent wrote in the *Winston Journal* that the report that William Jarvis, a prominent farmer living eight miles above Advance, had brutally murdered his son was "largely magnified." He did assault his son with a knife and also struck him over the head with a gun, but the boy was rapidly recovering.

1919: No More Emergency Teaching Certificates
The state superintendent of education, E.C. Brooks, received reports from different parts of the state showing that in every county, there were a few teachers who had made no effort during the past year to improve their professional status or to equip themselves to do a better class of work. After consulting with a number of county superintendents and the members of the Board of Examiners, it was decided that no more emergency certificates would be issued.

August 23

1918: FALSE REPORTS WIDELY SPREAD

It looked very much like "some unprincipled scoundrel" had set about deliberately to start lies to give pain to the parents of soldiers from Davidson County. The first report was that "John Essic [*sic*]," whose parents lived in Welcome, had died at Camp Jackson. Later, a telephone message came from Thomasville township inquiring about Carl S. Suggs. Someone had carried the report to his father that his son was dead. These were false reports. The call went out: "If anyone knows of a soldier or sailor from this county who did not leave with one of the military companies or was not sent to camp, but who had enlisted in some branch of the military or navel service, they should also send the same to Mr. W.F. Brinkley."

August 24

1814: DOLLEY MADISON

Dolley Madison, wife of the fourth president of the United States, grew up in New Garden, a Quaker community located in the area now known as Guilford County. The street on which she used to live is now named for her. Despite her Quaker upbringing, Dolley developed a vivaciousness and bubbling but sassy personality. She loved dresses with vibrant colors, rich fabrics and fancy feathers. Before British troops set fire to the White House on this date, Dolley's spunk surfaced again when she rescued valuable papers, sterling silver and a full-length Stuart painting of President George Washington from the White House. Purchased for $800 by the federal government, the painting represented an important symbol of the nation, and Dolley was determined to save it from destruction. Even though the picture frame was screwed tightly to the wall, she quickly had the frame cut loose from the portrait, thus saving this valuable work of art. Although she had earlier made dinner party preparations for forty guests, she fled before the British arrived. Reportedly, British soldiers ate the meal prepared and then looted and set fire to the White House. The Madisons never lived there again.

August 25

1918: A CALL TO ACTION FOR MASONS

A front-page newspaper plea went out to all Masons. Because nations were up in arms against nations, civil governments and societies were passing through a troublous time and unrest and uneasiness had come to take the place of comfort and pleasure, Masons needed to work in helping those boys who were making the supreme sacrifice know that this fraternal organization was with them "all the way." Although the Masons realized they were not with the soldiers in the thick of the fight, the soldiers should be made aware that this organization would support them in every way possible at home to make their burdens as light as possible and that it would "keep the home fires burning."

August 26

1953: FRONT-PAGE NEWS: COW HAS FOUR CALVES IN LESS THAN A YEAR

Two sets of twin calves were born to a Davidson County cow in less than a year. The cow, a registered Guernsey owned by Maegeo Farms, delivered the first two calves on September 1 of the previous year, and the third and fourth arrived on this day. Bob McLaughlin, manager at Maegeo, said that he had heard of only one other such occurrence of a cow giving birth to four bull calves in less than twelve months. The Maegeo cow was Valor's Luxury, eight years old, which held an outstanding record of 16,655 pounds of milk and 875 pounds of butterfat as a five-year-old. The two sets of twin calves were sired by different bulls.

1958: HE ALLEGEDLY SENT THREATENING LETTERS THROUGH THE MAIL

Willis Lee Payne, a fifty-two-year-old resident of Thomasville, was arrested for allegedly sending threatening letters through the mail to supporters of George Wallace. Payne was freed on a $1,000 bond on a charge of extortion for allegedly writing these threatening letters to Mr. and Mrs. Robert Clyde Suggs of Thomasville and to Eugene Queen of Lexington. Payne was also believed to have been the author of some obscene letters received by women, according to Thomasville police chief Paul Shore.

August 27

1938: Burris Hospital's First Set of Triplets

Annie Montsinger Sullivan Davis, thirty-three and obviously pregnant, walked with her thirty-six-year-old husband, Jesse Stanton Davis, into Burris Hospital in High Point on this Saturday night. No one knew that Mrs. Davis carried triplets because following the Depression, prenatal medical checkups were practically nonexistent in rural areas of the Piedmont Triad. After Dr. W.R. McCain delivered the babies, Annie Davis became extremely ill with uric poisoning and died of kidney failure. The triplets' Aunt Edna asked Mrs. Evie Gosset Thornton if she would board the infants. Mama Thornton did not hesitate. She offered to keep all three for one dollar per day. The triplets stayed with Mama Thornton for five and a half years. They went back to their father's house in time to enter first grade at Oak View School.

August 28

1914: IT LOOKED LIKE A MAP OF EUROPE

Piedmont Triad newspaper correspondent J.D. Newton and one other person were seated in a buggy on the Thomasville square about 10:00 p.m. The moon was shining down from a perfectly clear sky that had seemed like a "sea of glass" for weeks. A cloud the size of a man's hand appeared over their heads, glowing very rapidly and becoming very black in the central parts. Newton's companion remarked, "It looks like the map of Europe." Just then, another little cloud appeared and seemingly increased as rapidly as the first, only it did not assume large proportions. His companion spoke: "That is Japan." As they continued to watch the elements, another cloud began to form and grew larger than either of the others. As it developed, Newton remarked, "That is America." The great cloud made one mighty sweep around to the north and swung to the east, where it brushed the edge of an angry, boiling cloud. Then all flew apart, and the bright moon in the clear sky was all that was left. There was no rain or thunder.

August 29

1932: LABOR DISTURBANCE IN THOMASVILLE

Strikers marched to the square, where they held a quiet discussion and decided to close the Piedmont Veneer Company on Fisher Ferry Street. The following details described the labor dispute:

> *Those involved in the largest labor disturbance ever witnessed in Davidson County are, for the most part, natives of the county. Many come from rural homes to work in the plants and return to their homes at night. Others have moved into Thomasville. These workers formed a parade, "an orderly group, a long line of workers, double file, led by a group in a shiny new automobile from which an American flag fluttered in the breeze." They were drawing ample wages to provide every necessity and even luxuries. They have not reached the position when, they claim, a further reduction in the amount earned means actual deprivation.*

August 30

1968: Testimony in Murder Trial

Two Lexington police detectives, Lieutenant Jim Kimbrell and Assistant Chief Ed Weisner, took the stand in Davidson County Superior Court to relate details of their investigation into the shooting deaths of Terri Lewis, Charles Robbins and O.T. Nicholson. Daniel Lewis, a thirty-three-year-old High Point man, faced charges of first-degree murder for the deaths of these three persons last Christmas Day. Witnesses for the state included Lexington police officer Thomas E. Gibson, who testified that he had been at the police station last Christmas Day and that he received a call about 4:22 p.m. that there had been a shooting at O.T. Nicholson's Grocery on West Fifth Avenue. Glenn Taylor, a customer in the store, said Lewis entered right behind him and suddenly threw up the gun and shot Robbins. Taylor said he took cover behind the meat counter of the store. Miss Lillian Jones, seventy-one-year-old sister-in-law of Nicholson, said she had entered the store with a beer bottle she had picked up. En route to the back of the store, she said Lewis passed her and she hit him over the head with the bottle to keep him from shooting Nicholson, who was working in the stock room at the rear of the building. Sara Robbins testified she saw her father shot and thought it was a joke until she saw blood coming from under his hands. Mrs. Lewis received a fatal wound through her left arm and into her left side, just under her armpit.

August 31

1922: He Used a Hacksaw to Escape from Prison

Dr. J.W. Peacock was discovered missing from the criminal insane ward at Central Prison. He had taken all the linens from his bed and even written a note of departure to an assistant warden expressing his regrets that he could not say goodbye. It was soon discovered that the good doctor had taken a hacksaw blade to sever the bars of his cell window, tied his bed linens together and escaped into the dead of night. Prison officials figured out what had happened. Once Dr. Peacock was outside the prison compound, friends had picked him up in a car and driven him to an airport, where

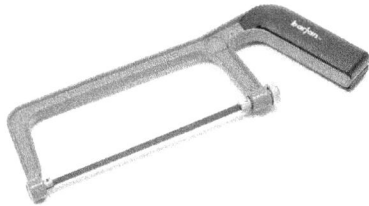

Hacksaws were sometimes used by jailed men to saw the bars of their cells and escape to freedom. *Wikimedia Commons.*

he was flown far away. Authorities later learned that he was in California, where his wife and children had joined him.

September 1

1962: SANFORD WILL VISIT PIEDMONT TRIAD

Announcements were made on this day concerning Governor Terry Sanford's visit to Lexington in October. Congressman Harold Cooley and other Democratic Party bigwigs planned to accompany the governor. That date was set for the Fourth Congressional District rally, and Lexington was "determined to be the selected site." No other plans for the gathering had yet been completed. A committee of local Democratic leaders would be named to make arrangements for the meeting. The Fourth District campaign committee was selected to determine the program, and details were to be announced as soon as these committees completed their functions.

September 2

1966: AMBULANCE FEE TRIPLED

Thomasville's desire to provide new and different ambulance service resulted in the town's desire to enter into an agreement with SurWay Ambulance Service. The following proposal included these specifics:

> *Under the proposal, no subsidy would be required from the city, but the city would have to provide a headquarters for the ambulance, including sleeping quarters for the attendants. Calls would be answered within a radium of about ten miles of the center of the city, and the fee would be $15—about three times the present ambulance rates.*

September 3

1968: Too Many Leaving the Farm

Smith W. Bagley, Democratic candidate for Congress from the Fifth District, made a speech at Denton. He declared that the exodus of young men from the farms posed a potentially worse crisis than the urban problem. Bagley suggested long-term, low-interest, government-insured loans for farm-operating expenses to make agriculture more attractive to young farmers of the Piedmont Triad. Because most farms were family owned and operated in the Denton area, the audience listened to his appeal for young people to stay on the farm. He closed by saying, "Our family farms have given this nation the finest agricultural system in the world."

September 4

1957: JOSEPHINE BOYD

Josephine Ophelia Boyd became the first black student at Greensboro High School. Wearing a brown dress with a white collar, Josephine walked toward the entry to become a member of the senior class. Students and adults shouted their objections to her decision to enter the previously all-white institution. "We don't want you here!" they screamed. "Go back to where you came from!" She crossed the threshold that day and every school day for the rest of the school year. She graduated from Greensboro High despite eggs being thrown at her, ketchup being poured in her lap, teachers ignoring her presence, boys spitting in her cafeteria food, snowballs being hurled at her, tacks being placed on her seat and ink being spilled on her books. Josephine persisted even though her family received Ku Klux Klan telephone curses, her mother Cora Lee Boyd lost her job as a housekeeper, her father's sandwich shop mysteriously burned to the ground, her brothers lost their yard-work jobs and someone killed the family's two pet dogs.

September 5

1956: DON'T DUMP NEAR OUR HIGHWAYS!
Piedmont Triad residents were reminded that the "dumping of garbage, junk, trash, and other unsightly refuse leads to the breeding of rats, mosquitoes, and other pests and creates unhealthy conditions and fire hazards." The reporter added his "two-cents' worth" by writing, "Such messes look like hell to strangers as well as homefolks." The report reminded readers that there were signs promising a fifty-dollar fine for tossing trash on highway rights-of-way. Public health and natural beauty must be observed, both legally and in good conscience and consideration.

September 6

1953: WHISKEY CUT WITH PAINT THINNER

Mankind Joyner, Johnny Sims and his wife, Dorothy, resided at 10 Finch Row in Thomasville. When officers searched the Finch Row home, they found paint thinner said to be used to cut whiskey. Johnny Sims, it was discovered, worked in a Thomasville furniture factory, where the thinner was obtained. Witnesses told Dr. David E. Plummer, Davidson County coroner, that the defendants had sold whiskey several times to Doris Barnes before her death. The one woman and two men were charged with murder and violating the prohibition law in connection with Barnes's whiskey-poisoning death. They were put in jail after failure to post $6,000 each.

September 7

1961: ALL IN THE FAMILY

A preliminary hearing was announced for Thomasville Recorder's Court for Henry (Pinto) Lewallen, who was charged with first-degree murder in the slaying of his stepfather, David McCoy Leonard. The following events preceded the murder hearing:

> *Leonard, 44, was shot twice in the back, once in the chest, and once in the arm. Dr. M.E. Block said that either of the wounds in the back would have caused death. The slaying occurred at the Leonard home on a dirt road in the Johnsontown community. Sheriff Homer Lee Cox said the killing climaxed a family argument, and it was reported that wives of both men witnessed the shooting. Reports were that the argument concerned advances by Leonard to his stepson's wife. The Lewallens are parents of five children.*

September 8

1955: Timber Thieves Arrested

Three men were arrested on charges of cutting and stealing timber from the property of a Southmont widow. The men—Henry Wall, Clyde Hargrave and Arthur Hargrave—were charged with larceny and receiving. They were accused of cutting timber from the property of Mrs. W.S. Beckner at Southmont and later selling the stolen timber to a veneer plant. All of the men were released on bond of $300 each.

1958: People Have Big Hearts

Goodness of people in a time of need was being displayed in an answer of assistance for Don Palmer, a young Davidson County farmer who had lost both arms in a tragic farm accident. Mrs. Katy Carrick Palmer, young wife of Don, referred to the kindness shown the entire Palmer family. "Everyone has been most considerate, and Don and I wish to express our deepest appreciation," she said in her note to the local newspaper. She referred to kind words and other considerations. "One never knows how kind people can be until something like this strikes," explained Katy.

September 9

1910: Stock Is Not for Sale!
It was rumored in Reidsville that the Honorable John Motley Morehead had purchased a controlling interest in the *Charlotte Observer*. In response to an inquiry, the *Reidsville Review* received the following telegram: "Neither Mr. Morehead nor any other individual who has not owned stock in The Observer Co. during the past twenty years has any stock now. Property is absolutely not for sale, in part or as a whole."

1961: Charged with First-Degree Murder in Shotgun Slaying
Fifty-four-year-old W.A. Dunning Sr. was charged with first-degree murder in the shotgun slaying of Hubert James Hedrick. Displaying a badly bruised and swollen left eye, in which he says Hedrick hit him before the shooting, Dunning quietly waived the hearing. No bond was set in the case, and Dunning was sent to jail. Dunning allegedly killed Hedrick with a single blast from a twelve-gauge shotgun, climaxing after an argument between the pair at Dunning's trailer home just off Rockcrusher Road. Although shot in the lower abdomen from a distance of less than two feet, Hedrick lived nearly seven hours and named Dunning as his assailant.

September 10

1910: BITULITHIC HIGHWAY

Notice was given on this day that a movement was scheduled to build a bitulithic highway between Greensboro and High Point. According to the newspaper report, there was already a fine macadam road that could be made a "bituminold" road for $700 per mile. Readers probably wondered about the terms used to describe this proposed new highway. "Bitumen" means that there is a combination of asphalt and tar, used for surfacing roads and for waterproofing. This would replace the "macadam" road currently in existence. A macadam road was one paved with layers of compacted broken stone, usually bound with tar or asphalt. I wonder how many citizens had to look up these terms in their dictionaries?

September 11

1862: William Sydney Porter
William Sydney Porter was born in Greensboro on this date. He graduated from the Greensboro elementary school run by his aunt, Evelina Maria Porter, and entered Lindsey Street High School. When he was nineteen years old, he earned his pharmacist license and began working in his uncle's drugstore, where he also demonstrated his artistic abilities by sketching the townspeople. Later, he adopted the pen name of O. Henry. A creative short-story writer and master of suspenseful endings, his stories had colorful, surprising and ironic twists. He acquired international recognition and credit for defining the short story as a literary art form.

William Sydney Porter, famous short-story writer, was also known by his pen name, O. Henry. He was born and reared in Greensboro. *Wikimedia Commons.*

1951: Domestic Quarrel Ends in Murder
David McCoy Leonard, forty-four, was shot once in the chest and three times from behind. He was taken to City Memorial Hospital in Thomasville, where he was pronounced dead at 8:00 p.m. Thirty-five-year-old Henry Lewallen, Leonard's stepson, was arrested and charged with

first-degree murder. Sheriff Homer Lee Cox announced the shooting allegedly took place following a domestic quarrel over Leonard's alleged attention to Mrs. Lewallen. Apparently, Lewallen had borrowed a .22-caliber target pistol from a friend because he had said he wanted to do some target shooting. A witness said that after Leonard had swung his fist at Lewallen, the stepson went to his car, grabbed the pistol and began shooting. When an ambulance and officers arrived, Leonard was lying in the yard, and Lewallen was standing in the yard. The pistol was inside the home on top of a cabinet.

September 12

1910: RANDOLPH BOY PRAISED

Charles Phillips, the sixteen-year-old son of Dr. C.H. Phillips of Fullers, Randolph County, was the sensation of the farmers' state convention that had recently met in Raleigh. According to press reports, the boy told his story well, making a fine impression and greatly pleasing the farmers present. Young Phillips, the champion corn grower of the state, told how he had raised 134 bushels on one acre of ground the preceding year. He said that it was a badge of honor to be known as a farmer.

September 13

1968: BEWARE DOOR-TO-DOOR SALESMEN

The Lexington Chamber of Commerce cautioned citizens about buying services or products from door-to-door salesmen without first checking on the reliability of the firm—or even its existence. Chamber officials reported that their office had received frequent calls from persons who made purchases from itinerant salesmen, signed contracts for goods and services and responded to "get-rich-quick" ads placed in various publications. The chamber was aware of the various schemes that were devised by unscrupulous operators to make a "fast buck at the expense of unsuspecting individuals." Citizens were urged to be extremely cautious if a salesman said, "You'll have to accept this offer now—I can't come back."

September 14

1910: CAMPAIGN LIES CIRCULATED
The opening paragraph of this page-one editorial is a classic example of Piedmont Triad reporting in 1910:

> *Someone stands a really fine chance of being caught, classified, ticketed and relegated to the Ananias Club for the rest of his natural life and all on account of a few dirty campaign lies that are going the rounds. This undesirable citizen, whoever he is, seems to have picked on Mr. S.D. McMillan, democratic candidate for sheriff, as a target for his shafts of falsehood, and is working overtime in his efforts to hurt him.*

The argument goes on to say that Mr. S.D. McMillan is not a "dissipated man; he is a devout Christian who loves his home and family with a beautiful devotion."

September 15

1911: VANDALISM IN THE NEIGHBORHOOD
Mr. Walter J. Fitzgerald of Thomasville said that someone set fire to a shock of corn in his cornfield and burned it down, destroying about three bushels. Then, some "scoundrel" broke into Mr. Ples Charles's springhouse, broke nearly all of the crockery and almost tore down the springhouse. After doing this, the criminal drove back to Mr. Fitzgerald's cornfield, this time tearing down another shock of corn and securing enough corn to feed his horse. "Fitz" offered a five-dollar reward for information leading to the identity of who "did the dirty work!"

September 16

1905: Dog Bitten by Rattlesnake Dies

On this afternoon while walking near the foot of Flat Swamp Mountain, going from Denton in the direction of what was known as the "Wild Cat's Den," Cleveland Doby, Charley Russell and two students of Denton High School came upon a large rattlesnake that was "peaceably slumbering" by the wayside. The boys attempted to kill the snake, and the reptile sought refuge in a cavity under a large stone. A valuable bird dog was with the party; it ventured too near the snake and was bitten on the head. When bitten, the dog gave one yelp, walked about fifteen yards away, fell over and was dead in fewer than fifteen minutes.

September 17

1980: DOCUMENTS OF GENIUS

Today is Constitution Day, a day unmarked on most calendars and one not celebrated by banks closing, a school holiday or even parades and speeches. And yet Constitution Day, which is celebrated by women who are members of the Daughters of the American Revolution, is remembered as a time when all Americans reflect, even if just for a moment, on this document of genius. For four months of a muggy Philadelphia summer, delegates to the Constitutional Convention in 1787 thrashed out great issues in political theory and practical politics. For more than 190 years, the Constitution has worked, surviving test after test. By reconciling unity with diversity, this practical application of the federal principle has undoubtedly become the most original contribution of the United States to the history of human liberty. It has enabled the nation to grow and to prosper as no other country ever has, and despite an image that occasionally becomes tarnished, the United States is still the shining example for the rest of the world.

The Daughters of the American Revolution held luncheons and teas as fundraisers. *Library of Congress.*

September 18

1955: Traveler Is Robbed of Over $400

The robbery made front-page news, the story beginning in the following way: "Transylvania County's Register of Deeds was a sadder, sorer, and poorer—but considerably wiser—man when he woke up in a wooded section near Lexington." Mr. Paul Whitmire, the victim, had delivered a patient to Butner Hospital and was on his way back home late in the evening when he picked up two men after he had stopped from his long trip to drink a beer just before midnight. The two men asked for a ride, and Whitmire obliged. One of the men said he had to go by his house in Lexington first. The man went to his car, and Whitmire and the other man followed in Whitmire's 1953 Mercury. Whitmire believed one of the men put something in his beer because he started getting very sleepy. The next thing he knew, Whitmire said, he awoke in some woods off a dirt road near Grubb Motor Lines. His face was bloody from a blow to the side of his head. He found his car about one hundred yards

An innocent traveler said he was drugged and robbed while on a business trip. When he regained consciousness in some woods near a dirt road, he realized he had received a blow to his head. He finally located his 1953 Mercury. *Wikimedia Commons.*

away and drove to the highway, where a helpful citizen gave him a towel to wipe the blood from his face and also directed him to the sheriff's office. Whitmire said his wallet, including about $10 in cash, and a number of valuable papers were stolen. In his pants pocket, he had $400, which was also stolen.

September 19

1905: LEFT FOOT GONE!
Gaines Winningham, a well-known young man of Greensboro, in attempting to catch a sleeper train at High Point lost his hold and had his left foot ground off under the car. He was on his way to Hot Springs, Arkansas, for treatment and had stepped off the train to bid goodbye to some relatives.

Another historical news item on this day indicated that certain repairs and changes were being made in the graded school building in preparation for the opening of the fall and winter sessions. It was decided, however, to use both the old graded school building and also the school building located near the Wenonah Mill. Unfortunately, statistics showed that there were 838 white children of school age in Lexington. The two buildings would not accommodate half this number, so the question was raised: What will be done with the more than 400 or 450 children who might desire to attend school? This was perceived as a real problem yet to be settled by the commissioners, who were scheduled to meet immediately to finalize some kind of satisfactory arrangements.

September 20

1905: Terrible Experience

Mr. and Mrs. Dupree Clodfelter arrived home on this day from northern cities, which they had visited on a wedding tour. They reported that they had had a terrible experience and a narrow escape from death while on their way from Boston to Norfolk by boat. They were passengers on the steamer *Juniata*, and during a dense fog, the ocean steamer was rammed by a schooner. The starboard side of the vessel was stove in by the collision and a great hole torn in the boat. A half dozen passengers were injured, and many others had narrow escapes, Mr. and Mrs. Clodfelter among them.

The luxury ocean steamer *Juniata* probably did not seem so luxurious after it was rammed by a schooner, injuring passengers. *Library of Congress.*

September 21

1913: MYSTERY UNEARTHED: SKELETON FOUND UNDER BURNED STORE BUILDING

After the fire that destroyed the stock and building of the Crawford-McGriff Grocery Company, rumors flew that a skeleton had been found in the basement under the store. Curiosity seekers visited the ruined store hoping to get a glimpse of the skeleton. The oldest inhabitants were called upon to ransack their memories for clues of missing men, but nobody could remember any disappearance—mysterious or otherwise. No one knew who the dead man was, and there was no mark on the crude box that contained the bones. Thinking that it might not be well to allow the folks

The Knights of Pythias was a lodge for Piedmont Triad men. Was the skeleton found in the basement of the grocery store part of initiation rites and rituals? *Wikimedia Commons.*

to take the discovery too seriously, seeing that the man "was dead beyond all hope of recovery," Mr. McGriff informed the crowd that the dead man was a friend of his whom he had brought from Alabama. The talk continued, and the mystery became a topic of conversation. Still, many folks were not afraid to creep up and "take a squint at the white bones displayed in the long box, lying in state in the unburned L of the store"; however, at night, they would walk around a block rather than pass near the building. It was a great mystery while it lasted, but it was discovered that the skeleton was part of the equipment for a Knights of Pythias lodge that had been shipped to the Piedmont Triad several years earlier by mistake and stored in the Crawford-McGriff building for safekeeping.

September 22

1918: SAFE HOUSING OFFERED
TO YOUNG GIRLS
The girls who had moved to
Winston-Salem during World
War I to work in the Reynolds
factories occupied their new
safe housing, called Reynolds
Inn. Their remodeled home
had once been the old Plaza
Hotel at Chestnut and Third
Streets. Katharine Smith
Reynolds and her sister-in-
law, Kate Bitting Reynolds,
spearheaded the renovations.
Before R.J. Reynolds died,
he had negotiated, through
his tobacco business, the
purchase of the Plaza Hotel,
opposite the railroad station
and across from Factory #1.

Katharine Smith Reynolds,
along with her sister-in-law,
spearheaded a drive to provide
"safe housing" for young women
who went to Winston to work in
the tobacco factories. *Forsyth
County Public Library.*

September 23

1913: CORN MAY BE GATHERED AND MEASURED AT ANY TIME
The Davidson County Agricultural Association adopted
the following rules and regulations for measuring the corn
of the various contestants in the 1913 Corn Contest:

> *1. The land and corn of each contestant shall be
> measured by two disinterested citizens.*
> *2. One acre shall be 160 square rods and shall be
> measured with a chain or rod pole.*
> *3. The measurers shall use a measure that will hold
> corn enough to shell out not less than one and one half
> bushels.*
> *4. Each measurer shall keep a separate score.*
> *5. The corn shall not be gathered until it is in dry,
> marketable condition.*
> *6. The measurers shall shell one measure full, weigh
> it and then compute the weight of the remainder of the
> corn by it.*
> *7. Any contestant not complying with the rules shall
> not be entitled to take part in the contest.*
> *8. The measurers shall mail their report duly signed to
> Arthur L. Leonard.*
> *9. The secretary shall not make public any of the
> reports so received until November 15th.*

September 24

1955: IMPORTANT TEXTILE MERGER

Announcements were made on this day concerning Lexington having a plant of the biggest merged textile concern in the world at this time. Burlington Industries Inc., as the concern was then known, had taken into its fold plants of several long-established concerns during the past year. The cotton textile industry in the South had long stood as one of the outstanding examples of free enterprise—competitive enterprise—in the industrial world. The trend of the past few years had been to steadily lessen the number of individual concerns, mostly locally owned. There were "chains" of mills, but one comprising more than two or three plants was regarded as a "whopper indeed." At this time, the big mergers included scores of plants and covered a wide range of textile operations.

September 25

1905: Cat Caught Mumps from Boy

The six-year-old son of Mrs. Bettie Woodring, who lived on Vine Grove Road, about five or six miles from Lexington, had a severe case of the mumps and, while the fever was high, took up in arms a pet cat and playfully blew his breath into its nostrils. In less than two weeks, the cat had a well-developed case of genuine mumps, with its jaws and throat swollen so badly it could scarcely eat. In due course, the disease wore off. The cat recovered and was as "fat and sleek as ever."

1939: Seized Booze Controversy

Judge Charles W. Gilliam of the Thomasville township court found himself enjoined from trying G.A. Randall, a High Point truck driver, on a charge of illegal possession and transportation of 230 cases of liquor. The case had to "go over" until after the restraining order could be answered before Judge John H. Clement in Guilford County Superior Court. It seemed that the confusion dealt with who actually owned the liquor being transported.

September 26

1903: RUNAWAY MARRIAGE
At the turn of the twentieth century, "runaway marriages" made the front page of Piedmont Triad newspapers. At Greensboro on this day, Miss Ollie Garrett, daughter of Reverend J.N. Garrett, of Yadkin College, was wedded to Mr. Albert Holder of High Point. The ceremony was performed by Reverend Dr. L.W. Crawford. The marriage was a runaway affair because the young lady's parents objected to the match. The young folks had kept up a regular correspondence and arranged to meet in Greensboro to get married. Mr. Holder went to Greensboro early Saturday morning and waited for Miss Garrett, who came in on the train from the east. A license had been secured, and the couple was married, leaving on the 1:20 p.m. train for High Point, their future home. The marriage was quite a surprise to the young lady's many friends in the county and especially those at Yadkin College, "where she lived and was highly respected."

September 27

1903: One Thousand People at Baptizing

One thousand or more persons attended the annual baptizing at Trading Ford Church on the Yadkin River. The pastor, the Reverend Mr. Summey, preached an "able sermon," after which fifteen candidates for church membership were baptized by immersion. Among the number were a lady eighty-six years old and a man sixty years of age. Reportedly, three candidates "backed out" because of the low temperature of the water, Sunday being a cool day.

1977: Mayoral Campaign Takes Last-Minute Twist

Democrat Carl Russell, who had lost in a primary runoff to Wayne Corpening, "threw a monkey-wrench" into the 1977 Winston-Salem mayoral campaign when he announced he would mount a write-in bid as election day neared. Russell, a funeral home operator, a sixteen-year alderman and the "dean of local black politicians," had signed a pledge not to run a write-in campaign. But he was reportedly "mightily upset with the Democratic Party's snub of him" when a group of business leaders secretly met to push Corpening, a Wachovia bank executive, to run. Early returns in the Democratic primary showed Corpening holding a comfortable lead over Russell. But the heavy turnout among black voters started to "change the tide." In the official results, Russell received 5,946 votes, 63 more than Corpening. Corpening immediately called for a runoff. Russell ultimately received 80.4 percent of the votes and Corpening 53.7 percent.

September 28

1892: SLATER INDUSTRIAL ACADEMY FOUNDED

Slater Industrial Academy, founded on this day in 1892, began as a 20-foot by 40-foot one-room frame structure with a full basement on a 50-foot by 140-foot lot. Francis L. Atkins, the school's first president, said he "remembered the building fondly because he had attended school there as a boy." Across the street from that building, the school had a large frame house used as an office and girls' dormitory. Male students lived at homes in the community. Simon Green Atkins, the founder of Slater Industrial Academy, served as head of the school from 1892 to 1904. In 1925, the school became the Winston-Salem Teachers College.

1905: QUACK DOCTOR FLEECING GOOD PEOPLE IN REEDS

A visitor to the regional newspaper office informed the editor of a quack doctor in Reeds. The quack claimed that he represented a northern medical firm. He approached his intended victims by telling them what ailed them, how their disease affected them and that he could cure them in a short time. He was always in a hurry, claiming his company required him to stay only a short time at a place, and demanded a fee of ten or fifteen dollars down, which he got at several places, promising to return in a week. Three weeks passed, and he did not return.

September 29

1955: WOMEN POKER PLAYERS

Word reached the Piedmont Triad from New York about an open secret concerning the fact that men found women puzzling. The one thing about women that most men felt surest about was this: women can't play poker well. Authority Jerry D. Lewis wrote the following in his book *Dealer's Choice*:

> *The average woman is too curious to play poker well. In an evening's play, she'll have a dozen hands where "calling the bet" displays a suicide complex. Yet she can no more resist throwing in the chips than she can help looking at the label in a friend's new coat.*

Lewis explored reasons why husbands didn't like to let wives into their poker games: 1) they win too often, 2) you can't bluff them, 3) they cheat and 4) after they win all the money, they expect the losers to walk home. They rarely offer to lend a man taxi fare.

September 30

1913: MIDNIGHT INTRUDER KILLED GROCER

A mystery that seemed to be composed of hopeless tangles became even more elusive of solution as it was investigated. Regarding the death of J.H. Taylor, the Greensboro grocer whose body was found with two bullet holes in it on the floor of his store, the circumstances were so strange and confusing that the coroner's jury, after sitting on the case for an entire day, submitted a verdict that death was due to bullet wounds fired by an unknown hand or hands. There were no eyewitnesses—nor was there any information as to the time Mr. Taylor was killed, although it was believed that the death occurred close to midnight. The crime scene indicated there had been a fierce struggle and that the muzzle of the pistol was close to the body of the dead man when one of the shots was fired, for there were powder marks on his hand, his clothing was burned and the right sleeve of his shirt was torn. A strip of molding had been pulled loose from the side of one of the counters, while articles packed in the central part of the store were scattered about the floor near the body of the dead man.

October 1

1912: SHORTAGE IN HIS ACCOUNT?

Taxpayers of Davidson County were informed in a front-page newspaper article that former treasurer Fitzgerald denied the shortage in his account with the county and then pleaded guilty by making some kind of deposit of money to cover some of the shortage. Whether the amount was $672 or $672,000, the public sentiment was adamant and labeled "crookedness" on the part of the public official. Publicity of such actions of "shortages or crookedness" was deemed important because politicians would be tempted to "take chances." Mr. Fitzgerald stated that "he was not quite done looking over the books." However, he had left office two years earlier and turned his books over to his successor. Interestingly, the article concluded by noting the following: "The books had been added up by a $500 adding machine in the office of G.W. Miller, and they were at the same time pronounced correct by the chairman of the Board of Commissioners of Davidson County, Mr. M.R. Harris."

October 2

1904: GREATEST WINSTON CATASTROPHE

The bursting of the brick-and-cement city reservoir was called the greatest catastrophe in Winston. A torrent of 180,000 gallons of water rushed east and then north, following the ravine to Belo's Pond and "carrying death and destruction in its path." Eight houses were swept away, the personal effects of the families living in them scattered everywhere. Nine persons were killed and many injured. The fire bells rang, and the firemen from both Winston and Salem rushed to the scene "to render heroic voluntary service." Winston's new water plant, at this time, had been running for just ten days prior to the flood, so the town did have clean drinking water.

1908: THE FIRST EVERYBODY'S DAY IN THOMASVILLE

The first Everybody's Day was held on this date, giving Thomasville claim to hosting North Carolina's oldest festival. The intersection of Salem Street and Main Street in the heart of downtown Thomasville formed a T-shape that was well suited for a street festival. Along the railroad tracks that gave Thomasville its start and nearby the historic Thomasville 1870 railroad depot (North Carolina's oldest), this event in Thomasville's downtown resonates its history. Incorporating local musicians and the representative music tradition of the region helped reinforce a sense of place.

October 3

1956: "GIRLIES" GET HOLIDAY

The four "girl shows" at the Davidson County Fair remained closed following orders from Sheriff Homer Lee Cox. Sheriff Cox and his deputies were at the fairgrounds as the big fair wound up its six-day agenda, and they reported no major trouble or complaints from any source. The sheriff and his men had earlier closed all shows and games except bingo on the Midway. For Saturday night, the grand finale, it was agreed that the games and certain shows would be permitted to operate, but a strict ban was ordered against the girl shows. The group of ministers, representing various denominations over the county, had protested against "indecency" and "vulgarity" in the girl shows. They objected to the public display of scantily clad women outside the shows as well as the nude performances inside. It was reported that some of the ministers returned to the fairgrounds on Saturday night and were satisfied that the agreement had been kept.

October 4

1910: GEORGE "YANK" HARGRAVE KILLED

George Hargrave, better known as "Yank," was declared dead, and the cause of his sudden demise was "too much corn whiskey and careless promenading of the Southern's deadly double tracks." His body was found on the tracks near the railroad bridge on Center Street in Lexington, part of it lying on the ties between the tracks and part of it outside. Coroner Peacock arrived from Thomasville and held an inquest. After careful examination, the coroner's jury found that "Yank" had come to his death by a northbound-moving train and that when it happened, he was under the influence of whiskey.

October 5

1918: INFLUENZA EPIDEMIC
As per the North Carolina Board of Health, Winston-Salem was ordered to close all public gathering places, including schools, churches, theaters and picture shows, because of the epidemic of Spanish influenza.

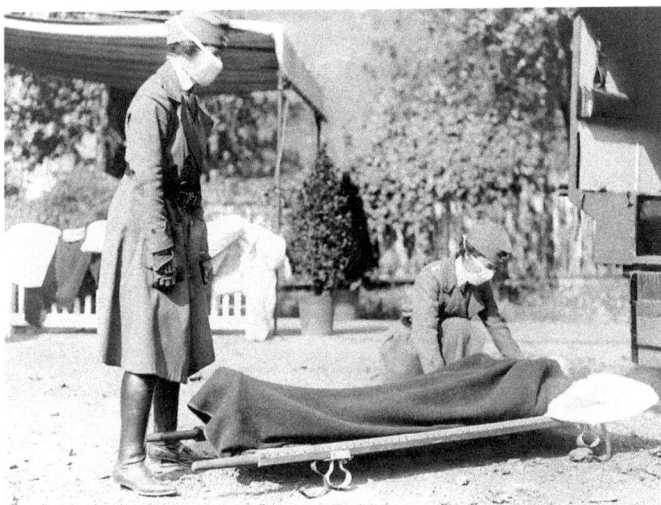

The 1918 Spanish influenza outbreak affected many men, women and children in the Piedmont Triad. *Wikimedia Commons.*

1944: OVERSEAS REPLACEMENT DEPOT (ORD)
The Overseas Replacement Depot in Greensboro during World War II played an important role in the logistics involved in deploying equipment and over 300,000 military

men and women. Recruit Corporal Rayman Williamson sent a picture postcard dated October 5, 1944, to his friend Jack, stationed in Selfridge, Michigan, with the following message: "Arrived here OK and they are giving us plenty of H…Stay at Selfridge as long as you can. Look to leave here real soon. Have you married your cousin yet? Regards, Rayman T.S.P.O.E. No fooling."

October 6

1910: COLONEL D.J. MADDOX DEAD

Colonel D.J. Maddox, a citizen of High Point who was well known to many people of the Piedmont Triad, accidentally shot himself, death resulting almost instantaneously. At about nine o'clock while sitting on his front porch, Colonel Maddox accidentally shot himself in the abdomen. The firing of the pistol was heard by two carpenters who were working near the Maddox home, and they went to his front porch, arriving there about the same time that Mrs. Maddox did from the back part of the house. For several days previously, Colonel Maddox had been working with an old pistol, trying to extricate a cartridge that had been fast in the gun for a long time. That morning, Mrs. Maddox saw him go out on the front porch with the pistol, a piece of wire and a small bottle of alcohol. It was supposed that Colonel Maddox was holding the barrel of the pistol just in front of his abdomen and that the ball entered the pit of his stomach, severing the aorta artery and causing almost instant death.

October 6, 1910, seemed to be a day of accidents. A horse driven by two gentlemen "of foreign extraction" created no small excitement on Main Street by dashing across the square at a pace that defied the speed limit. The horse ran across the sidewalk near Saleeby's store and threw out both occupants of the buggy. Several persons came to their aid, and the frantic horse was freed from the harness after it had broken it badly and smashed a wheel of the buggy. The outfit belonged to Hedrick's stables.

October 7

1912: REYNOLDA PRESBYTERIAN CHURCH
On this night, Katharine Smith Reynolds spoke to
the members of Class Number 4 of First Presbyterian
Church at a special meeting in the home of Mr. and
Mrs. Robert Critz. Katharine put her innovative idea in
the form of a motion. "I propose we sponsor a Mission
Sunday school in the Wachovia Arbor School building
located on the corner of 25th Street and Reynolda Road
in Winston," she said simply but elegantly. The class
enthusiastically accepted the challenge. This simple
motion became the nucleus for building the Reynolda
Presbyterian Church.

1915: ELEVEN HELD ON THE CHARGE OF RETAILING
One of the biggest hauls ever made by Lexington
officers was consummated in the arrest of nine suspects
on warrants charging the illicit sale of whiskey. Those
arrested were Sid Mize, Jesse Kepley, Clarence Ford,
H.I. Lopp, Walter Roan Scott, Rob Hayes, Stokes
Hargrave and Lois Mabry. Arch Green was caught in a
buggy with three gallons of liquor. Green was arrested,
and the horse and buggy, which belonged to liveryman
Pat Myers, were seized along with the whiskey. A story of
remarkable profits from "blind tigering" and of terrible
concoctions brewed came out in connection with this
cleanup of tiger suspects. It was reported that one man
took four bushels of corn, distilled eight gallons of liquor
and then added two hundred pounds of sugar "to the

slop left" and made thirty-five gallons of "monkey rum." Thirteen gallons of "the vilest possible sort of stuff" was made from four bushels of corn, and "the whole mess" sold for at least $172. The term "monkey rum" was derived from the similarity of the actions of those who imbibed to these of that hilarious animal.

October 8

1912: Old-Fashioned Pounding

The new Baptist pastor, Reverend J.M. Hamrick, was the recipient of an old-fashioned "pounding" at the hands of his congregation. The pastor's pantry was stocked with all sorts of good things to eat. While "pounding had gone out of fashion in some localities and in some churches," among the Baptists, it was still very popular and held in city churches as well as those in the country.

October 9

1956: SHERIFF LOOKING FOR DEER HEADS

The following announcement was published in the newspaper on this day: "If you see a deer head around anyplace, please call Sheriff Homer Lee Cox." Roy Link, honorary fireman and furniture worker, reported to the sheriff's office that someone had broken into his cabin at High Rock Lake and stolen four deer heads. Other items taken included a table lamp, pictures and some paint.

October 10

1901: CHARLOTTE HAWKINS RETURNS TO THE SOUTH

Charlotte Hawkins left Cambridge on this date for
North Carolina, headed for what she thought was
a well-established mission school. Upon arriving in
Greensboro, she took her letter of directions and began
to inquire about McLeansville. The station porter told
her that McLeansville was just a little stop about eight
miles from Greensboro and advised her which train
to board, for trains stopped there only when signaled.
Her first impression of the place was a signpost marked
"McLeansville" with high towering pines on one side
and sturdy oaks on the other and one small unpainted
ramshackle house, which she later found to be the post
office and country store combined. She went into the
store and commenced to inquire where the mission
station, Bethany Institute, was located. After much
questioning, walking and riding on a wagon behind a
mule, she arrived at her destination, which was four
and a half miles from McLeansville. When the mission
school was closed, Charlotte Hawkins was offered a
job teaching rural black children at Sedalia. Hawkins
founded the Alice Freeman Palmer Memorial Institute,
a day school and boarding school for African Americans.
She limited the curriculum at this time to domestic and
industrial sciences.

1960: LYNDON B. JOHNSON STOPS IN THOMASVILLE
Thomasville's famous chair gained national attention when vice presidential hopeful Lyndon B. Johnson stopped to greet local supporters from atop the chair while on a campaign whistle stop.

Lyndon B. Johnson visited Thomasville and stood atop the "big chair." *Wikimedia Commons.*

October 11

1912: A BOUDOIR SHOWER

The social event of the week in Lexington occurred when Mrs. Wood H. Dorsett entertained in honor of Miss Arline Trice, whose marriage to Mr. Edgar Eugene Jones would soon take place. The entertainment took the form of a "boudoir shower," and wonderful, indeed, were the beautiful things that were literally showered upon the bride-to-be. The party decorations were white and green and effectively carried out to the smallest detail. White and green blocks of cream with white cake and mints were served, and souvenirs of miniature suitcases filled with rice were distributed to guests by Master Wood Dorsett Jr. The pastime of the afternoon was a floral story consisting of twenty questions on placards placed conspicuously throughout the rooms. Each question was answered by the name of a flower.

1948: CENTRAL CAROLINA CONVALESCENT (POLIO) HOSPITAL

The Central Carolina Convalescent Hospital opened on land donated by the county at the intersection of Bessemer Avenue and Huffine Mill Road. The fund drive had produced sums more than double the initial goal. A total of 116 patients from the Overseas Replacement Depot and a second makeshift hospital in the former office of the *Greensboro Record* on North Greene Street "were transferred by ambulance—with the nurses hand-pumping iron lungs—to the new hospital."

October 12

1909: No Smallpox Here

A "very hurtful report" spread that Lexington was infested with smallpox, the claim being "absolutely untrue and without any foundation whatever." There was not a case or a suspected case anywhere around the town, and moreover, none was expected! There were two cases at a Southbound Railroad camp, six miles above town, where two men were sent to a pest house and guarded by four armed men. These men arrived at the camp and soon thereafter showed signs of the disease, so they were promptly "cooped up—and that is the situation in a nutshell."

October 13

1907: COTTON MILL FOR DENTON

The Denton Cotton Mills Company was the latest acquisition in the way of manufacturing. The company was incorporated for $50,000 with the privilege of increasing the capital to $100,000. The incorporators were Messrs. Berry and Davidson of Gibsonville, J.W. Noel of Lexington and J.A. Noel of Roxboro. The new mill planned to have five thousand spindles and would manufacture cotton yards. It would give employment to about one hundred people. Work began at once, and the factory would be in operation by spring. The company secured a twenty-acre site from the Hub Land Company of Lexington. The men behind the new enterprise were men "of great business sagacity and experience and were deemed some of the best cotton mill men in the Piedmont Triad."

October 14

1912: GRIMES-WILSON ENGAGEMENT
On this afternoon at four o'clock, Miss Julia Wilson entertained at her beautiful new home. The house was handsomely decorated for the occasion in the reception hall, where the guests were greeted by Miss Wilson. Magnificent white and yellow chrysanthemums were used with pleasing effect, while "loveliest bride's roses in purity and sweetness" adorned the living room. Attractive score cards showed the guests to their places at several tables, where cubical hearts held them in close interest. The biggest score prize was a beautiful and embroidered guest towel. At the close of progressions, vases of exquisite bride's roses were placed on the tables, and Misses Cassie Rose and Edna Wilson disclosed the joyous engagement secret as they distributed telltale cards enfolded in the napkins. These were dainty fans in the form of wedding bells and linked hearts that been hand painted with orange blossoms and true lovers' knots. They bore the interesting wedding secret: "Julia Lindsay Wilson, John Clarence Grimes, November 1912."

October 15

1915: REYNOLDA PRESBYTERIAN CHURCH
The Orange Presbytery Commission met and approved the
name that Katharine Smith Reynolds had proposed from
the outset: Reynolda Presbyterian Church. Ministers and
elders from the area attended the momentous celebration
and listened intently as Dr. Melton Clark of Greensboro
delivered a message based on Psalm 48: 12–13: "Walk about
Zion, and go around her/Count her towers/Consider her
ramparts/Go through her palaces/That you may tell it to
the next generation."

1951: HARRY TRUMAN VISITS THE PIEDMONT TRIAD
President Harry S. Truman attended the groundbreaking
ceremony for Wake Forest College in Winston-Salem.
Before the festivities on campus, he and "illustrious
residents" ate lunch at Reynolda House, the home of
Charles and Mary Reynolds Babcock, where John Carter
and his wife served him "turkey, ham, roast beef, peppers
stuffed with corn, pickled peaches, whipped potatoes, string
beans, peas, cherry tarts, and ice cream."

October 16

1907: Revenue Officers Encounter Moonshiners

A posse of revenue officers had an encounter with a couple moonshiners on Summit Avenue in Greensboro. One of the distillers was captured and the other "scared half to death by the volley of pistol shots fired at him." Since the recent destruction of an illicit distillery just north of White Oak in which one of the blockaders was captured, the officers had been continually on the watch for John Brame and George Vickers, two others known to have been connected with the distillery. Men guarded all the roads into Greensboro both night and day. Two squads of revenue officers went out, one stopping on the east

During the earliest part of the twentieth century, area moonshiners would station their daughters with shotguns to frighten away revenue officers if they came too near the supposedly hidden stills. *Wikimedia Commons.*

road near the county poor house and the other stopping on Summit Avenue just opposite Mr. Caesar Cone's residence. The posse on Summit Avenue was headed by U.S. Marshal Jasper M. Millikan. About eleven o'clock, Brame and Vickers drove along the avenue, and when they were under the electric light in front of Mr. Cone's residence, the officers rushed from concealment and seized Vickers. Brame jumped from the vehicle and at the same time drew his gun to shoot, but he was pursued by the officers, who began firing their pistols. Brame ran as fast as he possibly could and finally made good his escape.

October 17

1912: THE SHOW CAME TO TOWN

Amusement seekers and show goers of Lexington had the treat of their lives when a famous circus came to town. The promise was made: "Every dream of boyhood days will be realized. The peanuts, the camels, pink lemonade, the clowns, and the smell of the fresh shaving—the whole good atmosphere of the tented show will be there." Highlighted was an appearance of the famous Electrique De Kamos, a quintet of high-air artists. This act was promised to

The appearance of a circus in a Piedmont Triad town presented a tremendous spectacle when tents began to rise high into the air. *Wikimedia Commons.*

amaze, with "whirling Dervishes" floating through the air like "winged seraphs" and the only thing sustaining them being "wires gripped in their teeth." The act was considered one of the most amazing and superbly ornate height performances ever conducted. In the wild-beast department were many unique, strange and distinctly novel specimens of the animal kingdom and zoological creation, and all were exhibited in a classified manner and explained by competent keepers and lecturers.

October 18

1915: THE FIRST MOONLIGHT SCHOOL
The class of twenty-four adults met at the West End
Methodist Sunday school room for their opening lesson in
the moonlight school; they were given their first training
in reading from the pages of the *Dispatch*. Mr. L.A. Martin
was the teacher of this class, the first moonlight school
in Davidson County. He stated that the men were more
highly pleased than children to have the opportunity to
learn to read. They made excellent progress this first time
and "went at their task with earnestness, expressing much
satisfaction at being able to learn some of the world's news,
which heretofore had been as closed books to them."

October 19

1913: THE CAMELS CAME AND CONQUERED

R.J. Reynolds Tobacco Company introduced Camel cigarettes to the public. They eventually made Reynolds the "leading tobacco company in the world and Winston-Salem the leading producer of tobacco products." Effective advertising was responsible for the success of this new tobacco product. Camel, the first brand sold nationally, began with ads teasing that "The Camels Are Coming." R.J. had taken his family to the September Barnum and Bailey Circus, and he had taken pictures of an ill-tempered dromedary with one hump. The camel's name? Old Joe. Dromedary or camel, he became the famous image for Camel cigarettes.

1915: DAVIDSON COUNTY CANNING CLUBS

On one-tenth of an acre, a Davidson County girl of fourteen years grew 506 cans of tomatoes with a market value of $51.45. Had she planted a whole acre and obtained the same results, the proceeds would have amounted to over $500.00. Her expense was $19.85, leaving a net profit of $31.60. The little girl who did this and thereby established herself as the champion tomato grower among the forty-three girls enrolled in the Davidson Canning Clubs was Miss Mamie Lee Myers, daughter of Mr. and Mrs. R.L. Myers of Reeds. This was not all little Miss Myers did, for the canning was done at odd moments, and she had helped her father with his crop every working day of the past summer. As a special recognition of her prowess, Miss Myers won a trip to the Great State Fair at Raleigh.

October 20

1915: COLORED FAIR THIS WEEK

The "colored folks" of Lexington welcomed several thousand visitors to their county fair, designated as Educational and Agricultural Days. An appeal went out to businessmen and manufacturers of Lexington, Winston-Salem, High Point and Thomasville to allow all "colored employees" to have at least one day as a holiday. In addition, special excursion rates were made on tickets to Lexington. Those in charge reported that the colored farmers of Davidson County had taken much interest in the fair feature and that the exhibits were "more than creditable." The white citizens of Lexington were most cordially invited to attend and inspect the exhibits; those in charge appreciated their doing so.

1921: SOCIAL ACTIVITIES AT ERLANGER COTTON MILL COMMUNITY

Mr. W.M. Jolly organized the first band of the Erlanger community. A strict disciplinarian, Jolly insisted band members adhere to all his rules. He chastised them severely if they arrived at practice without their instruments. The band played at special events at Erlanger Village, and members received an invitation to play at a statewide convention. The band also performed at community Sunday school picnics.

October 21

1907: BOARD OF ALDERMEN BUSINESS
At the Board of Aldermen's regular session, two items of business were on the agenda. A barber, Mr. Strange, appeared to see about the tax on barbers. He was told that it was five dollars for the first chair and one dollar for each additional chair. Two colored barbers were also present. They thought they should not be taxed as high as white barbers, stating that they were open only one night a week and that the barber business in colored circles was very poor in winter. After the last of August, they said, few Negroes had their hair cut until summer came again, and those few wanted it done at half price. They were

Barber poles were popular downtown icons at the turn of the twentieth century. Some barbers objected to being taxed. *Wikimedia Commons*.

"let off" with two dollars annually. The second items of business concerned the unpaid bill for wiring the Methodist Church, owing to a contract made with the church that the wiring should be inspected before payment was made. The job was inspected once and turned down and was again completed but had never been inspected a second time. It was the sense of the board that the town could wait no longer for said inspection.

October 22

1905: THE NEW KNITTING MILL
Application was made to the secretary of state for a charter for the Nobby Hosiery Mill Company of Lexington, a corporation that would be organized for the purpose of the manufacture of hosiery for men and women. Among the stockholders and gentlemen who were behind the enterprise were Messrs. C.M. Thompson, Grimes Brothers and George W. Montcastle of Lexington; Ed L. Greene of Yadkin College; F.W. Patterson of High Point; and "a Mr. Alexander" of Kernersville. They were all successful businessmen, so the "the new enterprise was bound to succeed." This mill would afford employment to a number of women and children. The paid-in capital stock was $10,000, with the privilege to increase to $100,000. The company negotiated with the Town of Lexington for a site for the new plant on Foster Street near the electric light and waterworks system.

October 23

1912: NUMBERING OF HOUSES

Mr. D.F. Conrad, postmaster, wanted all residents to know that there must be no delay about the numbering of their houses if they were to receive free delivery of mail. The inspector was expected to arrive, and if things were not ready for him, "Lexington would lose." Mr. Conrad asked people to remember that unless they numbered their houses, as required by law, they could not have their mail delivered to them twice a day and would instead have to go to the general delivery window. In addition, the sidewalks must be put in shape. Mail would be delivered to those people residing on the outskirts of the city, even beyond the corporate limits, provided that they would see to it that sidewalks were provided and houses numbered. That meant that the people of the Nokomis and "Dakotah [*sic*]" villages, which were really parts of Lexington, would have free delivery of mail—if and only if they "numbered their houses and fixed up their sidewalks."

October 24

1967: RACIAL TENSION IN WINSTON-SALEM

Local NAACP chapter president J.P. McMillian called a meeting of his executive committee to discuss "serious tension" arising from the clearing of a policeman who was involved in the death of a Negro. McMillian said his telephone had been ringing "until 2 a.m. or 3 a.m." after a hearing found no probable cause to hold policeman W.E. Owens, twenty-nine, in the death of James Eller, thirty-two. Eller was arrested for public drunkenness. Police said he was struggling to get away when brought to city hall and was struck on the head with a blackjack. He died as a result. McMillian called the freeing of Owens by Judge Leroy Samm "deplorable" and added, "I cannot predict what the executive board will do. I do know that pressure from the people will be on them. Citizens from several sections have been demanding we do something because the civil rights of a citizen is being undermined." Police Chief Justice Tucker said Owens would continue on suspension until the department held its own investigation.

October 25

1909: THE MAGNIFICENT CIRCUS

Barnum and Bailey's "Greatest Show on Earth" visited Greensboro on this day. Never since the beginning of time had an amusement enterprise so tremendous in size been organized as this one. Its magnitude was almost beyond belief. All of America, together with every foreign country, had been scoured from end to end by agents of this big show in search of novelties, and the result was a performance "brim full of sensational acts new to the circus world." In the big Barnum and Bailey show were nearly four hundred stars, most of whom would be seen for the first time. A

Schoolchildren loved a parade, and so did their parents. This parade is coming down North Main Street, turning the corner at West Fourth Street in Winston in October 1910. *Forsyth County Public Library*.

new sensation was promised at every performance in "Jupiter, The Balloon Horse." This remarkable animal with its fearless rider ascended to the dome of the circus tent in a balloon and descended to the ground in a shower of fireworks. Nearly one thousand animal wonders were to be found in the big 108-cage menagerie: eight herds of elephants, including one herd that actually played musical instruments in time and tune; a group of giant giraffes; a trained hippopotamus; the only living bi-horned rhinoceros; and hundreds of other strange beasts. Barnum and Bailey's big, new, free street parade was the most gorgeous processional display ever attempted in the history of circus business.

October 26

1930: Charges Termed as "Propaganda"

Thomasville Republicans mailed a formal request for removal of three registrars in that township on the charge that the Republicans were not permitted to copy the books following the close of registration. Registrar David Hinkle said he did not know who "demanded" to copy the books. Registrar B.W. Stone stated that at the close of registration, he reported to his regular employment. At that time, someone Stone did not know wanted to take the book for copying. Stone said he could not legally permit copying of the books except in his presence and that he was forbidden by law to surrender custody of them. Registrar Snow Loftin said he stayed at the place of registration for some time after the closing hour but that no one appeared to him during that time. He left to attend to some personal business and then went home. During the night, he said he was aroused after retiring with a demand to then permit copying of the books. So why did anyone want to "copy the books"? It seemed that last names appearing in alphabetical order were copied to prevent anyone from being registered after the books had been officially closed.

October 27

1967: UNITED DAUGHTERS OF THE CONFEDERACY
Highlights of the seventy-first annual convention of the North Carolina Division of United Daughters of the Confederacy were discussed at the October meeting of the Lexington Robert E. Lee Chapter 324. Outstanding speakers for the convention were Glenn Tucker, contemporary historian of the War Between the States, and Senator Hector McLean. Each was presented a Jefferson Davis Medal. Crosses of Military Service were awarded to recipients having served in World Wars I and II and the Korean Conflict. The Lexington chapter received the certificate for superior rating. It also won the silver tray given annually in memory of Mrs. W.M. Parsley (founder of the North Carolina Division of the UDC), having had the largest increase in new members forty years of age and under.

October 28

1919: THE BUTLER DID IT!
A Forsyth County jury awarded $271 to Mrs. J.H. Reich "for damages of an automobile alleged to have been caused by careless driving on the part of the owner's butler." According to the newspaper article, there were interesting facts and comments connected with this incident, one of which follows:

> If the case is taken to the Supreme Court, it will be the first opportunity given that august body to write a ruling on the scope of the law generally termed "A Law Defining Responsibility of Automobile Owners." There has been an opinion handed down from the Supreme Court that an automobile owner is responsible for the negligence of any member of his immediate family, or any authorized agent handling or driving at the request or command of the owner. In the case just concluded, however, it was the contention of the defendant that the butler was using the car for his own personal pleasure, and not for or at the command or request of the defendant.

Consequently, according to the article, a question was raised but not answered: Did members of the family really mind household help using the vehicles?

October 29

1901: ANNIE OAKLEY'S TRAIN WRECK AT LINWOOD
Annie Oakley, the star of Buffalo Bill's Wild West Show, was a passenger in a train headed to Danville, Virginia, for the last performance of the season when the train wreck occurred at Linwood. The wooden cars became piles of kindling as people and animals cried out in pain. Legend says that Annie Oakley, then forty-one, was found pinned beneath the rubble and that just seventeen hours after the wreck, her brown hair turned totally white because of the horror of the accident.

1967: 29-70 TRUCK STOP AND MOTEL PADLOCKED
The trial in Davidson County Superior Court on the padlocking of the 29-70 Truck Stop and Motel got underway with the plaintiff's cross-examination of Lavena Daniels. Prosecuting attorney Charles Kivett questioned Mrs. Daniels in connection with several prescriptions from the office of Dr. Paul D. Rudd of Denton, which he alleged Mrs. Daniels had forged. Mrs. Daniels denied the charge and said that she had never heard of Dr. Rudd and that she did not take any of the drugs listed on the prescriptions. The witness also denied that Dermont Conrad, owner and operator of the motel, had threatened her life or pulled a gun on her. Both Mrs. Daniels and Conrad denied knowledge of any prostitution, gambling, selling of liquor, planning of crimes or any of the other things alleged in the complaint. Mrs. Daniels also denied that she had sent a death threat

to her husband, James R. "Shorty" Daniels, while he was in the Davidson County jail under protective custody. Daniels, who had been charged with murder in the death of Harvey Eugene Dryer Jr., was a key witness for the state.

October 30

1917: LIBERTY LOAN IN THE COUNTY
Davidson County lacked only $1,950 of its full quota of $275,800, which was considered "fine work" by the committee in charge. Reportedly, if not for the failure of Denton to respond in any creditable degree, the entire amount would have been raised, with a good margin above the credit line. Lexington led the county both in amount apportioned and the amount oversubscribed. Called upon for $188,860 as their proper amount, citizens replied with a total of $200,000 in round numbers, thus making an oversubscription of $11,140. Thomasville went over the amount "by a slight but safe margin, their total subscriptions being reckoned at approximately $73,500, with an apportionment of $73,360." Denton reported a total subscription of only $350, thus lacking $13,340 "of doing its bit."

October 31

1930: Famous Old Giant Coffeepot Was Blown Up
The "prank" threatened its very existence. The giant coffeepot (sixteen feet around and twelve feet high) in Old Salem was the brainchild of a man named Julius Mickey, a "would-be grocer and tinsmith" who opened a store in 1856. According to *Journal* reporter Scott Sexton, "To distinguish his tinsmithery, he constructed a giant coffee pot capable of holding some 740 Moravian-sized cups of coffee and stuck it on a giant wooden pole in front of his shop." The old coffeepot was safe until Halloween 1930, when it was blown up by a bunch of young fellows who made a homemade firecracker, lit the fuse and tossed it inside the pot. Not until years later were the names of the boys made public. They had made the firecracker out of black powder, a dynamite fuse, shellac and scrap paper—only the paper was the personal stationery of one of the boys' grandmothers and bore her address. The boys were caught, and each had to pay three dollars to make restitution. Their identities remained a mystery to the general public.

1940: Democrats Meet to Defend Roosevelt—Denounce Wilkie
Senator Robert R. Reynolds began his Democratic rally speech in Thomasville by saying that Franklin D. Roosevelt had done more for the masses of the American people than any other president. He continued with specific examples of Roosevelt's work, praising the policies resulting from Roosevelt's actions to prevent

"fifth column" activities in this country and also his action in securing vital bases in the North Atlantic. Congressman W.O. Burgin, too, praised President Roosevelt for helping the needy, his program of aiding banking institutions, the unemployment program, the NYA, the CCC and other worthwhile agencies. He declared that the American people "did not believe that Wilkie was capable of administering the affairs of the government in such a period as the present." His speech concluded with a challenge for everyone to vote on Election Day.

AUTHOR'S NOTE: *In 1940, polls showed that 71 percent of Americans believed a fifth Nazi column had penetrated the country. Almost 50 percent was convinced that spies, saboteurs, dupes and rumormongers lurked in their own neighborhoods and workplaces.*

November 1

1905: BUILDING NOTES
Mr. J.H. Alexander "commenced the erection" of a residence on Fifth Avenue. When completed, it would be a six-room cottage modeled after plans "gotten up" by Mr. Alexander himself. In addition to the six rooms, which would be of an average size of fourteen feet by fifteen feet, there would be a large reception hall and about sixty-five feet of porch. When finished, few homes in Lexington would be more conveniently and comfortably arranged.

1961: DYNAMITED MAILBOXES
Because there had been dynamiting of rural mailboxes in Davidson County, county officers, as well as authorities of the U.S. Post Office, launched a thorough investigation. Two mailboxes on Route 2 had been dynamited recently, and others had been molested. In addition, five mailboxes on Moore Drive in Lexington had been knocked down. Police picked up two juvenile boys, ages twelve and thirteen, who admitted pushing the boxes over. Their cases had no connection with the others, as explosive charges had not been used.

November 2

1919: RED CROSS RALLY

A most enthusiastic Red Cross rally was held in the high school auditorium and presided over by Mr. Charles F. Lambeth, who had charge of the drive for Red Cross members of the Piedmont Triad areas. The "commodious" auditorium "was taxed" to hold the large audience, which was addressed by the Honorable Cameron Morrison of Charlotte, who made an eloquent and vigorous appeal on behalf of the Red Cross. Various churches throughout the area dispensed with their evening worship, and the church choirs of various denominations were represented in the music of the evening. Interestingly, Mr. Lambeth alluded to the strong possibility that his hearers were facing their next governor in Mr. Morrison, and "judging from the enthusiasm with which he was received," audience members were in no mood to "take issue with him on that point!"

November 3

1919: TELL IT LIKE IT WAS: REEDS COMMUNITY NEWS
The oyster supper at the Junior Order Hall was well attended. "Lack of preparation and slow comin'" were the outstanding features; nevertheless, there were oysters. On an entirely different news matter, Mr. Avery Beck was the proud papa of twins—a boy and a girl. His friend Charles Foster was reportedly angry with him because Beck had been bragging about furnishing more support to the school than his neighbors. There was only one child at Foster's home. The community had vowed to keep these two gentlemen peaceable. They were both strong school men and doing their best for the new consolidated school project. The school committee on this day reported very favorably on the progress made for the consolidated school. There were only a few who were willing for their children to be put off with such "a poor excuse for a school as existed."

1979: SPIRITED MARCH THROUGH GREENSBORO
Ku Klux Klansmen and American Nazis opened fire on union organizers and civil rights activists in Greensboro, killing five. Sally Avery Bermanzohn recalled the scenario:

> We were black and white radical activists who had deep roots in the civil rights, Black Power, antiwar, and women's liberation movements. On that fateful day, we wanted to protest the 1979 reemergence of the Ku Klux Klan (KKK) in areas of North Carolina in which union drives were in progress. We planned a spirited march through Greensboro, followed by a conference. Instead, the KKK and Nazis attacked us as we were gathering to march.

November 4

1905: BREAKING THE GAME LAW

North Carolina had many laws regulating the sport of
hunting—laws that applied to counties in the Piedmont
Triad and those that applied to the state at large. Some
hunters at Winston had gotten into trouble by violating the
game laws, and some Lexington "gentlemen" were before
his honor, Squire Moyer, for breaking the law relating to
hunting on lands without the owners' written permission.
There was a law that stated, "You cannot hunt on the
lands of another without first getting the permission of the
owner in writing." Game Warden W.F. Thomason, who
found that it was his duty to enforce the law, "got busy"
and had Cicero Sheets, Harvey Koonts, Bradly Everhart,
Lee Everhart, Herbert Lanning, Policeman P.B. Taylor,
D.C. Hayes and Charles Yates (eight in all) hauled before
a magistrate. In each case except two, the minimum fine
of five dollars plus costs was assessed, the two exceptions
paying a fine of ten dollars. Although these gentlemen were
considered good, law-abiding citizens, they had unwittingly
broken a "pesky law and had to stand the consequences."

November 5

1816: Wright Tavern

Although no official records or historical documents denote the exact date of completion of Wright Tavern and its antebellum outbuildings, November 5 was set as the day for its Restoration Celebration. In the early days, salesmen, called "drummers," arrived in the Wentworth area to sell their wares. The tavern provided a place for the gentlemen to engage in conversation while they enjoyed their evening toddy; however, not all adult beverages came from licensed establishments. An old man named Jenkins sold "spirits" in small quantities without a license. Jenkins drove four forked sticks in the ground, laid his crossed pieces on a board and set his jug and a half-pint cup on his improvised counter. He sat on a white flint stone and was ready for business—in competition with the Wright Tavern.

1919: Uphold Moral Standards

As a means of letting the people of the Piedmont Triad know exactly where they stood with reference to indecent and immoral exhibition of all kinds, and especially with reference to the recent carnival brought into their midst under the "guise of a fair," ministers drafted a lengthy statement. Furthermore, the clergy announced that it did not condemn *all* carnivals. The Ferris wheel, merry-go-round and some of the shows they did not brand as "immoral or indecent." They said the vulgar shows were troubling events; these included gambling and general "gross immorality." Ministers urged all decent citizens to assist in every effort to make it impossible for future carnivals to be "immoral, irreligious, indecent and dishonest."

November 6

1905: HORRIBLE DEATH IN RANDOLPH

Mr. Causey Brown, a miller at Humble's Mill, was caught by a belt and dashed against a post and then fell several feet below to the floor, breaking several ribs and injuring himself so severely that he died two or three hours afterward. Mr. Brown was a son-in-law of Mr. Alson Humble, who owned the mill. While Mr. Humble's family was at the mill with Mr. Brown, their house was destroyed by fire. They had left a fire in an open fireplace, and it was thought that the fire popped out and started in that way. The house was nearly half burned when it was discovered that it was on fire; consequently, it was considered a complete loss.

November 7

1917: PEACOCK FACTORY BURNED

Just after midnight, fire destroyed the finishing department and storerooms of the Peacock Furniture Company, as well as a very large stock of manufactured products and raw material. In addition, two frame dwellings and three smaller buildings were destroyed. The loss was estimated between $60,000 and $70,000, covered by only $26,900 insurance. The small frame dwellings were owned by Mr. W.H. Moffitt and were occupied by Mr. Tim Byerly and a widow and family. The small building was used as the factory studio. Flames leapt seventy-five to one hundred feet in the air. Every possible line of hose was brought to play, and local firemen stood up against the awful heat until they were "almost blistered." Only their valiant work saved the machine department, some sixty feet away, from whose walls the new coat of paint was burned, as well as a quantity of cross ties stacked beside the tracks of the Southern Railway. Flagmen were put out on the railroad, as it was necessary to put hose lines over the tracks.

November 8

1904: EVIDENCE OF THE STATE

The official transcript taken by the court stenographer from the habeas corpus proceedings of H. Clay Grubb, being tried for the murder of O.L. Davis, was released on this day. Following is an except from the transcript:

> *Rev. J.M. Bennett, a Baptist minister who lived near the scene of the tragedy, said he saw Mr. Davis, Mr. Sam Crump, and Mr. Grubb walking, coming towards the church. Crump was between the two men. Grubb stepped around Crump and shot Davis. Davis was walking along with Crump towards the church with his hands hanging down "sorter swinging along. I saw Davis' head fly back at the first shot. He then turned right back the way he was coming and ran five or six steps, and Grubb stopped about three steps and shot again. Davis ran five or six steps further; Grubb followed two or three more steps and shot again. Then Davis fell. After the shooting, Grubb cursed around for a little while."*

November 9

1800: CHURCH WALLS THREE FEET THICK
Salem workers completed construction on their new church (now called Home Moravian) after two years of diligent work, and members consecrated the sacred building. The physical structure consisted of "144,000 bricks, measured 92 feet by 46 feet, with lower walls three feet thick and stood as a fitting symbol of the church's prominence and prosperity."

1910: CORONER FOUND THAT "SKIP" WAS THE CAUSE OF DEATH
Mr. Jacob Hedrick was found in a dying condition six miles south of Lexington; he never regained consciousness. No one seemed to know what had caused his death, and rumors flew "thick and fast." A messenger was sent to Lexington for the sheriff, and he sent a deputy down to investigate. Coroner J.W. Peacock of Thomasville arrived and summoned a jury, which went over the case thoroughly and examined many witnesses. There was evidence that Mr. Hedrick, "Little John" Young, Wiley Kepley and others had spent that morning in drunken brawling. Kepley took the news of Hedrick's death to town, and "his damaged appearance gave strength to the rumor of foul play." It was evident there was booze, "and some to spare," and the crowd indulged to the limit, supposedly allowing a very short time between drinks. To top off the load he had already taken, Mr. Hedrick drank two glasses of "Skip," a beverage distilled from the green skimming from molasses.

November 10

1981: DUNBAR TEACHERS HEARD

A special meeting of the Lexington Board of Education resembled a court trial more than the usually quiet board meetings as evidence was introduced, witnesses were called and cross-examined and lawyers dominated the five hours of proceedings. The meeting was called in an attempt to resolve a long-running dispute involving grievances filed by the teachers at Dunbar Intermediate School against the school's principal, Willard Moody. The meeting did not resolve the dispute because the board voted to adjourn the meeting until another evening because of the late hour; however, before adjournment, the board had heard four of the six teachers who filed grievances, as well as the principal.

November 11

1908: GO FIGURE!
It was said throughout the Piedmont Triad that that if there were a storm on November 11, there would be a mild winter. Yes, there was a storm with thunder and lightning and rain on this day. Why the eleventh? "Search us!" Mild winter or not, the year 1908 brought a fine and late fall, with little cold weather. An invitation was extended: "for fine falls, come to the Piedmont." One printed source reported that prior to that October, one citizen did not recall an October in which there was no killing frost. Another recalled that he had snap beans on November 8, 1900, and that there had been no killing frost to that date. Go figure!

November 12

1908: Two Boys Rob a Farmer Getting His Shoes Shined
Two boys, Thomas Morris and Jim Manuel, worked a
successful scheme on Arthur Jessup, a farmer living near
Westfield. Officials believed their originality probably
surpassed anything of its kind in the annals of criminality
in the entire state. The boys were about fourteen years
old and were confirmed vagrants. Mr. Jessup was robbed
of $68.03 after the boys "decoyed" him to the restaurant
of E. Hawkins, where the robbery was committed. Jessup
had been drinking and was considered an "easy mark."
On the pretense that they could show him where he could
get a good lunch, they towed him to the restaurant, had
him fed and, while his shoes were being shined by one
and his red mustache dyed black by another, went through
his clothing and escaped with his money. Herbert Bitting,
the man who was applying the black shoe polish to the
red beard, detected the robbery and gave an alarm. The
boys fled, and the man "cried like a baby over his loss." In
less than thirty minutes, officers had the boys behind bars
and the stolen money returned. The boys had buried the
money in a stable to the rear of Manuel's house on Pearl
Street in Winston and declared that they were innocent
of the charge.

The shoeshine boy was a popular figure in Piedmont Triad history in
the early 1900s. Often, these shoeshine boys worked on various street
corners or in cafés or restaurants. *Wikimedia Commons*.

November 13

1908: FRIDAY THE THIRTEENTH
Thieves paid a visit to the kitchen of Captain C.W. Trice. Entering his pantry, they took "a nice, large, luscious country ham." The thief, or thieves, entered the house early in the night, before nine o'clock, as the pantry had been locked at nine. The following warning was issued to the general public: "Enduring of this season of Republican hard times, those who had something to eat, especially those who had wood to burn, had better look out." Many citizens had complained of the loss of oaken sticks used for heating purposes. One man said he actually saw an old gent crawling through a hole in the fence and "toting off" his firewood. He said that when his wood got low, he might walk over and ask said gent to return a portion to make a partial payment on the debt.

November 14

1958: THEY DISTURBED CHURCH SERVICES

Attorneys for both sides were seeking an agreement in a church difficulty that was scheduled to be heard in county court on this day. Judge Joe H. Leonard said he had continued charges against two men in order that "something could be worked out." The men, Donald Starrett and Clarence Grace, were charged with disorderly conduct and disturbing services at West Side Baptist Church, located in the "Shotgun Hill" section off Besecker Road in Lexington. The pastor who preferred the charges, Reverend V.A. Young, was in court on this day—but the two defendants were not. Judge Leonard continued the cases indefinitely until lawyers would be able to reach an agreement and make some recommendation. Starrett and Grace were former members of the church, according to Reverend Young.

November 15

1905: QUAIL HUNTING SEASON OPENED

On this day, the hunting season for quails opened in Davidson County, except in Franklinville township, where quails could be killed only during December—and then only upon the written permission of landowners. In that part of Columbia township north of Franklinville and Ramseur Road and west of Ramseur and Liberty Road, there could be hunting for quails only by written permission of landowners during the open season from November 15 to March 15.

A quail fry often occurred at the end of the "opening-day hunting season" for quails. Some areas of the Piedmont Triad had very strict quail-hunting rules and regulations. *Wikimedia Commons*.

November 16

1918: RACIAL TENSIONS WERE HIGH IN WINSTON-SALEM
This building tension came to a head on Saturday, November 16, 1918, as white couple Jim and Cora Childress strolled toward Pulliam's store about a half mile from their home. As the couple reached the Southern Railroad trestle over what is now Inverness Street, they were accosted by a black man, who hit Jim over the head with a pistol, robbed Cora of $2.25, dragged her down into a ravine and allegedly raped her. The sheriff was summoned to the scene, and deputies began looking for a man fitting a somewhat vague description offered by Cora. They observed a man generally fitting the description, and a pursuit began. The sheriff joined in, and the man turned and fired, hitting the sheriff in the hand. The posse lost the assailant, and the sheriff ordered a roundup of suspects. A number of people were initially arrested but released. Police stopped Russell High on the corner of Fourth and Depot Streets for carrying a concealed weapon. High, a black man, had recently moved to Winston-Salem from Durham. He was arrested and charged with rape.

November 17

1753: Bethabara Park Founded
Historic Bethabara Park, located in what is today Winston-Salem, North Carolina, was founded on this day when fifteen Moravian brethren arrived after walking from Pennsylvania. These Moravians settled the region, which was a virtual wilderness, full of bears, wolves, Indians and outlaws. Even today, Bethabara has preserved the 1753 site of the German-speaking settlement nestled in a picturesque, wooded 183-acre wildlife preserve with 126 species of birds.

1771: The First Black in North Carolina Baptized a Moravian
He was a black man called Sam, and Moravian leaders were impressed with his honest desire "to find the Lord." After answering the questions posed to him by Moravians in Salem, he received absolution and was baptized Johann Samuel while three hundred people in attendance exhibited reverent awe. Johann Samuel had become a "brother" of the church.

1918: The *New York Times* Covers a Race Riot in Winston-Salem
The death toll in the riot that followed efforts of a mob to storm the jail and lynch a Negro prisoner had been increased at midnight to five: "a woman spectator, a city fireman, and three negroes." A score of persons were believed to have been injured, five or six of them seriously. The mob had

first formed about 3:30 p.m., at which time it stormed the jail. Three shots were fired. Hardware stores were broken into, and revolvers, shotguns and other weapons and ammunition were taken. As the mob marched, it increased in size, and when its objective was reached, it numbered several thousand. The mayor sought to address the crowd but could not be heard. After an hour or more, the mob left the jail and started marching through the business section of the town.

1960: PROHIBITION BROUGHT DEMANDS FOR CORN LIQUOR
ATU agent Bob Martin invited David Graham and a Davidson County deputy to Davidson County. Everyone took a position around the still, and it wasn't long before a fellow came in with his dog and a shotgun. He checked the mash to see if it was ready to run. The dog spotted Agent Martin and started barking. The bootlegger, James Shirley, started running. Martin, with pistol in hand, ordered him to halt. Shirley turned around and shot Martin's right forefinger and part of his thumb. His thumb was dangling, so Graham took the shirt from his body to make a tourniquet for Martin, picked him up, carried him to the car and took him to the hospital. Graham went back to the still and discovered that Shirley had shot himself. Graham had developed an unusual talent. He could shake a mason jar filled with the amber liquor, look at the bubbles coming to the top and predict the strength. After he guessed, he shook the jar again, took off the lid and dipped his index finger into the jar for a taste—which confirmed his test.

November 18

1904: CHRYSANTHEMUM TEA PARTY

The chrysanthemum tea and voting contest given under the auspices of the Robert E. Lee Chapter of the Daughters of the Confederacy took place in a room at the Hotel March. It was a complete success, the gratifying sum of $193 being taken for the monument fund. From 6:00 p.m. to 11:00 p.m., "a gay throng crowded the tables where tea and luncheon were served continuously." That which reportedly lent chief interest to the occasion, however, was not in the tea and refreshments but the voting contest for the prettiest tea table. Interestingly, many of the young men lost sight of the beauty and art of the "inanimate tables of wood," attractive as they were; they were influenced more largely by the real art and beauty of the "fair faces" presiding over them.

November 19

1908: THE CONTEST IS NARROWING DOWN TO THE FINISH
Front-page newspaper headlines read "Only Ten Days
More in Which to Hunt for Votes—Contestants Must
Measure Up to Conditions and Get at Least 40,000 Votes in
Order to Be Eligible—Time a Plenty to Get This Number."
If any young lady in the Piedmont Triad wanted a free trip
to New York, this was her opportunity. All she needed was
at least forty thousand votes to be eligible. Young women
were reminded that they still had ample time to get the
"requisite" number if they were willing to work to win. In
fact, any contestant could begin on this day and succeed
in securing an attractive prize of a memorable (and free)
ten-day visit to New York. Apparently, young women were
supposed to know how to secure votes because the rules
were not printed.

November 20

1902: Discovered Dead in His Covered Wagon
Mr. C.F. Leonard of Lexington was found dead in his
wagon near Surratt's store in Alleghany township. He had
left his home with others en route to the lower part of
the county to spend time hunting foxes. He was drinking
when he left town and continued to drink for several days,
according to reports. He had recently suffered terribly
with a throat problem and extreme nervousness, so before
he left on his hunting trip, he went to a physician and
had morphine injected into his arm. While on the hunting
trip, Mr. Leonard insisted
on sleeping in his wagon.
The crowd had camped
near Surratt's store, and
all except Leonard slept in
a nearby barn. The others
tried to persuade him to
sleep with them, but he
insisted that he would
be just as comfortable in
his covered wagon. They
reluctantly left him, first
seeing that he was well
wrapped up. In fact, one
of the hunters visited him
later in the night and added
another quilt to his cover. At
this time, he was warm and

An early covered wagon was
sometimes the perfect "sleeping
place" when men embarked on
fox-hunting expeditions at the
beginning of the twentieth century.
Wikimedia Commons.

sleeping quietly. The next morning, they went to arouse him and were horrified to find him dead. When death took place, no one knew, but the body was yet warm when they made the discovery. He was lying flat on his back and had one hand in his pocket and the other under his head. Frank Leonard was probably the largest man in Davidson County, weighing 360 pounds. A coffin large enough to enclose the body could not be secured in Lexington, and a special order had to be sent to Charlotte.

November 21

1904: Splendid Steel Structure to Be Placed Over Abbott's Creek

At a special meeting of the Board of County Commissioners, held in Lexington on this day, a contract was let for the erection of a steel bridge over Abbott's Creek, near Finch's upper mill and about two miles southeast of Lexington. Four bids from reputable bridge builders all over the country were submitted to the commissioners. The lowest, and the one accepted, was that of the Virginia Bridge and Iron Company of Roanoke, and the price to be paid was $2,625. The specifications said the bridge would be of steel and would have a total length of 220 feet, consisting of "1 span 100 feet long between centre [*sic*] of end pins, and 120 feet of steel approach." In addition, the bridge would be 12 feet wide in the clear, and the spans would rest on steel piers. The contract called for the completion of the bridge on or before the first day of April 1905. It was touted as "a splendid structure and by far the best bridge in the county."

November 22

1904: CAUSE OF FEVER AT ORPHANAGE
After weeks of investigating conditions pertaining to the epidemic of typhoid fever at the Baptist Orphanage at Thomasville, C.S. Julian, MD, physician in charge, and J.T.J. Battle, MD, member of the North Carolina Board of Medical Examiners, made their report. They concluded that it was not the milk or water supply but the water closets that were responsible for the spread of the infection. Alteration in this system with sewerage, so persistently urged for years by the general manager and the physician in charge, was not being pushed as rapidly as possible.

1968: CHRISTMAS PROJECT FOR DIX HOSPITAL
The Dorothea Dix Volunteer Service Guild sponsored a project of collecting Christmas gifts for all 2,500 patients at Dorothea Dix Hospital. The guild hoped to obtain enough gifts to make a package of at least five gifts for each patient. The most-needed gifts were cigarettes, deodorants and toilet articles for both men and women. Women's gifts were usually more plentiful than men's, so the guild asked that more concentration be given to men's gifts in 1968.

November 23

1903: NEWS AND GOSSIP: "WITH THE BARK ON"
A correspondent for the regional newspaper kept readers posted on the news of the day. What he sent didn't have "a rubbed and polished piano finish on it; it was rather split out in the rough and sent ahead with the bark on." Following is an example of religious life in this neighborhood:

> *This Holiness gang that has been whooping and yelling, making night hideous at Hoover's Grove for ten days or more, ended their harangues last week. Let the Lord be praised. That appears to be less respectful than devout, but according to the evidence, this correspondent appears to be partial to peace and good order at religious meetings.*

November 24

1892: FIRE AT THE ZINZENDORF HOTEL
The cry of "Fire!" came from the laundry room about eleven o'clock. The Zinzendorf Hotel, at the intersection of West Fourth and Glade Streets in Winston, was in flames. Both Winston and Salem sent experienced firefighters to the scene; however, there was not enough water pressure, so the entire structure burned in about two hours. The Zinzendorf had been built in 1891 and had one hundred rooms. Woods surrounded this grand wood and cedar-shingle hotel where guests had danced to a twelve-piece orchestra. Reportedly, the intense heat had broken windows two blocks away.

1944: HE DECIDED TO GET EVEN
Craig Chappell reportedly confessed that he had set fire to the Dr. C.A. Julian home, the boardinghouse where he and other men lived. Chappell admitted that he had engaged in a bitter argument with two other men occupying the room with him, so he decided to get even with them by burning their clothing. Chappell was quoted as saying he stayed away from the furniture plant where he was employed with that purpose in mind. The men kept their clothing in a closet next to a room occupied by another boarder, June Weir. The fire was set in this room, and Chappell said he decided to take a bath before putting on his clothing and leaving but that the fire took hold so quickly he also lost most of his belongings before escaping. June Weir was so severely burned that he died at the hospital. Chappell, who made a full confession, admitted having a prison record, including time served for larceny and other offenses.

November 25

1963: Magic Cure for Arthritis

> *Letter to the Editor:*
> *Apple cider, vinegar and honey—the best medicine I have ever found. After eighteen weeks of trial, I have less arthritis, more all-night sleep and plenty of energy. If everyone would try Dr. D.C. Jarvis's (MD) treatise on arthritis and folk medicine and read and obey every word of it, we might turn our hospitals into dance halls, our Haven rests into beauty parlors, and our drugstores into lunch counters. Send our doctors and nurses out rabbit hunting while the good Lord blesses the honeybees that sit in the apple blossoms.*

1963: Tribute to Kennedy

Lexington today joined the nation and other countries of the world in mourning the death of President John Fitzgerald Kennedy. Mayor C.V. Sink joined other Piedmont Triad leaders in issuing a proclamation similar to one made earlier by President Lyndon Johnson in declaring a memorial day and setting aside the hour between noon and 1:00 p.m., the time of the funeral, for all citizens to observe a period of prayer and, when possible, attend a memorial service at a church.

November 26

1981: TWO STORES CLOSING, ONE OPENING

In the face of tough 1981 economic conditions, two major downtown stores left Lexington: the A&P store and Stercht Brothers furniture store. Declining sales, prompted by high interest rates and a slowdown in new housing starts, forced the furniture company to close its store. The health of the retail furniture business traditionally had been linked to new housing starts. The A&P's closing was part of a nationwide effort to revive the financially struggling food chain, according to Mike Rourke, vice-president of communications and corporate affairs for the Great Atlantic and Pacific Tea Company. Rourke announced that the local supermarket was one of twenty-one stores closing, adding that the store's age and lack of profitability forced the decision. While these two stores were closed, a new bookstore, Wordly Goods, planned to open soon on North Main Street.

November 27

1927: SCHOOLCHILDREN TO BE GIVEN SCHICK DIPHTHERIA TEST

An important announcement was made on this day by the Davidson County Health Department that all pupils of the public schools would receive the Schick test to determine whether or not they were immune to diphtheria. Dr. C.N. Sisk of the North Carolina Board of Health, formerly of the Winston-Salem Health Department, would assist Dr. G.C. Gambrell, Davidson County health officer, and city and county nurses in carrying out this important testing. Many people, it was announced, were naturally immune to diphtheria, while others were subject to the disease. The Schick test was the approved scientific method of determining who may or may not contract diphtheria. Those who were indicated by these tests as being subject to the disease would be urged to take the anti-toxin treatment and thus wipe out diphtheria then existing and prevent its spread in the Piedmont Triad.

November 28

1911: YADKIN MAN SEEKS DAMAGES FOR ALIENATION

"Is the love and affection of a good-looking woman worth $5,000?" asked the *Yadkin Ripple*. The newspaper explained the question in the following way:

> *This question will in all probability be decided at the next term of Yadkin Superior Court, an action having been begun against K.M. Thompson, a very prominent citizen of Jonesville, this county, by John Spann, of the same place, in which he charges that the defendant alienated the affections of his wife and asks damages in the above amount.*

Spann and his wife, who were married in 1895 and had five children, had separated over the affair. Thompson was also a man with a large family, having several grown children. This is the first case of this kind ever begun in Davidson County, and it created a great deal of excitement, especially in the community where the parties lived. The defendant, a prominent merchant and justice of the peace, was required to give bond in the sum of $5,000 when arrested.

November 29

1906: Judge Submits Timely and Interesting Remarks
Phillip F. Hedrick was acquitted of the murder of Gray
Whitaker. The verdict reportedly came as no surprise, for
the testimony as given indicated plainly his acquittal. The
jury did not state upon what issues its verdict was reached,
whether of self-defense, conspiracy against him or insanity.
It evidently acquitted him because he shot a man who had
wrecked his home. The verdict did not appear to have met
with the approbation of Judge Ferguson, who was quoted
as saying, "This is the end of a tragedy and of...I won't
say a farce." He referred to the evils that surrounded the
human family and the danger of violating any of the
commandments. Upon hearing the jury's acquittal, Judge
Ferguson made the following poignant statement:

> *The law against lynching was promulgated at the first
> criminal trial when the Almighty turned the guilty Cain
> loose, a wanderer and a vagabond, and proclaimed
> whosoever harmed him should be avenged sevenfold.
> The jury in this case, by their verdict, have saved the
> defendant from punishment but have not, in my mind,
> taken away his guilt.*

November 30

1967: Betty Crocker Homemaker Test
The newspaper announcement made on this day issued a call for senior high school girls to participate in a written knowledge and attitude test touching on all phases of homemaking. Approximately fifteen thousand high schools across the county were urged to participate in choosing the Betty Crocker Homemaker of Tomorrow. The winner would receive a $5,000 college scholarship, while a national runner-up would be granted $4,000. Judging for national honors was based on original test scores, plus personal observation and interviews. This program, launched in 1954 to emphasize the importance of homemaking as a career, was the only national scholarship competition exclusively for high school senior girls. It was on the approved list of national contests and activities of the National Association of Secondary School Principals.

December 1

1911: TRIPHAMMER SILENCED

Judge Oliver H. Allen forwarded to the clerk of Guilford County Superior Court an order in the case of *Moorefield vs. the Standard Boiler and Machine Company of Greensboro*, making permanent the injunction against the company that prevented it from using its triphammer. The sheriff was required to give a bond in the sum of $2,000 to insure the payment to the defendant of any damages that might result from the injunction. The injunction proceeding was ancillary to an action brought by Moorefield against the corporation for $3,000 in damages to his residence property, which he claimed was on account of the triphammer. Presented to Judge Allen were affidavits to the effect that the hammer was "a nuisance, annoying, aggravating, harrowing," while others swore that it did not bother them. Some testified that Moorefield's property had increased in value recently, while others said it had been greatly damaged. What was a triphammer? It was a "massive powered hammer used for decorative pounding in agriculture to facilitate the labor of pounding, decorating, and polishing."

December 2

1911: EXCITEMENT AT WIDOW SHERRILL'S HOUSEHOLD
Considerable excitement prevailed on this day in the household of the Widow Sherrill when her young son, William, came into the home much excited over the capture and killing of an alligator three feet long. He was down at the riverbanks and observed an "unusually ugly looking object floating about in the water." The lad was curious enough to pursue the course of the object until he could get it in shallow water. He caught hold of and struggled with the animal until its death. The corpse became a curiosity in the neighborhood, and many youngsters visited the Sherrill home to view the remains.

December 3

1918: AUTOMOBILE BURNED

An alarm of fire on this date proved to be one of a rather curious nature. An automobile caught fire while receiving gasoline in front of a Lexington garage and was almost entirely consumed before the fire was extinguished. The car was a Ford sedan that had been stolen from the owner. There was a lit lantern in the car, and in some unexplained way, the lantern and gasoline came in contact, causing a sudden fire. Nobody was burned, but "the machine was left a wreck."

1927: TOBACCO THIEVES

Officers in Forsyth County reported that they had found an abandoned Ford with empty tobacco sacks in it and evidence that tobacco leaves had also been there. The robbers reportedly stole already-sold tobacco from warehouses and had cashed in the tickets. It was guessed that the "organized band of tobacco thieves" had stolen an estimated $1,800 worth of tobacco. In addition, one farmer said he had lost his truck, which had been parked outside a Winston-Salem warehouse.

December 4

1905: RABBIT ATTACK ON HOUND

A party of Piedmont Triad men went on a rabbit hunt. Mr. J.R. McCrary, an attorney, related that one rabbit, when attacked by his hound dog, deliberately "smacked the dog on the side of the head and made him yelp." The dog had gathered "a large bunch of the varmint in his mouth" and was getting ready to chew the rabbit when the latter hauled away and "delivered such a lick" that the dog dropped it. The rabbit made good its escape. Able authorities on natural history had frequently pointed out that the rabbit, contrary to popular opinion, was "really a most dangerous beast, courageous and cunning." It had been known to attack men without provocation and "when drunk on moonshine whiskey had often vanquished and pursued no less a fighter than the bull dog."

December 5

1958: GUILFORD COUNTY AND JUDGE A
Elreta Alexander-Ralston became the nation's first black female district court judge. For Ms. Alexander-Ralston, being "first" came naturally. She had received the honors of being the first black woman to be accepted to Columbia University School of Law, the first black woman to earn her degree there and the first black female lawyer in North Carolina's history. Remembered for her fairness and compassion on the Guilford County bench, Judge Alexander-Ralston, or "Judge A," pioneered two successful programs. She supported early first-offender and community service programs, and she originated what she called "Judgment Day," when first offenders would return to her courtroom several weeks after their trials. If they had stayed out of trouble, she dismissed all charges. Judge A also exhibited extreme candor. The following true story illustrates her honesty:

> One day, a white woman whose daughter had run away appeared in her court. The mother approached the bench and whispered, "The worst thing is that the girl's running around with colored boys," to which Judge Alexander-Ralston responded, "Darling, have you looked at your judge?"

December 6

1906: PRAYER BLOCKED THE CIRCUS

Persons who identified themselves only as "XYZ" from Asheboro sent this message, which was printed on page one of the regional newspaper:

> *Last Sabbath evening, a little band of Christians, after having fasted all day, met and prayed that God would prevent Sparks' circus from exhibiting in Asheboro. The day for the performance came, then tents went up—and those Christians were still not discouraged. They continued to trust and pray, and before the day closed, the tents were down and the effectual fervent prayers of the righteous had prevailed. To Him be all the glory.*

The editor's tongue-in-cheek response was as follows:

> *This puts some of the other brethren in a mighty bad light. If a circus is a bad thing, and ought to be prayed against, and if praying will prevent it from showing— and of course it will, for here is proof—then lots and lots of Christians have allowed their love of seeing the animals to overcome their duty to pray, for "suckeses" have been exhibiting in this country since the oldest inhabitant was a boy.*

December 7

1942: DEATH RULED A HOMICIDE

George Arnold Kemp, a Thomasville police officer, and his wife, Nellie Rose Kemp, were in their kitchen. Nellie was preparing supper when her husband said, "Nell, I'm gonna tell you something, and never, never tell anybody what I'm about to tell you. Don't tell the boys, don't tell your brothers, don't tell your sisters. Last night I walked in on a very prominent crowd of Thomasville men…" He then abruptly stopped talking when his two sons walked into the kitchen. Later, Kemp's body was found in the pit of the elevator shaft of the three-story First National Bank—the very building where it is believed Kemp must have walked in on that "prominent crowd" of Thomasville men. Searchers found Kemp's revolver and blackjack still intact on his body. His .30-caliber Smith & Wesson revolver was still in its holster, his eyeglasses were set correctly on his face and his hat was still on his head. His skull had received a blow, which caused a cut on the right side of his head. Was it possible that Kemp had sustained such a serious blow by falling into the elevator shaft, which was only three and a half feet deep? A coroner's jury ruled the death a homicide, but no arrest was ever made.

December 8

1916: What Was That Commotion?

There was an interesting commotion in and about the banking rooms of the Bank of Lexington. An official representing the Electric Bank Protection Company of New York City gave a practical demonstration of the workings of the Double Automatic Electrical Burglar Alarm System that was installed in the vault. The Bank of Lexington had the distinction of being the only bank in the county possessing this system, which furnished immunity from burglarious attacks of the best professional burglars for the funds, securities, books and entire contents of the bank's vault. Piedmont Triad citizens were assured that "no burglar would ever make an attempt to rob a bank provided with this system, as he knows it's working and the danger to himself in meddling with electrical appliances of this character."

December 9

1924: MAGISTRATE HAS BUSY TIME WITH LAW BREAKERS
Squire J.R. Stone of Thomasville township was in
Lexington to turn in $160 in fines to the county school fund.
The fines had recently been collected by his court, much
of the amount coming from the weekend trials of "many
drunks and gamblers." Mr. Stone had been a magistrate
for thirty-five years, but the past year had been the most
active since his court was established. He attributed this
both to the increase in misdemeanors and the zeal of the
present county officers for law enforcement. Many of the
cases coming before him for trial, said Mr. Stone, were
for offenses committed in Davidson County by citizens
of Guilford County, "who make Thomasville township a
stamping ground for their misdeeds." Gambling, drinking,
prostitution and violation of the state traffic laws made up
the bulk of these offenses.

December 10

1924: THE STILL WAS WELL CONCEALED

When Deputies Blaylock and Farabee visited Boone resident Dolph Jenkins near the banks of the Yadkin River, they found a still and several barrels of beer, which they destroyed. When they started toward the nearby canebrakes, Jenkins requested permission to go along, and he and his son accompanied the officers. The still was well concealed on the edge of the river, with heavy canebrakes cutting off the view from the land side, but Deputy Blaylock's "experienced olfactory nerves" soon led him to the barrels. Before Jenkins was taken away, he stated he would have to have a drink first. He told his son to go get him "a little nip," and then he turned to the deputy and asked, "You won't arrest me for this, will you?" Blaylock replied, "I won't do anything but arrest you both." Then, "a loud halloo brought the son back without the wet goods, but search as carefully as he might, the officer wasn't able to find a thing in the suspected straw stack."

December 11

1918: A Christmas Message to the People to Continue Red Cross Care

A heartfelt message to the readers of the regional newspaper reminded them that soldiers, freed from the prospect of service overseas, were still going to spend weary months in camp. In the depressing waiting, it was feared they might lose heart more easily than before. It was stated that Red Cross Home Service must continue: "We are pledged it shall last as long as families are deprived of the support of the soldier's presence." The task was peculiarly heavy because of the large rural districts the Red Cross chapters covered. The worried soldier with a letter telling of sickness or trouble at home often had to wait days until a Home Service worker could make a visit to a distant place and write back that medical or other relief had been given. The 1918 Red Cross Christmas message was one of goodwill. It meant further sacrifice to prove conclusively to an attentive world that America was permanently aroused to the needs of the new era.

December 12

1903: HE WORE OUT FIVE SWITCHES ON TWO YOUNG BOYS
The case against Professor Walter Ingram, teacher of
Fair Grove School, was decided by J.R. Keen, Esquire,
of Thomasville. The decision was that the teacher would
have to pay the costs, which amounted to "something like
$15." This was a case in which the teacher was prosecuted
by some of the indignant patrons for "wearing out five
switches on two small boys." One was eight years old
and the other eleven. The teacher resigned his position.

1906: TO THE FIREMEN
An article in the regional newspaper on this day assured
the Lexington firemen that the paper had not "jumped
on them in what it had to say in regard to the need of
more organization and system in the fire department."
Then the blatant statement was made: "The firemen are
wrong. The *Dispatch* has not criticized them at all, has
had no occasion to do so and certainly has no desire to."
In fact, on the contrary, the paper had tried "in its feeble
way" to point out certain defects that the firemen were
not responsible for and to stir in the breasts of the folks
appreciation of the unselfish and patriotic efforts of the
firemen. To clarify its objective, the newspaper printed
the following:

> *What we would like to see accomplished in this
> matter is a system of signals indicating the location
> of the fire; the absolute command of the fire chief*

at fires, so that excited people not needed can be kept from hurting themselves and other people and property, and finally, the united support of the citizens enlisted in behalf of the volunteer firemen who get nothing for their services, and who, because they have no funds, cannot give us a fire department like the town needs.

December 13

1903: A DISTINCTION WORTHY OF NOTE

The *Ladies' Home Journal* had been collecting thousands of photographs. These were then numbered and submitted to Mr. Walter Russell, the famous painter, and the *Journal's* staff artists. They selected the picture of little Miss Mary Noble Burkhead, daughter of Mr. R.L. Burkhead, cashier of the National Bank of Lexington, as one of the 112 to appear in the *Journal* during 1904. The selection was a compliment to Piedmont Triad children and a distinction worthy of note. Those who knew the winsome little girl heartily approved the excellent taste of the *Journal*.

1966: PANTS SUITS GAIN POPULARITY AMONG WOMEN

At this time, pants suits were very popular among Piedmont Triad women, and shops stocked coordinated slacks, jackets and skirts. The most sought-after colors ranged from heather to pinks in the solids and checks and pinstripes for variety. Then there were also blue orchids, plaids and butterscotches. Demands were so great that stores sold completely out of their stock they had ordered for Christmas shoppers. The pants suit was touted as being "as elegant and often expensive as a classic suit. On any well-bred pants suit, the jacket is cut long enough to hide the curvy rear view."

December 14

1903: NEW CASES OF SMALLPOX
Twelve new cases of smallpox developed in and around
Lexington, and three deaths had already occurred. Ten
persons were presently confined in the pest house with
smallpox. In addition to these, there were several who were
in the house of detention, having been directly exposed
to the disease. It was reported that a large percentage of
the population of the town had been vaccinated and that
all who had not would be forced to submit as rapidly as
officers and physicians could reach them.

December 15

1903: POLICEMAN HAD EXCITING ENCOUNTER

Unaided, Policeman Moyer Sink was escorting Shed Shaver to jail when the prisoner "bucked" and a scuffle ensued. Shaver grabbed the policeman's billy stick and struck him over the head two or three times. The officer pulled his pistol and shot Shaver twice. The latter ran but was later recaptured in a ditch near the branch at the end of Center Street. One bullet had struck him near the ankle, passing entirely through his leg. The other bullet had entered his body near the thigh. Shaver was delivered to jail in a buggy. His wounds were not considered very serious. The policeman's injuries were deemed "pretty severe, the scalp being peeled so that it was necessary to take a few stitches in sewing it up."

December 16

1850: NEW COUNTY SEAT AND COURTHOUSE

The state legislature created a new county by dividing the older, larger one. The new board of county commissioners was responsible for finding enough land for a county seat and new courthouse. Salem was not under consideration because "the Moravian Church objected to whipping—a common punishment handed out by the courts of the day—and didn't want whipping posts built in Salem." A new courthouse was built and opened on this date. But what was the new town's name? Finally, the town was named after Major Joseph Winston, a Revolutionary War hero from Germanton.

1903: NEARLY COMPLETED HOME BURNED

At about 5:00 a.m., fire was discovered in Mr. S.W. Finch's residence in north Lexington. The entire building was in flames; it was but a short time until it was totally destroyed. Plasterers had completed their work, so Mr. Finch had hired two men, "paying them in advance," to keep a fire to dry the plastering and watch the house during the night. One of the men never showed up; the other came, stayed a few hours and left. Logs rolled from the fireplace on the floor and fired the building. When completed, the new house would have cost $1,950. The building was only partly insured.

December 17

1965: BURGLARS SURPRISED BANK PRESIDENT AND WIFE
WHILE THEY SLEPT
Eric Sellers, vice-president of the Wachovia Bank and
Trust branch in Thomasville, underwent surgery for
a bullet wound to the groin. At the same time, Bobby
Sheffield, sixteen, of Harris Street, Thomasville, was being
held by police in Cheraw, South Carolina, awaiting the
arrival of police officers from the Piedmont Triad. Richard
Sutton, nineteen, was still at large and was the subject of a
general manhunt. Entrance to the Sellerses' home came by
removing a screen at a window and then raising the window.
The burglars allegedly went upstairs and surprised Sellers
and his wife while asleep in their second-story bedroom.
Sellers was shot, and the intruders escaped. Mrs. Sellers
fled the house by jumping from the balcony and running
for help.

December 18

1964: No Such Bank Account

Both Thomasville and Lexington were hit hard by a "darling young man on a check-writing binge." A description of the dark-haired young man estimated his age as about eighteen or nineteen years old. He was approximately five feet, nine inches tall and weighed about 240 pounds. One merchant commented on the young man's calmness and the amazing fact that he even took time to register for an automobile to be given away but added, "It's also likely that he won't bother to come back for the coat he had laid away." An officer saw checks in the possession of police marked "no account" and cashed at W.T. Grant Co., McLellans, Lanier Hardware, Seaford's and the A&P store—all in Lexington. All the checks were forged, machine-written checks on Wilson Construction Company of Thomasville. On the back of the checks, he endorsed the name David Henderson, giving his address as 214 West Fifth Avenue in Lexington, which turned out to be false.

December 19

1955: MURDERED BABY FOUND IN TRUNK

Mrs. Dorothy Broom, thirty-three, admitted that she had a baby boy on this date but that she did not have medical assistance. The baby's body was found by officers when they went to a home at 8 East Sunrise Avenue in Thomasville. The body was in a shirt-box packed away in a trunk on the back porch of the home where Mrs. Broom had an apartment. Dr. Milton E. Block, county coroner, described the baby as a full-term one and weighing about eight and a half to nine pounds. He said it was indicated that the baby had been delivered without medical assistance and that the body had been in the trunk for about five weeks, adding that the recent cold weather had apparently preserved it well. The porch was an open one and exposed to the weather. Charles Stoneman told authorities that "he could be the father of the child." Mrs. Broom's husband, Elmer Broom, was incarcerated in a South Carolina prison.

December 20

1958: Horribly Mutilated Body

Albert Workman died in the Thomasville hospital about two hours after being dragged for more than two miles under an automobile. His death was described as "gruesome, with his body horribly mutilated." Charged with manslaughter were Paul Culbreth, twenty-nine, and Donnie Ray and John Causey, brothers in their mid-twenties. Culbreth was charged with hit-and-run driving. Culbreth had gone to the Causey home, where he and the Causey brothers reportedly drank whiskey and beer. At 11:20 p.m., the three men left to go to the Southside Pool Room on Fisher Ferry Street in Thomasville. Culbreth was driving, and as they left the Causey place, the car backed over Workman, who was lying in the yard. Workman's right leg became hooked about the rear spring and fender. Culbreth then drove over two miles to the poolroom. When they arrived, Culbreth got out of the car and saw Workman underneath. At that time, he is reported to have said, "There's a man dead as hell under my car. Let's get out of here." Culbreth then got back into the car, drove two hundred feet down the street and backed into a driveway. The men got out of the car and found that the front end was over Workman's body. Workman was rushed to Thomasville Memorial Hospital by ambulance. He died the next morning.

December 21

1966: BABY GIVEN LIQUOR IN THOMASVILLE
Police were called by Thomasville hospital authorities
after it was determined that a one-year-old baby had been
given some type of alcoholic beverage. A thirty-seven-year-
old Thomasville woman, Ollie Mae Kenner of Highland
Avenue, was arrested and charged with giving liquor to the
young child. Also accused in the case was a babysitter who
was turned over to juvenile authorities.

1967: FIRE LOSS IN BARBECUE CAPITAL OF THE WORLD
A fire damaged the barbecue pit at the Old Hickory
Drive-In on South Main Street and ruined some fifty-
eight pork shoulders being cooked at that time. Firemen
said most of the meat belonged to the Old Hickory, with
only two shoulders being cooked on special order. The pit
was behind the restaurant and was covered by a structure
with a roof and open sides. The roof was hit by flames
but was not damaged badly enough that the pit could not
be used. After all, what would Piedmont Triad folks do
without Lexington barbecue?

December 22

1859: DANIEL WORTH, ABOLITION EMISSARY

On this day in 1859, Daniel Worth, a Wesleyan Methodist preacher in Greensboro, gave himself up. He had been accused of "inculcating, publicly and privately, his incendiary doctrines." This meant "exciting" a Negro to "a spirit of insurrection." The sheriff committed Worth to the Guilford County jail. His feet froze, and he became extremely feeble. Crowds surrounded the Greensboro jail, and it was feared he might be lynched.

1967: SUNDAY STORE OPENINGS/CLOSINGS: A HEATED DEBATE

Citizens voted in a public opinion poll, almost three to one, against permitting stores in Lexington to stay open on Sundays. A number of stores in the business district decided to be open for the second straight Sunday, as would other stores that had been opening on Sundays for quite some time. In addition to voting, citizens submitted their detailed opinions. Those in favor wanted to keep Lexington money at home and felt that "fanatics had made this a religious issue." Those against were quite adamant in their beliefs, saying, "If they can't make a living during the week, they'd better close up. I think it looks awful. I will not trade, any time if I can help it, with stores that open on Sunday." The lists of reasons, pro and con, went on and on.

December 23

1903: CURE FOR SMALLPOX
A letter was published on the front page of the *Lexington Dispatch* from a reader who "herewith appended a recipe which had been used to prevent or cure hundreds of cases of small pox." The letter writer referred to Jenner, who had discovered cowpox in England. Consequently, science hurled an avalanche of fame upon his head. When the most scientific school of medicine in the world—that of Paris—published this recipe as a solid panacea for smallpox, it passed unheeded although it was as "unfailing as fate and conquered in every instance." It was also harmless when taken by a well person and could also cure scarlet fever. When physicians said the patient must die, it cured. Following is the recipe:

> *Sulphate zinc. One grain; fox glove (digitalis), one grain; half a teaspoonful of sugar; mix with two tablespoonful of sugar; mix with two tablespoons of water. When thoroughly mixed add four ounces of water. Take a spoonful every hour. Either disease will disappear in twelve hours. For a child, smaller doses, according to age.*

The writer closed with the following prediction: "If countries would compel their physicians to use this, there would be no need of pest houses."

December 24

1904: ACCIDENTAL DISCHARGE OF SHOTGUN

Twenty-two-year-old Pearl Turner, described as "worthy and highly respected," was killed by what was supposedly the accidental discharge of a shotgun in his own hands. The Turner family had attended a Christmas service at Unity Chapel in Thomasville. The young man preceded the other members of the family home. When his mother entered the yard, she noticed the body of a man lying near the house. She called her husband, and they realized it was their son. The young man was lying flat on his back in an unconscious state and did not speak after he was found. The gun was about five feet in front of him pointing toward his feet. It was fired at close range as the "whole load of the shell" went in his abdomen at one place. His clothes were burned with the powder and were covered with blood all around the bullet hole. The young man had evidently entered the house and secured his gun for the purpose of joining in the Christmas shooting going on, but in coming down the steps of the porch, he stumbled and fell in such a way that the whole load entered his body. He was dead before the doctors could reach him.

December 25

1929: CHARLIE LAWSON AND MYSTERIOUS MASS MURDERS

On Christmas Day 1929, Charlie Lawson of Stokes County murdered his wife and six of his seven children, an event known in the Triad as one of the most horrible and mysterious mass murders in North Carolina history. On this snowy day, Lawson shot his wife, Frannie, and shot or bludgeoned with the butt of his rifle his children: Marie, seventeen; Carrie, twelve; Mae Bell, seven; James, four; Raymond, two; and Mary Lou, four and a half months old. Charlie Lawson then escaped to the woods and killed himself. The eldest son, Arthur, had walked in the six-inch snow to a Germantown store to buy shells for the Lawson males' traditional Christmas Day rabbit hunt. Sources indicate that a few weeks before Christmas, Frannie Lawson had confided to her closest kin the serious problems in her home. Charlie had impregnated his daughter Marie and warned her that if she told anyone, including her mother, there would be dire consequences.

A Lawson family portrait taken on their trip to Winston-Salem a short time before the murders. *Courtesy of Trudy Jones Smith.*

December 26

1966: PIEDMONT TRIAD HOUSEWIVES BOYCOTT SUPERMARKETS
Although food prices had been edging upward for some
time, increasing over 20 percent in ten years, about half of
that rise had occurred in the past three years, according to
U.S. Labor Department figures. The biggest jump in a single
year, nearly 6 percent, occurred in 1965. When housewives
realized how much less they were getting for ten dollars,
they rose en masse, wrote letters to public officials, argued
with storekeepers and boycotted supermarkets. In Davidson
County, the effect of the price increase over a period of two
years resulted in adding approximately eighty-four dollars
a year to the food bill of the average family. "Higher labor
and marketing costs, vanishing surpluses of wheat and
other commodities and increased demand" were among
the factors cited for the increases.

December 27

1968: ASSAULT WARRANTS AGAINST PATROLMEN

When Larry S. Tate of Thomasville went to the Lexington Police Station to get a warrant for the arrest of another man with whom he had been having trouble, he began acting disorderedly. Police were not able to quiet him and charged him with disorderly conduct. He later resisted arrest while being jailed, and it was reportedly necessary to use force to get him into a cell. The saga did not end there. Tate swore out assault warrants against Patrolmen Lonnie Calloway and Charles Harrison. The officers were charged with assaulting Tate by beating him with their fists and kicking him about with their feet, "inflicting serious injury." Tate claimed that he did not assault the police in any way to provoke physical restraint. His wife posted bond for him and took him to a High Point hospital, where he was given two shots for pain and told to see his doctor.

December 28

1949: GET READY FOR INCREASED POSTAL RATES

Uncle Sam found operating expenses increased, so the announcement was published on this day that postage rates would increase at the beginning of the new year. Postal rates would then be three cents per ounce for the letter rate, one cent for postcards and six cents per ounce for sending letters via air mail. As a warning to the general Piedmont Triad public, Christmas cards sent during the next holiday season would require a two-cent stamp instead of the former one-and-a-half-cent stamp. Furthermore, anyone wishing a return receipt for a piece of registered mail would be required to pay a five-cent fee.

December 29

1860: NOTICES FROM OLD GREENSBOROUGH AND WINSTON
An important notice came from old Greensborough, North
Carolina, on this date:

> *Be it ordained by the Board of Commissioners of
> the Town of Greensborough that all persons from
> the city of Columbia, S.C., or from any other place
> in the State, or any adjoining State, infected with
> Small Pox, are prohibited from coming into the town
> of Greensborough, under a penalty of $50, to be
> collected from any person in such case offending.
> And if any person from any place so infected, and
> not being informed of this ordinance, shall come
> into the town of Greensborough, he shall be required
> to depart immediately, under penalty of 10 for
> every hour he shall stay after being informed. This
> ordinance to lie in force until the danger of such
> infection shall subside.*

A placard in Winston announced another important
notice regarding a meeting on this day to discuss secession:

> *A meeting of the citizens of Forsyth County,
> irrespective of party, will be held at Winston on
> Saturday the 29th of December, inst., at 11 o'clock
> a.m., to take counsel together on the alarming
> condition of the country. South Carolina has seceded
> from the Union. Commissioners from Alabama and*

Mississippi are now at our State Capital, inviting North Carolina to do the same thing. A great question is now before the people—no less than Union or Disunion. Believing that there is safety in the voice of the people, all our fellow-citizens, without regard to party, are earnestly invited to attend.

December 30

1966: Big Medical Center Expansion

Announcements released from Winston-Salem confirmed the report that construction would begin the following spring on a $28 million expansion of the medical center made up by the Bowman Gray School of Medicine and the Baptist Hospital. This would increase existing facilities by 80 percent. The first construction would include an eighty-six-thousand-square-foot addition to the medical school, a four-hundred-seat auditorium and a new power plant to serve the entire medical center. A family foundation in New York had given a grant of $125,000 to purchase equipment for the expansion of the department of radiology's programs of teaching, research and patient care. The big fund in sight for the construction program was assured by federal sources, national foundations and pledges from Winston-Salem sources.

December 31

1966: ANNUAL BABY DERBY STARTS TOMORROW!
The annual "baby derby" produced much interest in
Davidson County. To be eligible, the baby had to have been
born at Lexington Memorial Hospital, and the parents
must be residents of Davidson County. Hospital records
were used to determine the winner. The previous year's
winner was Laura Amelia Wrenn, daughter of Mr. and
Mrs. Thomas Franklin Wrenn of Cotton Grove Road. She
was born at 8:57 a.m. on January 1, 1966. Gifts for the next
New Year's baby would be a five-dollar gift certificate for
the mother from Holiday Stores, a reminder baby's book
from Karosal, the baby's first prescription filled free at
Peoples Drug, a gold-toned piggy bank from Ellis Jewelers,
a gift certificate from Coble Dairy, four weeks of diaper
service from Dydee Supply and other wonderful presents.

BIBLIOGRAPHY

"About Mr. Fitzgerald's Statement." *Lexington Dispatch*, October 16, 1912.

"About Town." *Lexington Dispatch*, December 30, 1966.

"Advise Against Exhibitions." *Lexington Dispatch*, February 23, 1910.

"After the Tigers." *Lexington Dispatch*, February 24, 1920.

"Aldermen Pay Debt on Horse Rather Than Take Down the Bars to Objectionable Shows." *Lexington Dispatch*, April 19, 1916.

"Alleged Owner of Boone Still Put Under Bond." *Lexington Dispatch*, December 11, 1924.

"All Over the State." *Lexington Dispatch*, November 8, 1905.

"The Amended Amendment." *Lexington Dispatch*, June 20, 1900.

"Announcement." *Lexington Dispatch*, January 1, 1949.

"Another Bonehead Play." *Lexington Dispatch*, July 7, 1921.

"Anti Fly Campaign." *Lexington Dispatch*, February 26, 1913.

"A&P Advertisement." *Lexington Dispatch*, May 19, 1966.

"A&P Guarantees It." *Lexington Dispatch*, May 19, 1966.

"Arcadia Notes." *Lexington Dispatch*, February 18, 1980.

"Arm Severed by Train Shipped to Father Without News of Accident Creates Sensation." *Lexington Dispatch*, August 8, 1917.

"At Healing Springs." *Lexington Dispatch*, July 7, 1921.

"Automobile Burner." *Lexington Dispatch*, December 11, 1918.

"Baby Given Liquor at Thomasville." *Lexington Dispatch*, December 21, 1966.

"Bad Piedmont Roads." *Lexington Dispatch*, March 11, 1914.

"Betty Crocker Homemaker Test Scheduled Dec. 5." *Lexington Dispatch*, November 30, 1967.

"Big Circus at Greensboro." *Lexington Dispatch*, October 13, 1909.

"Big Easter Egg Hunt." *Lexington Dispatch*, March 18, 1940.

"The Big Game." *Greensboro Daily News*, June 20, 1963.

"Big Medical Center Expansion." *Lexington Dispatch*, December 30, 1966.

"Big Still Taken in Forsyth." *Lexington Dispatch*, April 19, 1916.

"Big Time at Daniels." *Lexington Dispatch*, April 19, 1911.

"Billy Sunday's Famous 'Booze' Sermon." http://www.biblebelievers.com/billy_Sunday_booze. html.

"Bitten by a Mad Cat." *Lexington Dispatch*, March 8, 1905.

"Blandwood: History of the Mansion." http://www.blandwood.org/history.html.

"Blue Laws Are Amended for Second Time." *Lexington Dispatch*, March 13, 1956.

"Board of Aldermen in Regular Session Transacts Routine and Other Business." *Lexington Dispatch*, October 23, 1907.

"Bob Thomas Kills a Man: Thomasville Man in Jail for Shooting His Landlord—Dead Man's Wife and Son Say Self-Defense." *Lexington Dispatch*, January 22, 1913.

"A Boudoir Shower." *Lexington Dispatch*, October 16, 1912.

"Boy Uses Axe in Defense of Mother." *Lexington Dispatch*, April 15, 1964.

"Breach of Promise Case." *Lexington Dispatch*, May 1, 1912.

"Bride 70, Groom 58." *Lexington Dispatch*, May 29, 1907.

"Bridge Breaks Down Under Team." *Lexington Dispatch*, March 28, 1906.

"British Troops Set Fire to the White House." http://www.history.com/this-day-in history/british-troops-set-fire-to-the-white-house.

"Broadnax Hanged Friday." *Lexington Dispatch*, May 27, 1903.

Broughton, Vikki. "Dunbar Teachers Heard." *Lexington Dispatch*, November 18, 1981.

"Building Notes." *Lexington Dispatch*, November 8, 1905.

"Burglars Monday Night." *Lexington Dispatch*, February 5, 1913.

"Business News Notes." *Lexington Dispatch*, April 15, 1914.

"A Call to Action for Masons." *Lexington Dispatch*, August 21, 1918.

"Cam Heitman in Trouble." *Lexington Dispatch*, April 19, 1916.

"Campaign Lies Circulated." *Lexington Dispatch*, September 14, 1910.

"Cannot Try Randall at Thomasville Today—State Endeavoring to Show Liquor Never Legally Shipped." *Lexington Dispatch*, September 25, 1939.

Capel, Wint. *Dethronement of Reason: The Travails of North Carolina's Murderous Dr. J.W. Peacock*. Chapel Hill, NC: CapeCorp Press, 1998.

"Captured After Seven Years." *Lexington Dispatch*, August 14, 1907.

"Carnivals Still Forbidden." *Lexington Dispatch*, April 19, 1916.

"Carolina Music Ways: Events—Everybody's Day in Downtown Thomasville." http://www.carolinamusicways.org/events/Davidson/events_everybodys_day.html.

"Cat Caught Mumps From Boy." *Lexington Dispatch*, September 27, 1905.

"Cause of Fever at Orphanage." *Lexington Dispatch*, November 23, 1904.

"Chamber of Commerce Here." *Lexington Dispatch*, September 14, 1968.

"Chang and Eng Bunker." http://en.wikipedia.org/wiki/Chang_and_Eng_Bunker.

"Charlotte Hawkins Returns to the South." http://www.nchistoricsites.org/chb/pmi-growth.htm.

"The Chrysanthemum Tea." *Lexington Dispatch*, November 23, 1904.

"Church Case Continued." *Lexington Dispatch*, November 14, 1958.

"Col. D.J. Maddox Dead." *Lexington Dispatch*, October 5, 1910.

"Colored Fair This Week." *Lexington Dispatch*, October 20, 1915.

"A Colored Woman's Gift." *Lexington Dispatch*, April 28, 1909.

"Coming Friday Night." *Lexington Dispatch*, May 8, 1901.

"Commencement at Children's Home." *Lexington Dispatch*, May 13, 1940.

"The Commencement at Reeds." *Davidson Dispatch*, March 30, 1908.

"The Contest Is Narrowing Down to the Finish." *Lexington Dispatch*, November 18, 1908.

"Convicted of Manslaughter." *Lexington Dispatch*, August 24, 1910.

"The Cost of Smallpox." *Lexington Dispatch*, February 10, 1904.

"Cotton Fire on Holt Fire." *Lexington Dispatch*, June 1, 1910.

"Cotton Mill for Denton." *Lexington Dispatch*, October 16, 1907.

"Court Cases." *Lexington Dispatch*, February 14, 1921.

"Court Makes Little Progress." *Lexington Dispatch*, January 19, 1910.

Cramer, Mrs. John T. *Chairtown News*, July 28, 1921.

"Cupid's Park: America's First Private Little Theatre." http://www.kornersfolly.org/history.htm.

"Cure for Small Pox." *Lexington Dispatch*, December 30, 1903.

"Dangers of a Movie Star." *Lexington Dispatch*, April 19, 1916.

"Date of the Great Yearly Meeting of Thomasville Baptist Orphanage Changed." *Lexington Dispatch*, June 27, 1906.

"Davidson County Canning Clubs Are Very Successful." *Lexington Dispatch*, October 20, 1915.

"A Davidson Divorce Case." *Lexington Dispatch*, March 2, 1904.

"Davie Youth Who Killed Mother to Be Examined." *Lexington Dispatch*, May 13, 1958.

Davis, Don. "Volunteers Lacking for Court Program." *Lexington Dispatch*, December 19, 1975.

"Death of County Man Under Probe." *Lexington Dispatch*, February 25, 1959.

"A Defective System." *Lexington Dispatch*, June 10, 1908.

"D.H. Blair Is Republican Candidate from the Fifth." *Lexington Dispatch*, August 24, 1910.

"Dispensary Not Wanted." *Lexington Dispatch*, January 4, 1905.

"A Distinction Worthy of Note." *Lexington Dispatch*, December 16, 1903.

"Dixie in Chicago." *Lexington Dispatch*, February 10, 1909.

"Document of Genius." *Lexington Dispatch*, September 17, 1980.

"Dog Bitten by Rattlesnake Dies." *Lexington Dispatch*, September 27, 1905.

"Draft This Week Likely." *Lexington Dispatch*, July 11, 1917.

"Dr. Peacock Is Tired of the Pen." *Lexington Dispatch*, July 21, 1921.

"Dr. William Black at Presbyterian Church." *Lexington Dispatch*, April 19, 1916.

"Dunning Waives Hearing." *Lexington Dispatch*, September 9, 1961.

"Easter Entertainment at Arcadia." *Lexington Dispatch*, April 19, 1916.

"Eggs and Chickens by the Parcels Post." *Lexington Dispatch*, October 26, 1912.

"838 White Children of School Age—Room for Only 450—What Will Be Done?" *Lexington Dispatch*, September 27, 1905.

"Elegant Party." *Lexington Dispatch*, January 4, 1905.

"Eleven Held for Trial on the Charge of Retailing." *Lexington Dispatch*, October 20, 1915.

"Elvis Seen as Way to Educate Public on Sex." *Lexington Dispatch*, August 3, 1956.

"End of Second Week of Voting Contest." *Lexington Dispatch*, June 27, 1906.

"Epistles to the Editor." *Lexington Dispatch*, January 31, 1900.

"Erlanger Baseball Opens." *Lexington Dispatch*, April 19, 1916.

"Erlanger Man Convicted of Retailing." *Lexington Dispatch*, May 19, 1919.

"Erlanger Wins in a Walk." *Lexington Dispatch*, August 1, 1917.

"Ernie Shore." http://en.wikipedia.org/wiki/Ernie_Shore.

"Estimated 190 Gallons a Day: County and Federal Officers Destroy Huge Liquor Still." *Lexington Dispatch*, June 9, 1950.

"Evidence of the State." *Lexington Dispatch*, November 23, 1904.

"Extensive Loss Brought by Fire at Old Hickory Drive-In Here." *Lexington Dispatch*, December 23, 1967.

"The Factories Will Not Stop." *Lexington Dispatch*, January 22, 1908.

"False Reports Widely Spread." *Lexington Dispatch*, August 21, 1918.

"Famous B.B.B. Medicine a North Carolina Product." *Lexington Dispatch*, August 3, 1910.

"Fell in the Fire." *Lexington Dispatch*, March 8, 1905.

"Fiddlers' Convention." *Lexington Dispatch*, May 1, 1912.

"55 Homeless Armenian Orphans Knock at the Door of Davidson County People." *Lexington Dispatch*, January 30, 1920.

"Fight Near Pomona." *Lexington Dispatch*, July 24, 1907.

"Figure on This." *Lexington Dispatch*, January 27, 1908.

"Fire in Winston." *Lexington Dispatch*, January 22, 1908.

"First Moonlight School." *Lexington Dispatch*, October 20, 1915.

"First Services Held in New Beulah Church House." *Lexington Dispatch*, July 7, 1921.

"First Time in History." *Lexington Dispatch*, May 27, 1966.

"First Train to Denton." *Lexington Dispatch*, January 27, 1906.

"Fisherman Pulls Destructive Grindle from High Rock Lake." *Lexington Dispatch*, July 1, 1954.

"A 505-Pound Hog." *Lexington Dispatch*, January 4, 1905.

"Flags Sold to Aid Belgium." *Lexington Dispatch*, April 12, 1916.

"Fletcher Cowans Arrested." *Lexington Dispatch*, March 11, 1914.

"Follow Scout Motto." *Lexington Dispatch*, May 19, 1966.

"For a Town Clock." *Lexington Dispatch*, June 6, 1906.

"For Breaking Game Law." *Lexington Dispatch*, November 8, 1905.

"For Robbing the Mails." *Davidson Dispatch*, March 30, 1898.

"The Force of Habit." *Lexington Dispatch*, January 8, 1908.

"Foreclosure Notices for Taxes." *Lexington Dispatch*, March 18, 1940.

"Former Surgeon in Confederate Army Lives Here." *Lexington Dispatch*, July 21, 1921.

"Forsyth County News." *Lexington Dispatch*, August 3, 1910.

"Forsyth Man in Luck." *Lexington Dispatch*, May 2, 1906.

"Forsyth Pulls a Surprise." *Lexington Dispatch*, March 19, 1968.

"Four Persons Accused in Unusual Abortion Story." *Lexington Dispatch*, July 16, 1942.

"Fouts Awarded $5,l50: Jury Gives Heavy Verdict Against Thomasville Druggist in Ammonia Water Case." *Lexington Dispatch*, May 7, 1920.

"Frank Leonard Found Dead." *Lexington Dispatch*, November 26, 1902.

"Free If It Fails." *Lexington Dispatch*, May 26, 1906.

"Friday the 13th." *Lexington Dispatch*, November 18, 1908.

"Gambling Charges." *Lexington Dispatch*, August 16, 1905.

"Gidding Bound Over." *Lexington Dispatch*, July 24, 1907.

"A Gift for the Year." *Lexington Dispatch*, January 3, 1900.

"Girl Guard Observing Its 50th Anniversary." *Lexington Dispatch*, May 19, 1966.

"Girlies Get Holiday." *Lexington Dispatch*, October 6, 1956.

"Go Figure." *Lexington Dispatch*, November 18, 1908.

"Grimes-Wilson Engagement." *Lexington Dispatch*, October 16, 1912.

Guest, Betsey Stoner. "A Brief Sketch of Early Lexington, North Carolina." *Lexington Dispatch*, September 12, 1968.

"Guilford County." www.ncgenweb.us/nc/Guilford/courthouses.

"The Gypsies Are With Us." *Lexington Dispatch*, April 19, 1916.

"Hargrave Heads Gas Rationing for District." *Lexington Dispatch*, May 7, 1941.

"Has Two Wives." *Lexington Dispatch*, January 25, 1905.

"Hedrick Not Guilty." *Lexington Dispatch*, December 5, 1906.

"He Knew How to Keep a Secret." *Lexington Dispatch*, March 11, 1914.

"Here's Your Chance." *Lexington Dispatch*, May 8, 1901.

"High Point 'Doctor' Is Sent to Superior Court." *Lexington Dispatch*, May 13, 1956.

"Hirsh, Mrs. S. Abigail—Reminiscences of Ye Olden Time." *Lexington Dispatch*, January 17, 1906.

"His Bride Is Miss Grace Daniels—The Event Took Place in Greensboro Last Night." *Lexington Dispatch*, June 15, 1904.

"Historic Bethabara Park." http://www.learnnc.org/lp/pages 2291.

"Holiness Preacher and Erring Wife." *Lexington Dispatch*, July 8, 1903.

"Honor Lee and Jackson." *Lexington Dispatch*, January 19, 1919.

"Horrible Death in Randolph." *Lexington Dispatch*, November 8, 1905.

"Horse Defied the Speed Limit." *Lexington Dispatch*, October 5, 1910.

Houck, Lucy Hamlin. "The Story of Rockford." Self-published, 1972.

"House Trailer Dumped by Wind." *Lexington Dispatch*, July 2, 1954.

"The Hyphen Turns 100." http://www.journalnow.com/news/local/article_fa3e1a02-53b4-11e2-b80b-001a4bcf6878.html.

"Inauguration Day." *Lexington Dispatch*, January 11, 1905.

"Incidents of the Excursion." *Lexington Dispatch*, June 3, 1903.

"An Industry in Change." *Lexington Dispatch*, September 29, 1955.

"In Superior Court." *Lexington Dispatch*, May 1, 1912.

"Interesting Case in Supreme Court." *Lexington Dispatch*, April 19, 1916.

"In the Boys' Corn Contest." *Lexington Dispatch*, April 19, 1911.

"Items of Interest of Passing Events in the State of North Carolina." *Lexington Dispatch*, January 18, 1905.

"It Was Rumored." *Lexington Dispatch*, September 14, 1910.

"Jacob Hedrick Dead." *Lexington Dispatch*, November 9, 1910.

"J.A. Walser's Stolen Car Recovered Near Linwood." *Lexington Dispatch*, July 7, 1921.

"Jesse Jackson: Chronology." http://www.pbs.org/wgbh/pages/frontline/jesse/chronology.html.

"Judgment Is Delayed in Trial of Shooting Case." *Lexington Dispatch*, May 1, 1962.

"Juice Begins to Flow." *Lexington Dispatch*, February 9, 1910.

"Killed an Alligator." *Lexington Dispatch*, December 6, 1911.

"Killed on the Southbound." *Lexington Dispatch*, August 3, 1910.

"King Snake and Rat Fight to the Death." *Lexington Dispatch*, August 16, 1905.

"Large Attendance Saturday—County Is for Glenn—Delegates to Convention." *Lexington Dispatch*, June 15, 1904.

"A Large Percentage of Deaths in Mills." *Lexington Dispatch*, June 24, 1914.

"A Larger Outlook for the Modern Woman." *Lexington Dispatch*, April 15, 1914.

"Leonard Turned Loose." *Lexington Dispatch*, August 16, 1905.

"Letters to the Editor." *Lexington Dispatch*, November 25, 1953.

"Lexington Doing Her Bit." *Lexington Dispatch*, July 11, 1917.

"Lexington People Join in Tribute to Kennedy." *Lexington Dispatch*, November 25, 1963.

"Liberty Loan in the County." *Lexington Dispatch*, October 31, 1947.

"Linwood Boy Injured by Dynamite Cap." *Lexington Dispatch*, January 30, 1920.

"Liquor Men Have Narrow Escape." *Lexington Dispatch*, August 20, 1919.

"List Your Taxes." *Lexington Dispatch*, May 20, 1903.

"Loafers' Advice." *Lexington Dispatch*, February 26, 1913.

"Local All-American Football Hero." *Lexington Dispatch*, March 19, 1919.

"Local Briefs." *Lexington Dispatch*, January 11, 1905.

"Local Items." *Lexington Dispatch*, August 1, 1917.

"Local Items." *Lexington Dispatch*, October 4, 1911.

"Local People Comment on Sunday Store Hours." *Lexington Dispatch*, December 23, 1967.

"Local Police Charged with Assaulting Man." *Lexington Dispatch*, December 30, 1968.

"A Locksmith Saved the Day." *Lexington Dispatch*, June 24, 1914.

"Lowe Crouse Was Hired Out." *Lexington Dispatch*, February 26, 1913.

"Luther Beasley Killed." *Lexington Dispatch*, January 4, 1905.

"Maegeo Cow Has Four Calves in Less Than a Year." *Lexington Dispatch*, August 26, 1953.

"Magistrate Has Busy Time with Breakers of Law." *Lexington Dispatch*, December 11, 1924.

"Mail Boxes Dynamited in County; Investigation Made." *Lexington Dispatch*, November 1, 1961.

"Major Crime Ring Believed Instigators of Fraudulent Checks." *Lexington Dispatch*, December 14, 1964.

"Make Plans to Attend the Wright Tavern's Restoration Celebration." http://www.rceno.com/RCENO/news/events-news/make-plans-to-attend-the wright-taverns.

"Man Accused as 'Paddler' Will Face Kidnapping Charge." *Lexington Dispatch*, May 24, 1966.

"Man Confesses He Burned House at Thomasville." *Lexington Dispatch*, November 30, 1944.

"Man Dragged for Two Miles under Automobile Dies." *Lexington Dispatch*, December 29, 1958.

"Man Guilty of Armed Robbery." *Lexington Dispatch*, February 28, 1980.

Mann, Steve. "Looking Back: Racial Voting Lines Critical in 1977 Mayor's Race in Winston-Salem." *Winston-Salem Journal*, October 30, 2012.

"Many Gifts Await Winner of Annual Baby Derby." *Lexington Dispatch*, December 30, 1966.

"Maple Tree 100 Years Old." *Lexington Dispatch*, January 10, 1908.

"Mass Meeting of Baseball Fans Held." *Lexington Dispatch*, July 21, 1921.

"Mayodan." http://www.westernrockinghamchamber.com/id22_m.htm.

"McKnight Again." *Lexington Dispatch*, February 12, 1902.

"The Meeting Closed." *Davidson Dispatch*, March 30, 1898.

"A Message to the People of Our Rural Districts." *Lexington Dispatch*, December 11, 1918.

"Met Death by Freezing." *Lexington Dispatch*, January 18, 1905.

"Methodist Evangelistic Services." *Lexington Dispatch*, March 7, 1917.

"Midnight Intruder Killed Groceryman." *Lexington Dispatch*, October 1, 1913.

"Midway Robber Is Identified as Wade Loflin." *Lexington Dispatch*, May 7, 1942.

"Mills Home Will Have Homecoming Reunion Sunday." *Lexington Dispatch*, August 5, 1956.

"Ministers' Association Calls on Citizens to Uphold Moral Standards." *Lexington Dispatch*, November 7, 1919.

"Ministers Hit Sunday Movies in Thomasville." *Lexington Dispatch*, July 25, 1951.

"Mocksville and Davie County." *Lexington Dispatch*, August 16, 1905.

"A Monster Rat or a Good Lie." *Lexington Dispatch*, August 3, 1910.

"More Federal Prisoners Moved." *Lexington Dispatch*, August 16, 1905.

"More Large Hogs." *Lexington Dispatch*, January 11, 1905.

"Mothers March on Polio Set for Monday Night." *Lexington Dispatch*, January 29, 1955.

"Moved to Salisbury." *Lexington Dispatch*, March 8, 1905.

"Mr. and Mrs. Dupree Clodfelter's Terrible Experience on a Steamer." *Lexington Dispatch*, September 27, 1905.

"Mr. and Mrs. McCrary Entertain." *Lexington Dispatch*, January 11, 1905.

"Mr. Finch's Residence Burned." *Lexington Dispatch*, December 23, 1903.

"Mr. J.C. Kimel Dead." *Lexington Dispatch*, August 16, 1905.

"Mr. Moyer Is Elected." *Lexington Dispatch*, May 6, 1903.

"Mrs. Bailey Commits Suicide." *Lexington Dispatch*, May 20, 1903.

"Mrs. Broom Returned to Thomasville by Officers." *Lexington Dispatch*, February 1, 1955.

"Mrs. Nation at Durham." *Lexington Dispatch*, July 24, 1907.

"Much Visiting at Shade Grove." *Lexington Dispatch*, December 28, 1948.

"Mule Lunched on $24 Check." *Lexington Dispatch*, June 7, 1908.

"A Murderer Caught." *Lexington Dispatch*, June 15, 1904.

"Murder Hearing Set for Friday." *Lexington Dispatch*, September 13, 1961.

"Mystery Unearthed." *Lexington Dispatch*, October 1, 1913.

"A Narrow Escape." *Lexington Dispatch*, June 15, 1904.

"NC Nurses and the Polio Epidemics of the 1940s." http://nursinghistory.appstate.edu/nc-nurses-and-polio epidemics-1940s.

"Negro Arrested for Safe Robbery at Thomasville." *Lexington Dispatch*, July 12, 1934.

"Negro Found Guilty on Rape Charge." *Lexington Dispatch*, May 1, 1959.

"Negro Working at Thomasville Killed." *Lexington Dispatch*, April 13, 1944.

"New Burglar Alarm." *Lexington Dispatch*, December 12, 1906.

"New Knitting Mill." *Lexington Dispatch*, November 8, 1905.

"New Lumber Company." *Lexington Dispatch*, July 8, 1903.

"New Manufacturing Concern." *Lexington Dispatch*, March 31, 1906.

"New Radio Station Here Soon on Air." *Lexington Dispatch*, May 30, 1966.

"News and Gossip with the Bark On." *Lexington Dispatch*, December 16, 1903.

"News from Greensboro." *Lexington Dispatch*, September 27, 1905.

"News from Newsom." *Lexington Dispatch*, April 29, 1916.

"New Special Town Taxes." *Lexington Dispatch*, August 1, 1917.

Newton, J.D. "Too Strange to Talk About." *Lexington Dispatch*, July 18, 1917.

"1948 Polio Epidemic." http://www.yesweekly.com/triad/article-4702-1948-polop-epidemic.html.

"No Emergency Certificates to Be Awarded Teachers." *Lexington Dispatch*, August 20, 1919.

"No Harm Would Follow." *Lexington Dispatch*, March 23, 1906.

"No Hope." *Lexington Dispatch*, February 16, 1904.

"No Indictments Returned in Motel." *Lexington Dispatch*, February 27, 1980.

"Nominations Begin Monday." *Lexington Dispatch*, August 1, 1917.

"No Refund." *Davidson Dispatch*, March 30, 1898.

"North Carolina Collection." http://www.lib.unc.edu/ncc/ref/nchistory/feb2009/.

"No Small Pox Here." *Lexington Dispatch*, October 13, 1909.

"Not Dead But Sleeping." *Lexington Dispatch*, July 3, 1907.

"Notice." *Lexington Dispatch*, June 6, 1906.

"Notice to Non-Residents." *Lexington Dispatch*, May 13, 1903.

"Not Murder, But Assault." *Lexington Dispatch*, August 24, 1910.

"Numbering of Houses." *Lexington Dispatch*, October 16, 1912.

"Office Hurts Many Men." *Lexington Dispatch*, July 21, 1921.

"O. Henry." http://en.wikipedia.org/wiki/O._Henry.

"Old Booze." *Lexington Dispatch*, April 15, 1914.

"Old-Fashioned Pounding." *Lexington Dispatch*, October 16, 1912.

"Old Maids Give Night of Comedy." *Lexington Dispatch*, August 3, 1956.

"One Thousand at Baptizing." *Lexington Dispatch*, September 30, 1903.

"One Wife Too Many." *Lexington Dispatch*, May 1, 1912.

"Padlocking Hearing Still Going On in Superior Court." *Lexington Dispatch*, October 31, 1967.

"Palmers Find People Have Big Hearts." *Lexington Dispatch*, November 14, 1958.

"Pants-Suits Gain in Popularity for Women." *Lexington Dispatch*, December 24, 1966.

"Parker Makes Address." *Lexington Dispatch*, April 30, 1920.

"Passenger Station to Be Built." *Lexington Dispatch*, March 7, 1917.

"Peacock Factory Burned." *Lexington Dispatch*, November 14, 1917.

"Pearl Turner Found Wounded and Dying in His Mother's Yard." *Lexington Dispatch*, December 31, 1904.

"People Will Petition for Good Roads Election." *Lexington Dispatch*, April 28, 1909.

"Plethora of Peaches." *Lexington Dispatch*, June 27, 1906.

"A Poisoned Branch." *Lexington Dispatch*, May 20, 1903.

"Policeman Hepler 'Treed.'" *Lexington Dispatch*, February 2, 1910.

"Police Testifying in Murder Trial." *Lexington Dispatch*, August 30, 1968.

"Poppies Will Be Sold on May 25." *Lexington Dispatch*, May 13, 1940.

"Postponing Court Discussed." *Lexington Dispatch*, February 2, 1910.

"Prayer Blocked the Circus." *Lexington Dispatch*, December 12, 1906.

"Preserve American Community: Thomasville, North Carolina." http://www.preserveamerica.gov/PAcommunity-thomasvilleNC.html.

"Problem Apparently Is Solved at Thomasville." *Lexington Dispatch*, September 2, 1966.

"Prof. Ingram Found Guilty." *Lexington Dispatch*, December 16, 1903.

"Prohibition and Law Enforcement." *Lexington Dispatch*, June 9, 1909.

"A Protest Against Dumping." *Lexington Dispatch*, September 5, 1956.

"Protocol Signed." *Lexington Dispatch*, April 28, 1909.

"Public Printed Notices." *Lexington Dispatch*, June 28, 1905.

"Quack Doctor Fleecing Good People at Reeds." *Lexington Dispatch*, September 27, 1905.

"Rabbit Attacks a Hound." *Lexington Dispatch*, December 12, 1906.

"Racial Tension Arises in Winston-Salem as Policeman Freed." *Lexington Dispatch*, October 31, 1967.

"Randolph Boy Praised." *Lexington Dispatch*, September 14, 1910.

"Red Cross Notes." *Lexington Dispatch*, March 19, 1919.

"Red Cross Rally." *Lexington Dispatch*, November 7, 1919.

"Reeds Community News." *Lexington Dispatch*, November 7, 1919.

"Registrars Deny Charges of Withholding Books." *Lexington Dispatch*, October 27, 1930.

"Reminiscences of Days Long Past." *Lexington Dispatch*, January 31, 1906.

"Republican Convention at Greensboro." *Lexington Dispatch*, February 5, 1908.

"Restaurant Manager Here Takes Case to High Court." *Lexington Dispatch*, June 24, 1965.

"Revenue Officers at Greensboro Waylay Two Offenders and Capture One." *Lexington Dispatch*, October 16, 1907.

"Reynolda Farm, Splendid Country Estate of Mrs. R.J. Reynolds: Its Origin and Development and the Aims of Its Owner." *Twin City Sentinel*, July 7, 1917.

Reynolds, Patrick, and Tom Shachtman. *The Gilded Leaf: Triumph, Tragedy, and Tobacco*. Boston: Little, Brown and Company, 1989.

"A Romantic Courtship." *Lexington Dispatch*, July 8, 1903.

"Rubbing Doctors Rob Aged Citizen at Welcome." *Lexington Dispatch*, May 20, 1948.

"Runaway Marriage." *Lexington Dispatch*, September 30, 1903.

"The Rural Free Delivery." *Lexington Dispatch*, May 12, 1903.

"The Sabbath." *Lexington Dispatch*, August 3, 1910.

"Sanford to Come Here October 11." *Lexington Dispatch*, September 1, 1962.

"Saws Steel Bars." *Lexington Dispatch*, April 6, 1920.

"School Closing." *Lexington Dispatch*, March 28, 1906.

"Sea Scouts Rendezvous on Lake Attracts Many Folks." *Lexington Dispatch*, May 14, 1940.

"Senate." *Lexington Dispatch*, January 11, 1905.

"Senator Stevenson at High Point." *Lexington Dispatch*, February 9, 1976.

Sexton, Scott. "1930 Explosion Mystery Solved." *Winston-Salem Journal*, December 30, 2013.

"She Demanded Morphine." *Lexington Dispatch*, July 8, 1903.

"Sheriff Looking for Deer Heads." *Lexington Dispatch*, October 10, 1956.

"Shooting at the Erlanger." *Lexington Dispatch*, April 15, 1914.

"Short Stop in Greensboro." *Lexington Dispatch*, August 16, 1905.

"Shot Resisting Prisoner." *Lexington Dispatch*, December 23, 1903.

"Shut Up in Cold Storage." *Lexington Dispatch*, August 14, 1907.

Sink, Alice E. *Hidden History of the Piedmont Triad*. Charleston, SC: The History Press, 2009.

———. "Katharine Smith Reynolds: The Story of Her Life." Unpublished manuscript.

———. *Wicked Greensboro*. Charleston, SC: The History Press, 2011.

———. *Wicked High Point*. Charleston, SC: The History Press, 2011.

———. *Wicked Lexington*. Charleston, SC: The History Press, 2011.

———. *Wicked Winston-Salem*. Charleston, SC: The History Press. 2011.

Sink, Alice E., and Nickie Doyal. *Boarding House Reach: North Carolina's Entrepreneurial Women*. Wilmington, NC: Dram Tree Books, 2007.

Sink, Dave. "About Town." *Lexington Dispatch*, May 13, 1940.

"Slater Hospital." http://www.digitalforsyth.org/photos/stories/slater-hospital.

"Slater Industrial Academy and Cottages." http://www.wssu.edu/cg-okelly-library/archives/buildings/cottages-m.aspx.

"The Slayer Is Released." *Lexington Dispatch*, January 20, 1905.

"Slayer of Thomasville Man Is Committed to Dix Hill." *Lexington Dispatch*, June 21, 1962.

"The Smallpox Situation." *Lexington Dispatch*, December 23, 1903.

"Snazzy New Cars." *Lexington Dispatch*, April 15, 1914.

"Soldiers' Picnic Tomorrow." *Lexington Dispatch*, August 8, 1917.

"The Southbound Railway." *Lexington Dispatch*, March 28, 1906.

"Southern Race Riot Costs Five Lives." *New York Times*, November 17, 1918.

"Spicy and Saucy." *Lexington Dispatch*, March 18, 1940.

"A Statement from Supt. Vann." *Lexington Dispatch*, October 16, 1912.

"Story of a Numerous Family." *Lexington Dispatch*, February 5, 1971.

"Story of General Leach." *Lexington Dispatch*, June 27, 1906.

"Strike at the Wenonah." *Lexington Dispatch*, January 17, 1906.

"Strikers March in Thomasville, Most Are Natives." *Lexington Dispatch*, August 29, 1932.

"Struck by the Train." *Lexington Dispatch*, May 6, 1903.

"Suit for Alienation." *Lexington Dispatch*, January 19, 1919.

"Sunday School Excursion." *Lexington Dispatch*, May 27, 1903.

"Superior Court in Session." *Lexington Dispatch*, February 24, 1915.

"Swiss Bell Ringers." *Lexington Dispatch*, April 15, 1914.

"Take a Little Salt with This, Please." *Lexington Dispatch*, January 11, 1905.

"Tanks and Gatling Guns Defending Salem—1918." http://walkingthroughsalem.blogspot.com/2010/12/tanks-and-gatling-guns-defending-sale.

"Tax Locker Clubs $5,000." *Lexington Dispatch*, February 23, 1910.

"Telephone Lineman Falls Thirty-Five Feet." *Lexington Dispatch*, March 19, 1919.

"Theft of $6,000 in Stocks, $130 Cash Is Reported." *Lexington Dispatch*, June 28, 1950.

"Thieves Paid Visit." *Lexington Dispatch*, November 18, 1908.

"Thirty-Five Years from Now." *Lexington Dispatch*, August 1, 1917.

"This and That from Winston-Salem." *Lexington Dispatch*, June 6, 1906.

"This and That from Winston-Salem." *Lexington Dispatch*, March 26, 1906.

"Thomasville Banker Is Shot at Home Today." *Lexington Dispatch*, December 17, 1965.

"Thomasville Department." *Lexington Dispatch*, October 31, 1940.

"Thomasville Man Confesses to Killing Estranged Girlfriend." *Lexington Dispatch*, August 13, 1951.

"Thomasville Man Is Charged with First Degree Murder." *Lexington Dispatch*, September 11, 1951.

"Thomasville Ministers Protest Show." *Lexington Dispatch*, June 23, 1954.

"Thomasville Pays Tribute—French Memorial Certificates Awarded." *Lexington Dispatch*, April 6, 1920.

"Thomasville's Population 2,224." *Lexington Dispatch*, May 20, 1903.

"Those Funny French Customs." *Lexington Dispatch*, July 3, 1918.

"Those Who May Be Exempt." *Lexington Dispatch*, July 11, 1917.

"Three Held for Murder in Whiskey Death of Thomasville Woman." *Lexington Dispatch*, September 9, 1953.

"Thursday Services Grace Episcopal." *Lexington Dispatch*, May 13, 1940.

"Timber Thieves Are Arrested." *Lexington Dispatch*, September 29, 1955.

"Tobacco Crop Forecasted as Shortest in Ten Years." *Lexington Dispatch*, July 7, 1921.

Tomlin, Jimmy. "Murder Mystery: After Nearly 70 Years, Death of Policeman Remains Unsolved." *High Point Enterprise*, July 29, 2010.

"Tom Sheets Is Dead." *Lexington Dispatch*, January 15, 1913.

"Too Many Leaving the Farm." *Lexington Dispatch*, September 11, 1968.

"To Round Dozen Club." *Lexington Dispatch*, April 29, 1945.

"To the Firemen." *Lexington Dispatch*, December 12, 1906.

"Tragedy at Thomasville: Mrs. Sallie Thomas Burned to Death—Widow of Dr. R.W. Thomas." *Lexington Dispatch*, March 6, 1912.

"Traveler Is Robbed of Over $400 in County." *Lexington Dispatch*, September 29, 1955.

"The Trial a Warm Number." *Lexington Dispatch*, January 22, 1908.

"Trip Hammer Silenced in County of Guilford." *Lexington Dispatch*, December 6, 1911.

"Trouble at Thomasville." *Lexington Dispatch*, March 7, 1917.

Tursi, Frank V. *Winston-Salem: A History*. Winston-Salem, NC: John F. Blair Publisher, 1994.

"Two Boys Rob a Farmer." *Lexington Dispatch*, November 18, 1908.

"Two Cases in Juvenile Court." *Lexington Dispatch*, August 20, 1919.

"Two Killed by Shifting Engine." *Lexington Dispatch*, September 27, 1905.

"Two Stores Closing, One Opening on Main." *Lexington Dispatch*, November 18, 1981.

"Two Year Old Is Driver of Auto in Accident." *Lexington Dispatch*, March 13, 1956.

"U.D.C. Hear Highlights of State Convention." *Lexington Dispatch*, October 27, 1967.

"The 'Unknown Tongue' Business." *Lexington Dispatch*, July 24, 1907.

"Up $84 Per Family in Two Years." *Lexington Dispatch*, December 24, 1956.

"Various Local Items." *Lexington Dispatch*, May 29, 1907.

"Volunteer Service Guilds Begins Christmas Project for Dix Hospital." *Lexington Dispatch*, November 25, 1968.

"Walkertown News." *Winston Republican*, January 30, 1902.

"Wants the Streets Cleaned Up." *Lexington Dispatch*, May 29, 1907.

"Wants to 'Corry Spond.'" *Lexington Dispatch*, May 29, 1907.

"Was Awarded 37 Cents." *Lexington Dispatch*, March 4, 1904.

"Welcome Stages Gymnastics Meet." *Lexington Dispatch*, February 4, 1980.

"When Coon's Good Eating." *Lexington Dispatch*, June 10, 1908.

"When the Show Comes to Town." *Lexington Dispatch*, October 16, 1912.

"Who Were They?" *Greensboro Patriot*, May 6, 1903.

"Why November 11ᵗʰ? Search Us." *Lexington Dispatch*, November 28, 1908.

"Will Build County Home." *Lexington Dispatch*, March 9, 1910.

"Will Build New Bridge." *Lexington Dispatch*, November 23, 1904.

"Wins Double Header." *Lexington Dispatch*, August 20, 1919.

"Winston and Forsyth." *Lexington Dispatch*, August 16, 1905.

"Woman Killed by Southern Freight in Thomasville." *Lexington Dispatch*, January 13, 1936.

"Woman's Traducer Arrested." *Lexington Dispatch*, April 24, 1907.

"Women Poker Players Are Too Good at It." *Lexington Dispatch*, September 29, 1955.

"Would-Be Killer Killed." *Davidson Dispatch*, January 18, 1905.

"Would Poison a Family." *Lexington Dispatch*, July 12, 1905.

"Would Welcome Them." *Lexington Dispatch*, June 30, 1950.

"Wrightsville Beach." *Lexington Dispatch*, August 16, 1905.

"Yadkin College Notes." *Davidson Dispatch*, February 11, 1902.

"Yadkin College Notes." *Davidson Dispatch*, January 31, 1905.

"Yadkin Got Thaw Money." *Lexington Dispatch*, February 5, 1908.

"Yadkin Man Seeks Damages for Alienation." *Lexington Dispatch*, December 6, 1911.

"Yank Hargrave Killed." *Lexington Dispatch*, October 5, 1910.

ABOUT THE AUTHOR

Alice E. Sink is the published author of numerous books, short stories, articles and essays. She earned her MFA in creative writing from the University of North Carolina at Greensboro. For thirty years, she taught writing courses at High Point University in High Point, North Carolina, where she received the Meredith Clark Slane Distinguished Teaching/Service Award in 2002. The North Carolina Arts Council and the partnering arts councils of the Central Piedmont Regional Artists Hub Program awarded Sink a 2007 grant to promote her writing.